D1204556

Scottish
Country Houses & Castles

Culzean Castle, Ayrshire

Scottish Country Houses & Castles

SHEILA FORMAN

Introduction by **GEORGE SCOTT-MONCRIEFF**
Illustrations by **SCOTTISH FIELD** *Photographers*

COLLINS · Glasgow and London

First Published 1967

Printed in Great Britain by GEORGE OUTRAM & CO. LIMITED, PERTH

Introduction

by **GEORGE SCOTT-MONCRIEFF**

FOR MANY YEARS SHEILA FORMAN'S ARTICLES on old Scottish houses provided the most welcome reading in our illustrated magazines. Welcome is very much the word one chooses, because, just as I believe she was always a welcome guest at the homes she visited, her descriptions had a quality of welcome about them. It was as though she herself were for the moment a hostess rather than a guide. This I think was because of her very genuine enthusiasm for her subject.

She had not only a feeling for and a delight in the varied architecture that came under her purview, such as a man might have, but also a truly feminine delight in furnishings, in gardens, and in the individual qualities that make a home out of a house. It was plain to see, too, the sympathy of her appreciation of those who made the home. Her natural delicacy was such that she did not intrude upon the privacy of the owners of houses, yet she was able to convey something of their individuality, so that it was never museum pieces into which we were invited but real homes, lived in and living places.

In consequence I do not believe that Sheila Forman ever wrote about ruins. To her they would only have had an academic interest. It was continuity of occupation that appealed to her in her subjects, the changes made by successive generations, even when these were sometimes architecturally unfortunate.

Thus Sheila Forman would never have claimed that the present collection of her writings covers all phases or constitutes a history even of one element of Scottish architecture. For that there are other books to which we can refer. Her purpose was different, and more personal, and she fulfilled it admirably. In writing an introduction, I have only to add a brief historical outline that may help to relate the architectural aspect of Sheila Forman's portraits of Scottish homesteads to the main traditions that guided their building.

Little enough remains of the earliest of our castles, established by Norman immigrants in the twelfth century. They were not built of stone but of timber and earth and clay so they could not be expected to survive except as grass-grown foundations, and, occasionally as the ground plan for later stonework. They were in a sense almost more offensive than defensive in character, spearheads of an occupying force. William the Conqueror ordered one to be built immediately upon his arrival at Hastings, and the Bayeux Tapestry shows us clearly what they were like. They were quickly constructed, but for permanent occupation masonry obviously provided a more satisfactory residence: nevertheless there is evidence that some timber castles of similar type continued in occupation for long enough.

These Norman castles are known as motte-and-bailey castles: the motte, or mote (not to be confused with moat), being the small circular mound usually within a bailey, the enclosure formed by ditch and embankment and containing lesser buildings than that on the motte.

They were succeeded by the castle of enclosure in which a high curtain wall of stone, defensive, with few apertures, was built round a courtyard. Against the inside of the containing wall, residential buildings were erected of stone or timber with perhaps a free-standing chapel in the centre, so that a small community could be fully provided for within the enclosure.

With the re-introduction of siege weapons similar to those of classical times, various refinements and elaborations had to be introduced. Notably this involved the construction of large towers at the angles of the curtain wall, giving the defenders a better opportunity to observe and repel the enemy.

These castles of enclosure, built from the twelfth into the fourteenth century and now all ruinous, usually massive and capacious, could of course only be afforded by royalty and the most powerful nobles. But they are the forerunners of the much smaller tower houses that were to be the homes of even modest lairds for the next three centuries—and some of which are homes to this day.

In their simplest form the building of these tower houses overlaps with the building of the great castles of enclosure. Sheila Forman has written of one of the earliest and most interesting of them all, the original square tower of the Castle of Drum in Aberdeenshire.

Although one of the earliest, having been built around the year 1300, the old tower of Drum is not of the most primitive construction. For its building, there must have been available masons accomplished and experienced enough to incorporate some of the lessons learnt in making the enclosure castles more defensible. In the most primitive tower houses the walls rise sheer to the parapet, but at Drum the parapet is projected on corbels, with open rounds at the angles, giving vantage points to the defenders.

Drum Castle gave particular pleasure to Sheila Forman in having been the constant home of the Irvine family since King Robert the Bruce gave the property to their direct ancestor in gratitude for his loyal services. Moreover, the family fortunes seem to have been at their peak not—as was so often unfortunately the case—in Victorian times, but in a far happier architectural age. So it is that the relatively little-altered addition made by a highly cultured laird in 1619 is as good of its kind as the original tower itself, an asset and not an embarrassment.

An immediate development of the free-standing foursquare tower consisted in building a shallow wing against it to contain the newel stair. Walls were thinner now and it was generally no longer possible for them to contain a convenient intra-mural stair like that in the twelve-foot thick walls of Drum. This projection of a stair tower formed the L-plan which, with various modifications, is the predominating type amongst surviving Scottish towers.

A good unaltered example of the simplest L-plan tower may be seen at Scotstarvit in Fife, which, although well preserved, being unoccupied was not described by Sheila Forman. At Scotstarvit the whole of the projecting wing is occupied by the stair, but quite early on the advantage of the additional wing for obtaining extra accommodation was appreciated, and the stair might be contained in another tower built within the re-entrant angle, or, alternatively, start in the stair tower but reach the uppermost storeys in a turret carried out on corbels, so that the top of the stair tower could be used for chambers. At Balmanno, described in this book, both adaptations may be seen where there is a square stair tower in the angle of the L and also a turret stair above the first floor.

While the long-persisting unease of Scotland's history and the depredations of the 'auld enemy' to the south made defence remain a consideration far into the seventeenth century, gradually its demands became less insistent. It was doubtless appreciated that since, with the increasing effectiveness of weapons of assault, a determined attack could no longer be resisted, while casual raids could be held off by a simple thrawnness of construction, more scope might be allowed for comfort and convenience.

There ensues a transition period, the tower house looking forward to the mansion, becoming less militant, more genial, and producing what many consider the finest and most characteristic achievements of Scottish architecture. The change is immediately apparent in the rooflines, where parapets and open rounds give place to roofs that oversail the wallhead, garnished with pepperpot turrets at the angles.

The late Dr. Mackay Mackenzie used to express his irritation with writers who too freely bandied the word 'functional' when describing Scottish tower houses. He insisted that much of their detailing was not strictly functional but carried out with a keen eye to decorative effect. A little observation will endorse his view. A wonderful natural artistry seems to inspire the building of the tower houses. I use the epithet 'natural' because the final effect seems far less deliberative than that achieved in the more formal mansions that succeeded them.

Yet basic function was always present, checking any confused elaboration such as was liable to betray the Victorians in their efforts to recapture the 'Scotch Baronial' style. But the underlying basic forms of the L-plan and the less-common Z-plan (in which the central block is flanked by two towers set at diagonally opposite angles) could be developed in a delightful variety of ways.

The massive nobility of Borthwick Castle, unique in its scale, is based quite simply on a double L-plan. For its beauty Borthwick depends upon the austerity of its honey-coloured ashlar masonry. On the other hand the great castles of the north-east, Glamis, Fraser, Crathes, Craigievar, the final flowering of the tradition and all described by Sheila Forman, depend upon elaboration kept under control by simple planning.

It is hard to realise, looking at the glorious flourish of turret and lum and balustrade which crowns Craigievar, that it all springs from an L-plan at ground level, while Castle Fraser, starting with a modest tower grew, in time, into a Z-plan house.

The extraordinarily felicitous detail of turret and corbelling of these great Aberdeenshire castles seems to have been the work of one family of master-masons, the Bells, about whom little is known, but their works pay them a more expressive tribute than any biographical detail.

However, the remarkable qualities of the Scottish castellated tradition are by no means confined to these major works. Totally different from the English tradition, deriving from the French but early developing its own character, the medieval Scottish home achieved a true, poetic beauty even when built to the most modest scale. Notable examples visited by Sheila Forman include Traquair, Barra, Stobhall, Barcaldine and Aldie: all of them little lyrics of building.

Before turning to the classical manners of our mansion houses, a word should be said about three castles 'born out of due time' and described in this book.

The earliest of these and by far the finest is Drumlanrig. The building was begun in 1679 when masons trained in the castellated tradition must still have been available. Moreover the plans were based upon others drawn up sixty years earlier, presumably by William Wallace, who was responsible for Heriot's Hospital and belonged essentially to the older school. They were revised by Sir William Bruce, the first and the greatest of our architects in the modern sense of the word, although, as Sheila Forman tells us, the work seems actually to have been carried out by James Smith. Smith was himself the son-in-law of Robert Mylne, sixth of his family to hold the post of King's Master Mason, by whom he was doubtless also influenced.

Despite its varied genealogy, Drumlanrig achieves

homogeneity as well as originality and, as Mr. John Dunbar says in his *Historic Architecture of Scotland*, 'the overall effect is one of immense dignity and splendour, a unique alliance of the Castellated and Renaissance styles in which Scottish Baronial is unexpectedly translated into Baroque'.

By 1745, that fatal and romantic year in Scotland's history, when Roger Morris was drawing up his plans for the Duke of Argyll's castle at Inveraray, there was a complete cleavage between the two traditions. Inveraray is one of the earliest of Gothic Revival buildings, pure revival and pastiche. About its exterior there is none of the sweetness, the aptness of line and detail that distinguish the old castles. There was nobody left to whom the tradition came naturally. The best of Inveraray Castle is to be seen in its interiors, distinctively classical in character, the work of a later generation of the Mylne family.

Even a much finer architect than Morris, Robert Adam, could not recapture the old style when he built Culzean Castle some thirty years later. All Culzean's real merit lies in its classical interiors, which in the great oval stairway achieves brilliance of design.

From the end of the seventeenth century until well into the nineteenth, when Gothic and Baronial Revivalism began to dominate, the architecture of the Renaissance holds sway. Even small houses are influenced by the classical idiom, sometimes rather rustically misconceived but not necessarily any the less attractive for that, indeed not infrequently all the better for not being derived too mechanically from the design book.

Emanating from the classical revival of the Italian Renaissance (although in fact we now know that the revival was more 'classical' in the sense of being regular than the original), the new manner of building was cosmopolitan, but inevitably received modifications from the varying conditions, climates and proclivities of the different countries adopting it.

As we have observed, its first fully qualified practitioner in Scotland was a man of genius. Sir William Bruce was something of an amateur, but in the supremely good sense of that word. He had other interests besides architecture, and seems at times to have been reluctant to accept employment in the art in which he was a master. We have too few of his buildings—tragically, two of them were destroyed by fire since the last war.

Generally, as at Balcaskie, Bruce was engaged in reconstructing earlier buildings to suit the new taste for a greater amplitude of domesticity. But at Kinross he built for himself an entirely new house, his masterpiece, comparable in its perfection to the great Renaissance châteaux of France, and mercifully preserved by a discriminating family from the decay that has befallen so much of our heritage.

Bruce's pupil and immediate successor was James Smith, the range of whose work is only now becoming known and appreciated. A better-known architect who also learnt from working with Bruce is William Adam, senior. It was he who continued Bruce's house of Hopetoun, not, be it said, to a design so grand as Bruce's own—probably for reasons of economy, although it was ultimately finished and somewhat redeemed by his sons, John and Robert.

Robert Adam is now the most celebrated of all Scottish architects, although for a time his work fell out of favour. Settling in London, with his brothers, John, James and William, he built up a large practice in the southern kingdom, and bequeathed his name to a whole style of Renaissance architecture. Many buildings are called 'Adam' that are not actually his, and some of which hardly merit the association.

Nevertheless, in spite of settling in England, Robert Adam still did much work in Scotland, and Sheila Forman gives us descriptions of several country houses which are his or partly his.

At Mellerstain he built the finely-proportioned central block: quaintly enough the little wings were built first, by his father. Like Culzean, Mellerstain contains a decorous staircase, and the ornamental plasterwork has all the exquisite elegance of the Adam style—quite distinct from the robust plaster motifs favoured by the older Adam. Father and son were also both employed in the building of Yester, and John and Robert Adam built Paxton, where the fine collection of original furniture gave particular pleasure to Sheila Forman.

Smaller, and with none of the slight concessions to the baronial conceit made at Mellerstain, Newliston is a charming example of Robert Adam's own work, although the elaborate lay-out of garden and policies is earlier, and the wings to the house are a later addition.

Where, in my opinion, Robert Adam does not quite measure up to his great predecessor, Sir William Bruce, is in a certain preoccupation he shows for façade. He does not generally achieve the same satisfactory sense of mass that is ever-present in Bruce's work. This doubtless is a danger inherent in the increasing dependence upon the drawing-board, with its linear limitations, amongst the later architects.

Floors Castle, Achnacarry and Abbotsford are nineteenth-century houses visited by Sheila Forman. Abbotsford if not deservedly for its architecture, is famous at least for its contents and its association with Sir Walter Scott, who contributed so greatly to restoring the national self-confidence when that was much needed. Architecturally Abbotsford reflects only too well a mistaken antiquarian zeal that brought a decline in our buildings during the century, when mock Gothic and 'Scotch Baronial' were liable to be heavily and pompously handled by architects and many a fine old building lost its distinction through rebuilding or through lavish additions that were to become a headache to future generations.

Finally, this book includes two modern houses. Both are the work of Sir Basil Spence. Gribloch, built in collaboration with an American architect, reflects a new cosmopolitan fashion. Broughton invokes the castellated tradition, but with a fresh appreciation of the fundamental simplicity that is the real source of its merit.

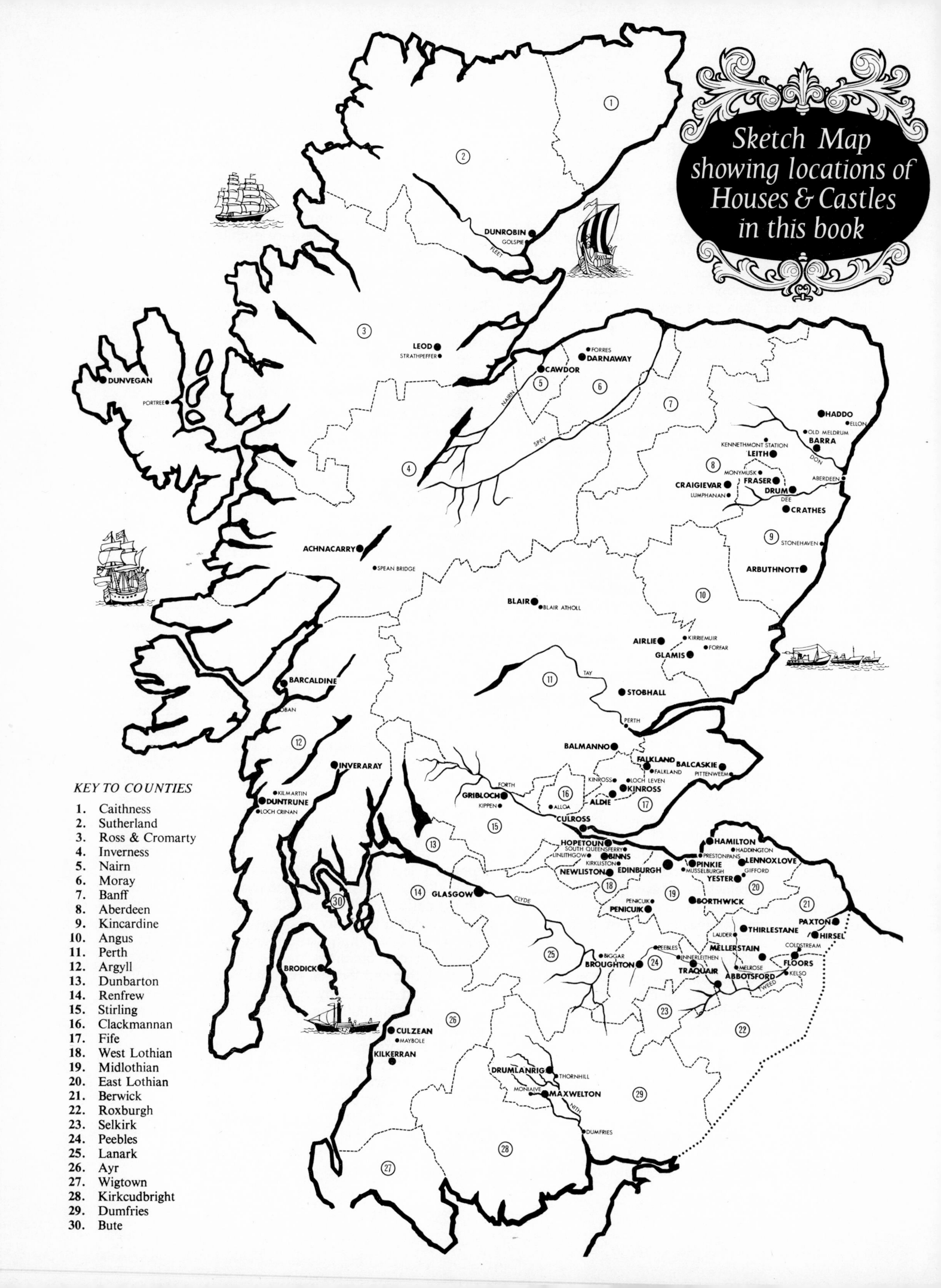

Sketch Map
showing locations of
Houses & Castles
in this book
DUNROBIN
GOLSPIE
FLEET
LEOD
STRATHPEFFER
DUNVEGAN
PORTREE
CAWDOR
FORRES
DARNAWAY
NAIRN
SPEY
HADDO
ELLON
OLD MELDRUM
BARRA
KENNETHMONT STATION
LEITH
DON
MONYMUSK
FRASER
ABERDEEN
CRAIGIEVAR
LUMPHANAN
DRUM
DEE
CRATHES
STONEHAVEN
ARBUTHNOTT
ACHNACARRY
SPEAN BRIDGE
BLAIR
BLAIR ATHOLL
AIRLIE
KIRRIEMUIR
FORFAR
GLAMIS
TAY
STOBHALL
PERTH
BARCALDINE
OBAN
BALMANNO
FALKLAND
BALCASKIE
FALKLAND
PITTENWEEM
INVERARAY
KINROSS
LOCH LEVEN
KINROSS
ALDIE
FORTH
GRIBLOCH
KIPPEN
ALLOA
KILMARTIN
DUNTRUNE
LOCH CRINAN
CULROSS
HOPETOUN
SOUTH QUEENSFERRY
LINLITHGOW
BINNS
KIRKLISTON
NEWLISTON
EDINBURGH
HAMILTON
HADDINGTON
PRESTONPANS
PINKIE
MUSSELBURGH
LENNOXLOVE
GIFFORD
YESTER
GLASGOW
CLYDE
BORTHWICK
PENICUIK
PENICUIK
PAXTON
THIRLESTANE
LAUDER
HIRSEL
COLDSTREAM
MELLERSTAIN
BIGGAR
PEEBLES
INNERLEITHEN
BROUGHTON
TRAQUAIR
MELROSE
FLOORS
KELSO
ABBOTSFORD
TWEED
BRODICK
CULZEAN
MAYBOLE
KILKERRAN
DRUMLANRIG
THORNHILL
MONIAIVE
MAXWELTON
NITH
DUMFRIES
1 2 3 4 5 6 7 8 9 10 11 12 13 14 15 16 17 18 19 20 21 22 23 24 25 26 27 28 29 30
KEY TO COUNTIES
1. Caithness
2. Sutherland
3. Ross & Cromarty
4. Inverness
5. Nairn
6. Moray
7. Banff
8. Aberdeen
9. Kincardine
10. Angus
11. Perth
12. Argyll
13. Dunbarton
14. Renfrew
15. Stirling
16. Clackmannan
17. Fife
18. West Lothian
19. Midlothian
20. East Lothian
21. Berwick
22. Roxburgh
23. Selkirk
24. Peebles
25. Lanark
26. Ayr
27. Wigtown
28. Kirkcudbright
29. Dumfries
30. Bute

Contents

For centuries earlier castles stood on the same site, true bastions secondary to the main Kennedy stronghold of the now ruined Dunure Castle farther up the coast. In the late 17th century Culzean was described as "standing upon a rock above the sea, flanked upon the south with very pretty gardens and orchards, adorned with excellent tarases, and laden with peaches, apricotes, cherries and other fruits; and these gardens are so well sheltered from the north and east winds and ly so open to the south that the fruits and herbages are more early than in any other place in Carrick." Nearly a hundred years later additions were made to this tower house for the 9th Earl of Cassillis and in 1777 his brother, the 10th Earl, commissioned Robert Adam to reconstruct the interior and add the turreted wings facing the gardens. Adam continued to elaborate and extend the house until his death in 1792 and work went on till the end of the century. Various alterations were made to the house in late Victorian times and in 1953 The National Trust for Scotland carried out a restoration of the interior. Thus Culzean has grown and developed continuously for some 600 years since the Kennedys first acquired the lands of Cassillis in 1350, gathering legend and history and changing in outline and purpose on its rocky site above the unchanging sea.

The old Earls of Carrick are believed to be the ancestors of the Kennedy family. There is the story of Marjory, daughter of Earl Neil, who lost her husband in one of the Crusades and later, in 1271, married the man who was sent to break the news to her—Robert Bruce, Lord of Annandale. He found her, it is said, out hawking near Turnberry Castle and was so enchanted by the young widow that he stayed on to court her. Their son became King Robert the Bruce. Documentary history begins with John Kennedy, son of Gilbert Kennedy of Dunure, who owned Culzean, then known as The Cove, Coiff or Coff, and who died in 1409. Gilbert, 1st Lord Kennedy, was brother to the famous Bishop of Dunkeld and St. Andrews who founded St. Salvator's College and was entrusted with the education of the young King James III. David, 3rd Lord Kennedy, who in 1509 was made Earl of Cassillis, died four years later on the field of Flodden. The 2nd Earl was murdered on the beach at Prestwick for his bid to rescue James V from the Earl of Arran's party, and his grandson, the 3rd Earl, was poisoned at Dieppe on his way back from the wedding of Mary Stuart and the Dauphin of France in 1558, after a difference of opinion with the French Court. The 3rd Earl's brother, Quentin Kennedy, who was Abbot of Crossraguel Abbey, is remembered for his public dispute with John Knox in 1562 at Maybole on the Sacrifice of the Mass.

Nor was violence abated in the 17th century when the Kennedys, a large and powerful clan, warred among themselves in continuous feuds for position, land and money. On the death of the 8th Earl in 1759 without issue, a dispute arose for the Cassillis title and honours which was finally settled by the House of Lords in

Culzean Castle

favour of Sir Thomas Kennedy, Bt., of Culzean. Thus he became the 9th Earl and Culzean the family seat. Now, at long last, the fighting Kennedys settled down to the more constructive activities of farming, estate management and horticulture. Before Earl Thomas died in 1775, he had not only greatly improved his property but, with a typically 18th century interest in architecture and the arts, had begun to enlarge the old castle. It was his brother, David, the 10th Earl, however, an advocate and M.P., who employed Robert Adam to rebuild the present house.

For Robert Adam, the brilliant classicist of European fame, the castle style of building was a late and unfamiliar essay into the Romantic. Culzean, the largest and most spectacular of his castle-buildings, triumphs in spite of its demerits—Adam's lack of historical form and detail and the difficulty of welding piecemeal additions into a concise whole. Inspired by the magnificent site, he recreated the whole pattern of the place with pleasing and imaginative boldness. Without exactly imitating any feature of the traditional Scottish castle, he used towers and turrets—which he arranged in tidy Georgian symmetry—to build up his romantic theme.

In 1787, 10 years after Adam had begun work on the south front, a contemporary traveller reported that ". . . His Lordship, not content with the present extensive pile, intends adding a similar front to the sea, which will be a most arduous undertaking from the vast depth of the foundation necessary to be formed. At present it does great credit to Adam, the architect and his Lordship's peculiar taste, and will, when complete, stand unrivalled in its way." Earl David, who had made the Grand Tour of Europe and was even more intrigued with architecture than his brother, is said to have had a hand in the building himself. By this time the low range to the north (later built over by the Victorian wing) was completed and finally the splendid round tower was added, dominating the whole range of buildings.

Characteristically, Adam's interior at Culzean excels the outside composition. If the exterior of the Georgian castle was a tentative venture for him, he was more than master of the planning and decoration inside. Here are all the familiar marks of his genius, emboldened by space and a mood of romantic expansion. The great oval staircase which is the central point of the various groups of buildings is one of the most successful and scintillating of his so-called "space compositions." With its double flight of steps descending from the colonnaded gallery on the first floor, below successive tiers of pillars linked by gilt balusters, the staircase achieves a grand and perpetual movement.

The round drawing room on the first floor of the great tower, with its six tall windows overlooking the sea, for all its superb elegance, has a fairy-tale quality evocative of "charm'd magic casements opening on the foam of perilous seas... forlorn." On a background of pale green, delicate shades of egg-shell blue, turquoise and sugar pink are introduced into the decoration of the modelled ceiling, contrasting with the bolder design and colour of the round carpet, woven in Ayrshire. Most of the fittings too, were designed by Adam for the room, including the gilt mirrors and beautiful candle-holders on the walls, although the original furniture has been dispersed. Over the chimneypiece hangs a portrait of Susannah Kennedy, a famous beauty who became Countess of Eglinton and died at the age of 90 in 1780, just before Robert Adam had started on the new castle.

Also opening off the first floor gallery are the long drawing room with its exquisite ceiling, the green drawing room, the Adam room where a collection of drawings and photographs of Adam's works in Scotland is now displayed, and the Kennedy room which is decorated and furnished in the Victorian manner. On the ground floor, the library is one of the first rooms Adam completed and was originally used as the "eating room," the rounded ends being designed for freedom of movement while the servants waited at table. The present dining room, adapted for that purpose in 1879, was then somewhat altered in the process.

ABOVE: *Adam's oval staircase.*

LEFT: *Old eating room, now the library.*

A large body of craftsmen worked under Adam's direction on the decoration of Culzean and the plaster ceilings were carried out by a local firm who are still in business today and were able to help with paint and materials for the 1953 restoration. William Cairncross, a well-known contractor of the time, was mainly responsible for the building and woodwork and Patrick Henderson of Leith Walk, Edinburgh, executed most of the marble fireplaces, except for those in the round and long drawing rooms, which are by the Dutch sculptor, P. M. Gelder. Among other things, the mirrors

TOP: *The round drawing room.*

BOTTOM LEFT: *David, 10th Earl of Cassillis painted by Pompeo Batoni.*

CENTRE: *Captain Archibald Kennedy, 11th Earl of Cassillis.*

RIGHT: *The dining room has a fine set of Chippendale chairs.*

were made in England.

Throughout the house there are portraits of the Kennedy family, their kinsmen and connections by marriage and friends, tracing their history from one generation to another. The builder of Culzean, the 10th Earl, died in 1792, the same year as Robert Adam. Cassillis was unmarried and succeeded by a distant cousin, Captain Archibald Kennedy, R.N., whose great-grandfather had settled in America. Captain Kennedy, who lost most of his considerable American property in the Revolutionary War, died in 1794 and was followed at Culzean by his eldest son. This 12th Earl was created Marquis of Ailsa by King William IV in 1831, taking his title from the island rock of

RIGHT: *Adam's Gothick archway.*

BOTTOM LEFT: *The round sitting room in ex-President Eisenhower's flat.*

Ailsa Craig which stands out clearly on the seaward horizon from Culzean and which has been owned by the Kennedys since the Reformation. It was the 3rd Marquis who made the Victorian alterations and additions to the castle, including the new west wing. He also developed the gardens and grounds and fostered the now famous collection of trees and shrubs which thrive so well in the mild climate.

Beyond the walled garden, the outer policies were probably laid out by Alexander Naysmith (1758-1840), the landscape-gardener and painter. These are, in themselves, an entrancing maze of orderly fantasy, characteristic of the Gothic Revival, woodland paths winding from the formal Fountain Court on the south side of the house, with its terraces, palm trees and glory of rainbow-coloured azaleas, to the wilder aspects of Swan Lake, through the great trees and giant rhododendrons of Happy Valley, past the Gothick splendour of Camellia House, and back to the main approach to the castle, over the bridge designed by Adam in the approved rustic manner. His neo-Gothic archway leads into the courtyard of the castle between the stable block and the main entrance. Here, on the neat round plot of grass, stands the battery of guns. These guns were purchased for protection against the Americans in the War of 1812.

In 1945 the 5th Marquis presented Culzean to The National Trust for Scotland and today the present and 7th Marquis and his family live at Cassillis in Ayrshire. The following year, the top flat of the tower, a charming suite of rooms, was given to General Eisenhower for his lifetime as a thank offering from Scotland for his services as Supreme Commander of the Allied Forces in the Second World War. As President of the United States, he visited Culzean in 1959 and the flat has been used to put up his friends from time to time. Recently he gave his approval for its use for Government hospitality, and under this arrangement the first visit made was that of Prince and Princess Hitachi of Japan in November, 1965. On the basement floor of the tower, the old billiard room has been adapted to make a gay restaurant with enchanting glimpses of the sea from the deep-set windows. Last year, the Victorian west wing was converted into three flats, one of which is now let to Jimmy Logan, the actor, and another to the botanical artist, Miss Bessie Darling Inglis, who arranged an exhibition of her flower paintings there in May, 1966. More people visit Culzean than any other stately home owned by The National Trust in Scotland, the total for 1965 being 92,180. But the cost of maintaining such a place is enormous and an appeal for an endowment fund for Culzean was launched in 1966.

This sturdy Scottish mansion stands out clearly, high above Brodick Bay. A fortress of some kind has stood on this site since the days when the island was occupied by the Danes.

Brodick Castle

In 1958 the National Trust for Scotland was asked by the Treasury to accept the responsibility of taking over, on behalf of the nation, Brodick Castle and grounds, which had been offered by the family of the late Duchess of Montrose in lieu of death duties. To make this possible, a public appeal was launched to raise £10,000, the sum required to supplement the amounts available from various special funds and provide sufficient endowment for the undertaking. This figure was reached successfully, and the castle and its gardens are now among the most popular attractions of the Isle of Arran.

Every historic castle has its own particular character. Brodick, to begin with, has the reserve, the romanticism and the comparative inaccessibility of an island fortress. Arran, the most southerly and best known of the Western Hebrides, and within two hours reach of Glasgow by train and boat, is hardly remote. Yet there is always something a little apart and mysterious about a small island and as one approaches Brodick Bay, dominated by the rose-red castle standing high among dense woods and backed by pointed, rocky peaks, the scene is, without doubt, romantic and picturesque.

But probably more than a thousand years ago, the site was chosen by the Vikings to build a fortress from a more practical point of view. The Arran coast provided these intrepid Norse invaders with shelter for their galley fleets and fortifications were a necessary part of their manoeuvres against the mainland Scots. A stronghold on Arran and the Castle of Rothesay formed the outposts of the Norwegian possession of the Hebrides just before the final cession of the islands to Scotland in 1263 after the Battle of Largs. Nothing remains of the Viking fort at Brodick today, nor of the next castle, said to have been built by James, the High Steward of Scotland to whom the Island of Arran belonged. During the War of Independence the castle was alternately held by the Scots and the English. Robert the Bruce landed on Arran in 1306 and, it seems, besieged and took the castle from Sir John Hastings, the English Governor and his " squyers and yeomanry " and here waited for the kindling of the beacon at Turnberry, the signal for his re-conquest of Scotland.

The castle which with the rest of the Island became crown property when Robert I came to the throne, was attacked and partially destroyed by Donald Balloch of Islay, in league with the rebellious Earl of Ross and the Lord of the Isles. In 1503 James, Lord Hamilton, first cousin to James IV, had " so distinguished himself by feats of strengt hend valour at Holyrood during the rejoicings at the King's marriage, that he was created on the spot the Earl of Arran, and presented with the crown lands of the Island and the Castle of Brodick." A large part of the present castle dates from about this time when began the long connection with the Hamilton family which lasted, with only a few years break, till The Trust took over the property in 1959. The oldest part of the building, where Bruce's tiny room may be seen, is certainly of the 14th century.

It was James V, determined to quell the rebellious chiefs of the Isles, who made frequent journeys to the Hebrides in person. On one of these expeditions in 1540, he stayed with his Hamilton kinsmen at Brodick Castle for a few days. In his train was a French courtier who has left the following record of the Islanders clothing at the time:—" They wear, like the Irish, a large, full shirt coloured with saffron," he wrote, " and over this a garment, hanging to the knee, of thick wool, after the manner of a cassock. They go with bare heads, and allow their hair to grow very long; and they wear neither stockings nor shoes, except some who have buskins, made in a very old fashion which come as high as to their knees." After the death of James V the castle was twice harried by the English—first by the Earl of Lennox, under orders from Henry VIII, in an attempt to force a treaty of marriage between his son Edward and the young Queen Mary. Lennox sailed up the Clyde with a considerable fleet and succeeded in sacking the castle and plundering the island, but he was eventually resisted. No sooner had Brodick been rebuilt than it was battered to a ruin once more by another English expedition under the Earl of Sussex.

In the Civil Wars the Hamiltons were staunch Royalists and James, 3rd Marquess, commanding King Charles' army in Scotland, was in 1643, created Duke of Hamilton. He was executed by order of Cromwell in 1649, only a few weeks after Charles I had suffered the same fate. During this time Brodick

The dining room is in the older part of the castle and contains many sporting prints and trophies collected by the 12th Duke of Hamilton.

The drawing room on the first floor of the Early Victorian wing.

The library with its fine round inlaid table.

Castle was seized, first by one side and then the other. Cromwell's garrison occupied it long enough to build the strong quadrangular tower at the western end in 1652. The old library is housed in this part of the building. The 2nd Duke who was killed at the Battle of Worcester, was succeeded by his sister " Good Duchess Anne " who restored the estates in the early 18th century and was much beloved for her philanthropic and practical improvements to the island, including the building of a pier at Lamlash.

From now on, Brodick Castle grew and developed in peace instead of by wars and the suppression of the lawless Highland and Island chiefs after the '45 Rising brought security at last to the people of Arran. The magnificent family collection of furniture, pictures, books, china and ornaments which may be seen in the castle today belong mainly to these last two hundred and fifty years, although the 17th century is well represented and there are older relics. The difficulties of arranging such a splendid collection in a castle without creating a museum, have, at Brodick been admirably overcome, the main rooms being kept as far as possible as private apartments, with notes about the important items set up in each. Another excellent feature of The Trust administration is the particularly good snack restaurant on the ground floor. French windows in this room open on to the long grass walk on the south side of the castle, where visitors may bring their meals on a tray, and sit overlooking the woods and the village to the firth beyond the bay.

The present entrance at the west end of the castle opens into the Early Victorian wing, built by the architect James Gillespie Graham for the future 11th Duke of Hamilton and his wife, Princess Marie of Baden. In the drawing room which is part of this addition, hangs a charming portrait of the German Princess whose influence seems to linger perceptibly in the northern castle she learnt to love so well. The elaborate heraldic ceiling in the drawing room is typical of the period and in keeping with the unselfconscious grandeur of the room and the furnishings. Through double doors, the old library in the 17th century building houses some of the very fine collection of European and Oriental porcelain. The ceiling in the long dining room also dates from 1844 but the medieval panelling was brought from Letheringham Abbey, a Hamilton estate in Suffolk, and the structure of the room itself belongs to the 16th century. There are many other rooms on view, including the delightful boudoir and bedroom suite lived in by the late Mary, Duchess of Montrose who, as a daughter of the 12th Duke of Hamilton brought the Brodick property to her marriage. In her latter years she made her home at Brodick till her death in 1957. One of her greatest achievements was the planning and creation of the superb gardens as we see them today. From 1919 up to the last years of her life she built up the shape and substance of both the enchanting formal garden at the east end of the castle and the fascinating and far-flung wild garden, now one of the finest in Great Britain, sloping down to the water's edge. Rhododendrons species of bewildering variety, colour and height which bloom from January till August are the main glory of the shrub collection, but there are others as well as many plants and trees from all over the world to delight and astonish both amateur and connoisseur. As one of the former I found this wild garden the most beautiful I had ever seen.

Brodick Castle has been a home for many hundreds of years and more particularly so in this century up to 1957. Nothing has been changed so that even the casual visitor sees and feels something of the Montrose home as it was lived in so lately. In a foreword to The Trust's guide book to the castle, Lady Jean Fforde records her own impression of her former home:—" Brodick Castle, with my mother and father, was home to us, their family. They were homely people, with an intense sense of humour and complete unity one with the other which could not fail to build a home where we returned from school, or on leave and from abroad, for we are a scattered family. How could the walls of this house fail to imbibe some of this happy atmosphere? Some are apt to think of a Duke and Duchess living with a permanent Hollywood backcloth—the Duke and Duchess of Montrose were real people—highly civilised; my mother was an artist and played the piano and violin beautifully. Both were great readers. Both had their feet placed firmly on the ground and so knew there was no chance of any of their family being able to retain a Castle of this size . . . Brodick belonged to my mother and for years she tried to make it possible for the National Trust for Scotland to accept it . . . now her endeavours have borne fruit and no-one would have been more thrilled than she. . ."

Kilkerran House

THE FAMILY HISTORY OF THE Fergussons of Kilkerran, paints an almost complete picture of the Scottish Lowland laird over the last three hundred years. Other families may boast a more spectacular past, ancestors of greater national or romantic fame or a longer pedigree, but few can show with such full documentary evidence, a pattern of living so characteristic of the Lowland laird from the middle of the 17th century to the present day.

The Fergussons of Kilkerran, a family described by a former Lord Lyon King of Arms as one of " the most ancient in Carrick," held lands in Ayrshire from at least the mid-15th century. Impoverished by their adherence to the Royalist cause, the elder branch of the family eventually sold their property—a number of hill farms and the stone Tower of Kilkerran—in 1700 to a first cousin, Sir John Fergusson, who had also bought the adjoining estate and House of Barclanachan with the proceeds of five " eminently successful " years at the Scots Bar. Sir John transferred the name Kilkerran to his new house, rebuilt at the turn of the 17th century and now the centrepiece of the present house. He built over an earlier dwelling, known to have been in existence in 1517 and for nearly two centuries the home of a family of Kennedys of Barclanachan. Parts of the walls and the vaulted cellars of this building are visible today. A distinguished advocate as well as a considerable landowner by the end of the 17th century, Sir John was created a Baronet of Nova Scotia by Queen Anne in 1703. His new house reflected the rise in fame and fortune of the Fergussons of Kilkerran.

Set at the foot of a wooded hill in the valley of the Girvan Water and overlooking wide lawns and a sweeping vista of green parkland trees and rolling fields, the house today has all the restrained grandeur and serenity planned, no doubt, by Sir John, and carried out by the excellent craftsmanship and innate good taste of the builders and masons of the time. Tall and stately, with large symmetrical windows and important chimney-stacks, the original house, built of light greyish-pink local stone, faced north, the entrance set back from a little forecourt formed by the matching east and west elevations. These were joined at right angles by a shorter, central block containing the old Barclanachan Tower. Without the Regency wings added by Sir John's great-grandson, the building looked rather more austere and imposing and may be compared with other William and Mary and Queen Anne houses such as Melville in Fife and Edgerston near Jedburgh. Inside, the rooms are high, spacious and well lighted with panelled walls and—on the first floor—coved ceilings. In this grave and charming house Sir John lived for many years, taking part in some public work in Ayrshire and managing his estate, and here he died in 1729 and was buried in the old disused Tower of Kilkerran.

Long before Sir John's death, his eldest son James, afterwards Lord Kilkerran, had become an ardent " improver " of the estate and in particular was enthusiastic about the tree planting begun here as early as 1715. " I came pretty early to take a liking to planting," he wrote, " and which my father gave me full latitude in, tho' little disposed to it himself . . . I begun in the spring 1711 to sow nurseries—the very year I was admitted advocate and came to live with my father in the country—and spring 1715 begun the hill planting and soon made great progress with it." He was also interested in landscape-gardening and in the new agricultural experiments which were then being introduced to the Lowlands in the teeth of much opposition. He must have been more successful in converting his tenants and neighbours to new ways than many of his fellow lairds for it was said of him that " . . . the common farmers in the neighbourhood who, until they saw what he did, and what crops he got, never so much as once fancied that such barren-like ground was a subject proper for agriculture, begin now to copy after him."

In this age of specialisation and deputation, it is difficult to imagine how Sir James managed to carry out such large scale improvements to the estate, much of it under his own eye, and at the same time to build up his brilliant career at the Bar, to sit for Sutherland in Parliament (if only for a few months) and to take an active part in the bringing up and education of his fourteen children. In 1735 Sir James was raised to the Bench, taking the title of Lord Kilkerran. He had married Lady Jean Maitland, grand-daughter of the 5th Earl of Lauderdale, to whom he was devoted as indeed the whole family were to one another. A liberal education was very near the heart of the Scottish gentry in the 18th century. While his eldest son John (who died of tuberculosis at the age of twenty-three) was spending a year at a well known Dissenting Academy in England but not applying himself with any great ardour to the classics, Lord Kilkerran wrote to him, " Should you, in return for all this, return to me a mere country squire, I ask yourself how you think I ought to take it?" His letters to his son on education and on conduct in general might well instruct many parents today.

LEFT: *The drawing room in the south Regency wing.*

RIGHT: *Five family portraits in the drawing room — top left, Charles Fergusson by Raeburn; bottom left, Adam Fergusson by Pompeo Batoni; centre, Helen Boyle, wife of Sir Charles Fergusson, 5th Bt., by William Dyce; top right, bottom right, Jean and Mary Fergusson by Allan Ramsay.*

LEFT: *The Kilkerran bedroom in the William and Mary part of the house.*

Besides the alterations to the grounds, Lord Kilkerran added to the decoration and furniture of the new house, founding the large library of books, ordering " marble chimneys " (i.e. chimneypieces) from William Adam and employing Allan Ramsay to paint portraits of himself and two daughters. Lady Jean also brought several good portraits of her Lauderdale and Sutherland relations to Kilkerran and the set of embroidered chairs worked by her and her daughters are among the most elegant heirlooms in the house.

Lord Kilkerran was succeeded in 1759 by his second son Sir Adam Fergusson who had followed his father to the Bar and later became Member of Parliament for Ayrshire. " A diligent, honourable, cultivated, kindly man, he was unshakeably orthodox in all that he did, and might stand as the regular type of all conscientious Lowland lairds of the middle and late 18th century." He was disliked by James Boswell, Dr. Johnson's biographer, probably for these very reasons, but respected and admired by most of his contemporaries. Planting and farming with experience and prudence, in his time he made Kilkerran a prosperous and model estate as well as adding much of cultural interest to the house. Painted at different times by Pompeo Batoni, Raeburn and George Watson, all three portraits hang in the house today.

Sir Adam never married and when he died in 1813 he was followed by his nephew Sir James, 4th Baronet, who immediately launched out into large schemes of alteration to the house and grounds. By 1815 the west front of the house had been flanked by two Regency wings with rounded ends, designed by the architect James Gillespie. The present delightful drawing room on the first floor of the south wing remains today predominantly Regency in character with its great triple bow window and pale green watered wallpaper,

The straight staircase added in 1815. In the centre of the north wall hangs a portrait of the Rt. Hon. Sir James Fergusson, 6th Baronet, M.P.

although the pictures and furniture are mixed in date. Sir James also moved the entrance to the west side of the house, adding the straight staircase to the vestibule. Sir Adam "had never spent more than £2,000 a year, including not only his household and personal expenses" but also the large sum needed for maintaining the estate. After two years at Kilkerran Sir James found himself £70,000 in debt. With the help of his uncle, Lord Hermand, a Lord of Session, however, financial matters, in time, were put again on a sound basis.

The final Victorian additions to the house, made by Sir James Fergusson, 6th baronet, include a billiard room designed by David Bryce in 1854, and some twenty years later an enlargement to the dining room, the addition of attics, a porch over the front door and various offices on the east side where a back door was thrown out. In 1956 Kilkerran received a government grant through the Historic Buildings Council for restoration and redecoration which has been used with skill and imagination to bring out the character of each period of building. The advising architect was Mr W. Schomberg Scott. In the dining room, among a gallery of family portraits, hangs Philpot's painting of the late General Sir Charles Fergusson, 7th baronet, who after a long and splendid military career became Governor-General of New Zealand between the years 1924-30. His son, Sir James, the present Laird of Kilkerran who lives there today with his wife, is already one of the most eminent of a remarkable succession. Like some of his ancestors, he not only excels but achieves much in several different spheres. Now Keeper of the Records of Scotland and a leading member of many Historical and Arts Committees, he is well known to the public as a historian, writer and broadcaster. As Laird of Kilkerran and Chief of the Fergussons today, Sir James has a great heritage to which he brings great gifts, not least that scholarship which he has used to put it on record for posterity.

Maxwelton House

A few miles from the village of Moniaive, on the north side of the Cairn valley, Maxwelton House stands above sloping lawns and a formal garden of box-edged parterres, commanding a magnificent view of the wooded heights climbing to the peak of Bogrie Hill, which marks the boundary between Dumfriesshire and the Stewartry. The house, harled a dazzling white against a sombre and rugged background, forms three sides of a square round the courtyard now open to the south. Part of Glenkairn Castle, which stood on the site some five hundred years ago, still remains within the present house—a tower at the south-west corner, a small turret in an angle of the courtyard, two arches in the eastern wing and walls, in places twelve feet thick. This castle or tower was probably built in the 15th century and later enlarged and spread round the courtyard.

ABOVE: *The marriage stone of Anna Laurie's parents, Sir Robert Laurie and Jean Riddell.*

LEFT: *Anna ("Annie") Laurie.*

RIGHT: *Alexander Fergusson of Craigdarroch, husband of Anna Laurie.*

BELOW: *The marriage stone of her grandparents, John Laurie and Agnes Grierson.*

In the year 1373 a royal grant of the Maxwelton and other lands in Glencairn was conferred on Sir Robert Dunyelston, whose daughter inherited them as part of her dowry when she married Sir William Cunningham. Their grandson was created 1st Earl of Glencairn in 1488 by James III, the title being taken from the property. The Cunninghams, descended from Hugh de Morville, Constable of Scotland in the 12th century, continued to live at Maxwelton till it was sold in 1611. They were a powerful family and took a leading part in Border history. When Henry VIII made plans to invade Scotland, William, 4th Earl of Glencairn, was able to guarantee the English army a free passage from Carlisle to Glasgow "without stroke or challenge." Early in the 17th century, James, 7th Earl, implicated in a long standing feud with the Montgomeries found himself on the wrong side of the law, for which he had to pay out large sums of money. This and other material losses may account for the sale of Maxwelton, then a much larger property than it is today, only a small plot of land being retained for the sake of the title.

The estate was bought by Stephen Laurie, a prosperous Dumfries merchant. His wife, the daughter of Provost Corsane of Dumfries, the Member of Parliament for the county, was well endowed and no doubt her fortune was also invested in the new property. The name of the house was now changed to Maxwelton, possibly because Mrs. Laurie had Maxwell forbears or perhaps after a nearby farm on the estate. The new Laird and his wife lived in the heart of the Covenanting country and they themselves supported the Dissenters, but like many other families in Scotland at that time, they were to be split by divided religious loyalties. In 1630 their son John married Agnes Grierson of Lag, daughter of the feared perse-

ABOVE: *Maxwelton from the south, showing the 18th-and 19th-century additions to the old house.*
BELOW: *A view of the drawing room with Anna Laurie's boudoir seen through the archway.*

cutor of the Covenanters who has been immortalised in Scott's novel *Redgauntlet*. Their marriage stone is set over one of the windows in the house today. Stephen Laurie's grandson, Robert, following in the footsteps of his Royalist grandfather, became one of Claverhouse's most active helpers, being made a Baronet of Nova Scotia by the king in 1685.

In 1674 Robert Laurie had married, as his second wife, Jean Riddell of Minto, who bore him nine children. On a December morning in 1682 their fourth daughter was born. "At the pleasure of the Almighty God," Robert wrote, "my daughter Anna Laurie was born upon this, the 16th day of December, 1682, about six o'clock in the morning, and was baptised by Mr. George Hunter, Minister of Glencairn." Little is known of Anna's childhood but as one of a large family brought up in a country house, there is nothing to suggest it was not happy and uneventful. She grew up to be "the most beautiful Dumfriesshire lady of the day," it is said, and as the heroine of the best known love song in Scotland and famous far beyond, this may well be true. Her portrait, which hangs in the house today, describes an oval face, a straight nose, fine dark eyes and hair, and an expression both proud and gentle.

William Douglas of Morton Castle, Fingland, the writer of the song, was ten years older than Anna and, one can hardly doubt it, very much in love with her. But the true story of the wooing has been lost in the mists of tradition, imagination and fantasy. There are so many different versions of their meeting and parting, of the duels Douglas fought for her and the reasons why Anna refused to marry him, that no one story can claim the truth. Douglas, however, seems to have survived his disappointment for he did not "lay him doun and dee," but shortly afterwards married another lady, Elizabeth Clerk of Glendorth, Lanarkshire, the daughter of a flourishing Edinburgh merchant. Three years later, when she was twenty-eight, Anna herself married the son of a neighbour, Alexander Fergusson of Craigdarroch.

It seems certain that Douglas *did* write the original verses to Anna Laurie but they are not exactly the familiar words of the song we know today. The following is the true version

ABOVE: *The library in the 18th-century part of the west wing.*

BELOW: *The dining room.*

The drawing room has some fine pieces of Georgian furniture.

"in a style wonderfully tender and chaste for their age," although the detailed wording of the second verse has been disputed:—

> "Maxwelton Braes are bonnie,
> They're a' clad ower wi' dew,
> Where I an' Annie Laurie
> Made up the bargain true;
> Made up the bargain true,
> Which ne'er forgot s'all be,
> An' for Bonnie Annie Laurie,
> I'd lay me doon and die.
>
> She's backit like a peacock,
> She's breasted like a swan,
> She's jimp about the middle,
> Her waist ye weill may span,
> Her waist ye weill may span,
> And she has a rolling eye,
> And for Bonnie Annie Laurie
> I'd lay me doon and die."

The authenticity of the first verse may perhaps be confirmed by an anecdote related at Maxwelton House towards the end of the last century by an elderly lady who was staying there. While visiting the Rev. Mr. Murray at Morton Manse in Dumfriesshire one evening in 1854, when she was a young wife, she had been asked to sing, and chose from her music *Annie Laurie*. She was afterwards complimented by a Miss Clerk Douglas, an old lady of 90, who said "but those are nae the words my grandfather wrote." Upon request next day, she wrote out the words of the first verse in a shaking hand. When asked how she could be sure they were correct the reply was indignant —"I mind it fine. I have remembered them a' my life. My father often repeated them to me." She signed the verse, below which she wrote, "I mind n' mair." Miss Clerk Douglas was a granddaughter of William Douglas of Morton Castle, Anna Laurie's ardent suitor.

The two verses were first published in 1823, more than a century after they were written by Douglas, in *A Ballad Book*, edited and privately printed by Charles Kirkpatrick Sharpe who added the note "Anne was much celebrated for her beauty, and made a conquest of Mr. Douglas of Fingland, who is said to have composed the verses under an unlucky star. . . ." In 1825 the verses were included in Allan Cunningham's *The Songs of Scotland* where they came to the attention of Alicia Jane Spottiswood of Spottiswood, afterwards Lady John Scott of Buccleuch, a talented musician who composed many of the Scottish songs we know today. Ten years later she altered a few words of the original version to suit the gentility of the time and added a third verse, setting them to music. The song gained instant popularity although Lady John Scott did not divulge her part in it till half a century later. In 1899 she wrote to a friend telling her that she had first sent the song to be published for a bazaar in aid of the widows and orphans of soldiers who had been killed in the Crimean War.

There are no indications that Anna regretted her choice of husband. They seem to have spent a happy married life at Craigdarroch, one of the loveliest country houses in Dumfriesshire. They had several children, one of whom, Alexander, was the hero of Burns' ballad *The Whistle*. Anna long survived her husband and died at the age of 80 at Friar's Carse, the home of her grandson, Robert Riddell, the antiquary and collector of ballads. Anna's brother Robert had succeeded her father at Maxwelton in 1698 but four years later was killed by a fall from his horse. His younger brother Walter became the 3rd Baronet and it was in his time that the west wing of the house was partially destroyed by fire. Presumably either he or his son, who succeeded in 1779, rebuilt part of the present west wing. There is another reconstruction dated 1823 and various later additions in Victorian times. The top floors of the north and east wings date from about 1850 when the porch and conservatory at the present front door were added and certain extensions made to the hall and study. The interior of the house, embracing so many different periods, has also been altered from time to time. The drawing room in the south-west tower overlooking a long and peaceful view of the Cairn valley is a charming room, and is now connected by an archway to the little boudoir where Douglas is said to have proposed to Anna.

Lt.-General Sir Robert Laurie, who died in 1804, was M.P. for Dumfriesshire and Knight Marshal of Scotland. The next generation brought the baronetcy to an end, for Admiral Sir Robert Laurie died without issue in 1848. Through his sister, Mrs. Fector, who married into a Hugenot family living in the south of England, the line was continued. The Rev. Sir Emilius Bayley, Bt., who succeeded to the estate (but not to the baronetcy) in 1887, assumed the name of Laurie by royal licence.

Major-General Sir John Laurie, Bt., C.B.E., D.S.O., late Seaforth Highlanders, who succeeded in 1936, and Lady Laurie, live at Maxwelton today.

Drumlanrig Castle

DRUMLANRIG CASTLE, SURROUNDED BY formal gardens and great woods and magnificently set among high hills bordering the Nith valley, is one of those rare houses which seems to grow in stature and beauty each time it is seen. Built of rose-red sandstone round an inner courtyard, the exterior is square on plan, four tall towers rising at each corner above the intervening wings. A perfectly devised approach to the north front, the long, straight lime avenue allows an unhurried first view of this very grand facade with its double flight of stone steps leading to the main entrance, the richly carved ornament over windows and doorways and the bold outline carried up to a flourish of turrets and chimneys on the skyline.

Built between the years 1679-90 by the 1st Duke of Queensberry, Drumlanrig stands on the site of two older castles, the earlier raised by William de Douglas, first of Drumlanrig, who was knighted by James I in 1424. More than a hundred years later, after English raiders had devastated the lands and the castle, Sir James Douglas, 7th Lord Drumlanrig (1498-1578), set about restoring his property and "beildit the haill hous and pallice of Drumlanrig." Practically nothing remains of this second stronghold except a cellar in the present house.

Although first and foremost a man of war, Sir James left Drumlanrig richer in lands and power. He was followed by other lairds who showed an interest in the cultivation of their growing property and skill in its administration. In 1617 James VI was entertained at the castle by Sir William Douglas, who was later created Earl of Queensberry by Charles I. The 2nd Earl supported the king in the Civil War and Drumlanrig was again attacked, this time by the Parliamentary party. In spite of £2000 compensation, paid after the Restoration of Charles II in 1660, the damage seems to have been too great to repair and William, the 3rd Earl, demolished the remains of the castle in 1675, a few years before the present house was begun.

As early as 1618, however, plans for a new castle had been drawn up by the 1st Earl. Upon these designs his grandson based the outline of the existing house, begun more than half a century later. A note by the Duke on the old plans "to be looked over and advised by Sir Wm. Bruise" had established a likelihood that Bruce was, at least in an advisory capacity, concerned with the building. Although the actual drafts and contracts have disappeared, recent research has uncovered some fresh facts of interest. From Queensberry's letters it is clear that James Smith (according to Colin Campbell's comment in *Vitruvius Britannicus* "the most experienc'd architect in that Kingdom"—i.e. Scotland) was the directing architect under whose orders worked William Lukup, the builder.

James Smith was the son-in-law of Robert Mylne, the sixth of his family to hold the post of King's Master Mason, and had worked with him on various projects including, in 1678, Holyroodhouse. The Queensberry correspondence also reveals that Robert Mylne (referred to as "Mr. Mills") had worked for the Duke on plans for a bridge and other items at Drumlanrig. This information opens up new possibilities about the architect of the castle. While James Smith seems the more likely claimant, he may merely have carried out designs by his father-in-law, Robert Mylne, who was certainly the leading exponent of the Scottish Baronial style to which Drumlanrig is most nearly related. Finally, going back to the basic plans of 1618, so reminiscent of the contemporary Heriot's Hospital in Edinburgh, built

ABOVE: *Drumlanrig from the north and from the south-west.*

by William Wallace, the conjecture arises as to whether he might be responsible for the original Drumlanrig design.

Although Drumlanrig is traditionally Scottish in feeling, it marks a new departure in building. While the spirit of the medieval castle has been subtly recaptured in such features as the corbelling of the main tower turrets, the angle turrets of the courtyard and in the massiveness of the building as a whole, the emphasis on symmetry and the baroque enrichment of the exterior show the influence of Renaissance ideas. Some of the most brilliant and original houses in Scotland are of this period when the old Scottish Gothic merged with the classical style.

The building of Drumlanrig cost the Duke a fortune and it is said that on the bundle of accounts he left a curse on any of his descendants who should pry into the extravagance—"The Deil pike oot his een wha looks herein." It is also said that he spent only one night in the castle and retired for the rest of his days to Sanquhar Castle in greatly reduced circumstances. There is a touching letter from his Duchess to a kinsman, imploring him to buy her a silk gown as she was penniless. The Duke held various state appointments under Charles II from whom he received his title in 1684 while the work on Drumlanrig was in progress. But when James VII and II succeeded and it became obvious that he was resolved to re-establish Papacy, Queensberry resigned his public posts in disapproval, retired from court and gave his whole attention to the finishing of Drumlanrig.

Another pointer to the earlier theory that Bruce had a hand in the building plans was the fact that two Dutch workmen employed at his home, Kinross House, were sent to Drumlanrig to carry out some of the resplendent carving which embellishes the north front. Originally the entrance hall was divided from the inner courtyard only by an open arcade, the present closed-in hall having been altered in preparation for a visit by Queen Victoria which, in fact, never materialised. Four round stair towers stand at the corners of the central courtyard, the turrets soaring above the roof-line. The interior of the castle is closer to English planning of the time, the wide straight staircase and passages connecting the rooms being then rare in Scotland. All the state rooms, lit by long windows, are panelled in oak (renewed in the 19th century, as were most of the panelled ceilings, with careful workmanship) and there are some beautiful wood carvings by the great Grinling Gibbons and one of his pupils. Almost every window frames an enchanting vista—of the formal gardens below, set among green lawns, wooded hills rising on all sides, or a quiet reach of the river.

Today, these handsome rooms make a stately setting for one of the most princely collections of furniture, paintings, silver and

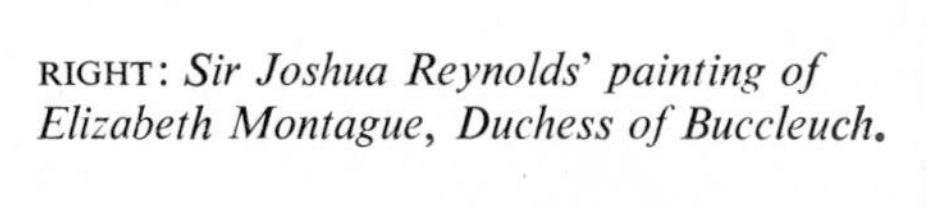

RIGHT: *Sir Joshua Reynolds' painting of Elizabeth Montague, Duchess of Buccleuch.*

RIGHT: *The Regency bed, brought from Dalkeith Palace.*

china in Scotland. French and English pieces of the 17th and 18th century, many of them presents to the family from both Courts, hold pride of place, but there is much else of wide interest. An excellent collection of paintings from almost every European country and period include family portraits by many of the great English painters of the 18th and early 19th centuries and by Raeburn and Allan Ramsay. A number of these have been inherited from the Buccleuchs as well as the Queensberries and brought from family homes on both sides of the Border. One of the loveliest things in the house is the superb Charles I silver chandelier which hangs above the staircase today. In the drawing room are two exquisite Louis XIV cabinets given by the French King to Charles II and by him, as a wedding present, to his son, the Duke of Monmouth and Buccleuch. Such a collection, in itself a combined art gallery and museum, is set in ideal surroundings, for Drumlanrig remains a family home where the present is still more important than the great pageant of the past.

The 2nd Duke, who succeeded in 1695, was made Secretary of State under Queen Anne and was jointly responsible for the Union of the Scottish and English Parliaments in 1707. Powerful and purposeful, he is said to have ruled Scotland for ten years. Queen Anne rewarded him for his service with gifts including portraits of herself and William of Orange and his Queen, which now hang above the staircase at Drumlanrig.

His son, Duke Charles, continued to support the House of Hanover and in December, 1745, Drumlanrig was invaded by Prince Charles Edward's army on the retreat from Derby. The chamberlain wrote to inform the absent Duke of the incident. ". . . . they laid straw in all the rooms for the private men to lye on, except Your Grace's bedroom (where the Prince lay) . . . they killed about 40 sheep . . . most of them in the vestibule near the low dining room and the foot of the principle stair which they left in a sad pickle, as indeed they did the whole house. Under the gallery, they keeped several of their horses which they made shift to get up the front stair. . . . By the nearest computation I can make, at least 2000 of them lodged in the house and stables. Drink money 10 gns." Some of the pictures in the house still bear the marks of the Highlanders' claymores.

Duke Charles, who was much beloved in the countryside, married Lady Kitty Hyde, famous for her beauty, high spirits and wit, and for a rumbustious eccentricity which livened Court circles as well as her friends and enemies. Her manner of flouting decorum was, for instance, to appear at Court dressed as a Scottish peasant, to send her husband to a royal fancy

RIGHT: *The oak staircase. The portrait on the right is of Queen Anne by Kneller.*

The panelled drawing room has a wood carving by Grinling Gibbons set above the chimneypiece.

dress ball in the kilt after George II had banned the wearing of Highland dress, and to suspend a ball at Drumlanrig one evening as she could not bear the noise of the band. She was cured of both headache and whim this time, however, by her son, who pushed her round the floor in an armchair and eventually persuaded her to allow the festivities to continue.

Her circle of friends included Horace Walpole, Jonathan Swift, William Pitt, Pope and John Gay, who wrote *The Begger's Opera*. The roaring success of this piece was not altogether approved of in court circles in view of the caricaturing of various public figures, and Gay was refused a licence to produce his second opera, *Polly*. This so provoked the Duchess that, much against the King's will, she touted for subscriptions among her friends at court to help the penniless playwright. Finally, after a spirited correspondence with His Majesty on the subject, she was asked to withdraw herself from Court. Flouncing off to Drumlanrig, she entertained Gay there while he was convalescing after an illness. He evidently spent his time going through the library, picking out books which pleased him and dispatching them to London—whether for the Duke or himself is not known.

Duke Charles was predeceased by both his sons and when he died, in 1778, the long succession of father to son, stretching over nearly four hundred years, was broken. He was succeeded by the Earl of March and Ruglen who died unmarried in 1810. "Old Q.," as he was known, a gambler and bon viveur of extravagant tastes, not only neglected the estates but denuded them of trees to pay his debts. Both Burns and Wordsworth have left laments for this "unworthy deed". In 1810 the 3rd Duke of Buccleuch succeeded to the Queensberry estates and titles (through his grandmother, Lady Jane Douglas) and these two great houses were joined. Seldom in Scotland has such much in land, titles and property devolved on one family. The Scotts of Buccleuch, themselves an old and renowned Border family, brought to the Douglas story another equally long and dramatic as well as connections far beyond Scotland. Royal blood ran in their veins through the marriage of Anna, Duchess of Buccleuch, to the ill fated Duke of Monmouth, illegitimate son of Charles II and Lucy Walter, a descendant of Edward I of England.

Many old familes who rose to power and held their lands at the point of the sword in early days have since disappeared. Not so the Buccleuchs, who turned from fighting to take up responsible leadership on the Borders and later in national affairs. With this change of direction went an ever-growing skill in the cultivation and administration of their lands. For many years now the Lairds of Drumlanrig have been pioneers in progressive agriculture, forestry and estate management. The preservation of Drumlanrig's immense beauty and rich historic interest today owes much to this practical gift.

In the morning room hangs Van Dyck's portrait of Queen Henrietta Maria, wife of Charles I.

The oval hall with the wide staircase curving across the long windows.

Gribloch

Gribloch from the south-west.

GRIBLOCH IS ONE OF THE RARE MILEstones in 20th century domestic architecture. The last sixty years or so in Great Britain has been a time of scientific revolution largely at the expense of artistic achievement, and architecture has fared worse than any of the arts, not so much for lack of talent as of funds and (in the case of the country house) of demand. The few houses of this sort built in Scotland since the First World War have tended to look back to the past for inspiration. We have not been sure of a new form or what to fashion from the more established ideas of various other European countries.

Gribloch, built in 1938-39, is new not only in time but also in design. Yet even the eye accustomed to " functional " building will not discern any precise modern " ism " in the house as a whole. There is nothing stark or crude about its bold outline, and the broad wings and flat roof are skilfully balanced by sweeping curves and rounded windows which subtly suggest sustained movement.

First of all, it is a house with a view—surely one of the most magnificent in Scotland. Near the village of Kippen on the edge of Gribloch Moor, the house, in a high situation, commands a splendid panorama of the blue-tinged Grampians from the giant peak of Ben Lomond in the west to Ben Vorlich, and stretching away to the Ochils on the eastward horizon. To the south, the wide valley is bounded by Fintry and the Gargunnock Hills.

Arriving at the front door, it is difficult at first to take one's eyes off this spectacular semi-circle of natural grandeur. The north entrance of the house, a shallow concave curve, with the door set in the centre under a pillared balcony of wrought iron (the little windows on either side of the porch also have wrought iron grilles) is disarmingly simple and unpretentious. Walking round the bow-ended west corner, another aspect appears—rounded windows overhung by a verandah swerving away from the solid south-west wing—which suggests something of the Regency period in building. The south front—and you must walk quite a long way across the lawn and down the birch-bordered avenue to get a full view—is impressive. Two angled wings run out from the central convex portion, which consists of long vertical windows reaching from just under the roof line to the ground. A swimming pool surrounded by a flagged stone pathway is sunk in the sheltered enclosure thus formed, and lawns sweep outwards to make a green level foreground to this very grand, very dignified southern facade.

A sense of space is, I think, one of the main enchantments at Gribloch. The splendour of the mountainous, almost Alpine, panorama, ever present but ever changing in colour and contour, is perhaps the dominant factor. But the setting and design of the house, although constructed in a completely different medium (there is not the faintest reflection of the upward movement with which the towers, turrets, the spires and domes of the old Scottish style of building echoed their surroundings), suggest, first and foremost, space, light and expansion.

This is emphatically carried out in the interior, which is remarkable not only in form but above all in the bold and exciting use of colour. Mr and Mrs Colville, for whom Gribloch was built and who live in the house today, spent a year discussing the plans with Sir Basil Spence and Mr Perry Duncan, a New York architect who gave some assistance to the project. Various firms of designers in decoration and furniture were also consulted, but Mrs Colville, who is an American by birth, may be responsible herself for many of the best ideas. The Americans are acknowledged colourists, but not until I had seen the interior of Gribloch did I realise how revolutionary their conception appears compared to ours. Beside the neutral tones, the subdued chintzes and self-effacing pastels we are addicted to in Britain, the treatment of Gribloch stands a world away in vigour, in decision and in vivid, unimagined beauty. You are aware of this the moment you enter the oval hall with its turquoise blue wall, deep mauve carpet and curtains and white detail (all three colours are woven into the feathered pattern of the carpet). Here the main feature is the wide staircase curving across the long windows like a cascade of water pouring into a pool below. The wrought iron balustrade is painted white.

The living room, where the wide bow of windows frames the north-westerly chain of Grampians (here a mahogany kidney-shaped writing table commands the full roving view), is another study in colour. Against a background of oyster-shaded walls and pale-blue ceiling, an off-white, faintly pink carpet with lime green and charcoal chair covers make an impressive composition. Once again the four colours are repeated in gaily-patterned curtains. It is a restful, confortable room, inviting study and ease. Completely different in character is the more traditional drawing room, where Queen Anne furniture and an Adam mantelpiece harmonise with the heavy satin rose-pink curtains and beautiful Aubusson carpets.

Upstairs, in all the bedrooms, the nursery

ABOVE: *The drawing room.*

LEFT: *The red bedroom, where red and grey provide a study in colour contrast.*

and the service suite, contrasting colour and form make each room a fascinating subject. The many ingenious labour-saving devices (like the tip-up doors in every fire-grate which lead to a chute down which the ashes descend to a basement ash-bin, and the oil-fired central heating (which supplies hot water and also warmth for the swimming-pool) explain the possibility of running such a house today.

One last word about colour—in the oldest setting of all. Gribloch garden, with its vistas of brilliantly coloured flowering shrubs and the strong colour-grouping in the more formal flower arrangements beyond the garden gate, shows how well such heightened effects can become the Scottish countryside. Thirty years ago, heather and bracken roamed over this bare rocky moor, which was a favourite place to picnic in Mr Colville's childhood. Ever since then, the idea of building a house on the site had simmered in his mind. Now the day-dream is fact, the idea reality, a heartening thought in a century of broken dreams.

Falkland Palace from the north-west.

Falkland Palace

Of all the royal palaces in Scotland, Falkland is the least altered in aspect since the days of the Stuarts. Before the building of the Forth Road Bridge, this palace was a little remote from the main lines of traffic, but this situation has been notably changed in the last few years.

Under the green Lomond Hills, on the edge of the Howe of Fife, the little Royal burgh of Falkland clusters round the palace as if it had no pretensions to an independent life of its own, white-washed cottages with red pantiled roofs jostling each other under the very shadow of the great stone gatehouse. Reminiscent of a medieval French village built round its château, Falkland came into being by a king's command to supply the palace with food, drink and service. This was in the time of James II, but the setting remains much the same today.

In June, 1952 The National Trust for Scotland acquired the Palace of Falkland—in so far as royal property can be acquired by any person or body. With legal advice on the point, Major Michael Crichton-Stuart, Heritable Constable, Captain and Keeper of the Palace, who has endowed it for the future, was able to appoint the Trust Deputy Keeper of Falkland Palace. Her Majesty the Queen was informed and replied that she had "taken note of it."

It is thought that the site of the palace dates back to the beginning of the 12th century, and the foundations of the 13th century Falkland Castle, which was the home of the Earls of Fife, can be seen today. It was here that the Regent Duke of Albany imprisoned the Duke of Rothesay then heir to the Scottish throne. Sir Walter Scott, in his novel *The Fair Maid of Perth*, elaborates the popular legend of Rothesay's murder in the castle prison, and if documentary evidence disclaims such dark melodrama, it is not the first time that Scott has willingly been granted poetic licence. The present palace, begun by James II in 1451, was designed as a country residence rather than a military stronghold, and the King's household enjoyed good hunting as well as such pleasures as music and dancing, painting and poetry. For the Stuarts had a fine appreciation of the arts. James IV and V were both much attached to Falkland, and it was after the disastrous battle of Solway Moss that the latter died here—it is said, of a broken heart. Being told of the birth of a daughter just before he died, the King made his comment on the Stuart dynasty—"It cam with a lass and it will gang with a lass." But before her tragic end, Mary Queen of Scots found some of the happiest days of her life at Falkland.

Meantime the palace grew in stature. The magnificent gatehouse and archway and the chapel date from the beginning of the 16th century.

James V is responsible for the lovely court-

ABOVE: *The drawing room in the gatehouse where the present Keeper of the Palace, now lives.*

BELOW LEFT: *On the second floor of the gatehouse is a bedroom with a Shakespearian aspect.*

RIGHT: *The tirling pin on the wicket door.*

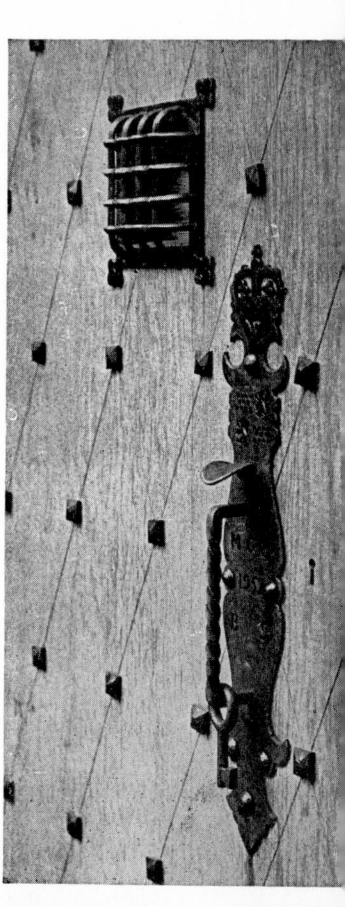

LEFT: *In the drawing room of the gatehouse is a unique portrait of James VI, dated 1586.*

yard exterior of the south front with its Renaissance columns and circular panels containing carved heads—probably of court characters. No other important building in Scotland shows such fine Renaissance detail so early, although the corbels supporting the roof are similar to those of the Banqueting Hall at Edinburgh Castle. James V spent some time at the French court and passionately admired the Renaissance châteaux of the Loire country. He brought back with him French workmen to carry out designs on his own buildings, for at Stirling also there is evidence of such handiwork.

James VI, too, added his contribution to the palace—at very little personal expense. Proclaiming a royal levy among his subjects in Fife, he commanded his tenants to provide slates, lime, sand and timber for the restoration of the building, making known that he would accept this assistance as a "gratitude." When completed, the palace surrounded three sides of the courtyard, the fourth being enclosed by a high western wall. Standing on the green courtyard lawn today, one can visualise the extent of its ancient grandeur. The south front, of mellow greyish-golden stone, remains whole and beautiful. Traditionally the home of the Palace Keeper, the gatehouse is now lived in by Major and Mrs. Crichton-Stuart. The east wing, a superb facade, largely restored by the late Lord Bute, was partially gutted by fire in the reign of Charles II, which completely destroyed the north wing. Only the foundation stones of this remain, now planted with a rose garden.

With the death of James VI, Falkland ceased to be a regular retreat for the royal family, although both Charles I and II visited the palace. Nearly three hundred years later, Her Majesty Queen Mary spent a day there. In the interim the palace gradually fell into disrepair, and was not rescued from ruin until the 19th century. During the 1715 Rising, Rob Roy Macgregor occupied it, after the battle of Sheriffmuir, as a base for plundering the countryside. In 1887, the 3rd Marquis of Bute acquired the property and carried out thorough and skilful restorations on a large scale. At a time when doubtful taste, backed by wealth, disfigured much good old Scottish building, Lord Bute achieved outstanding results on traditional lines. His family continued the immense task of building up the palace, and his grandson, the present Keeper, has made great progress in a comparatively short time. Already the gardens, replanted on the original site and following the 16th century lay-out, make a delightful vista, and the interior of the gatehouse has been transformed into a charming home. Within the palace gardens stands the unique royal tennis court, the only one of its kind remaining in Scotland, where the old game of tennis was played within four high walls. This tennis court is now in play, a club having been formed in 1965.

The historic interest and ancient setting of Falkland Palace make it one of the more important of The National Trust's properties. But perhaps most exciting of all today is the realisation that life stirs once more in a palace which is a home and not merely a relic of the past.

ABOVE: *A view of Falkland from the east by the 17th-century engraver John Slezer. Falkland has changed little since Stuart times and the little royal burgh of Falkland still clusters round the palace.*

The eastern facade of the palace from the courtyard. This was partially destroyed by a fire, in the reign of Charles II, which completely destroyed the north wing.

The spiral staircase in the south wing.

ABOVE: *Balcaskie from the south-west.*
LEFT: *The south face overlooking the terraced gardens and the Firth of Forth.*

Balcaskie

SIR WILLIAM BRUCE IN HIS LIFETIME literally changed the architectural face of Scotland by establishing the Renaissance style of building. Before his time Scottish Baronial, the last phase of individual national building, was supreme and scarcely touched by outside influence. When Bruce died in 1710 the purely Scottish idiom had been all but abandoned. Balcaskie, rebuilt by Bruce about 1670, is probably his earliest house. Although the exterior is almost certainly an enlargement and elaboration of an older building, his experiments, both outside and in, make a fascinating study. In many ways Balcaskie was the workshop in which Bruce discovered his talent and scope.

A long straight drive leads up to the house, which stands about two miles inland from the village of Pittenweem in the East Neuk of Fife. The north entrance front, an oblong centrepiece connected to outlying wings by curving screen walls and facing a wide semi-circle of green lawn and grey gravel, foreshadows many of Bruce's later designs. As it stands, the main block is three-storeyed with, at each corner, a projecting pavilion, the two northern ones flanking crow-stepped gables. The porch and Venetian window above are early 19th century additions, and later Victorian work stands not very obtrusively at the east and west ends of the house. The tall rugged gables remain solidly Scottish, but the whole north front is dignified and restful with the new, more precise charm of symmetry and classical proportion. The south aspect of Balcaskie, overlooking the great terraced gardens, turns its back even more decisively on the medieval past, expanding in the new grand manner from the Italian statues on the lawn to the distant Bass Rock at the far end of the long vista across gardens, parkland and sea. Such a far-flung yet care-

ABOVE: *The buttressed walls and terraced gardens below the house.*

RIGHT: *Portrait of Janet Anstruther, wife of Sir Thomas Strang, by Raeburn's master Owen.*

fully calculated vista is a hallmark of Bruce's designs, as at, notably, Hopetoun House in West Lothian and Kinross House on Loch Leven.

In the house today hangs a charter of 1223 confirming the house and lands of Balcaskie to one Juan Cook, son of Nigel Cook, whose family probably assumed the name of their property. They remained there for more than a century. The next owners were Strangs, and by 1362 John Strang was married to Cecilia de Anstruther, which is the first connection with the present Balcaskie family. The estate was next acquired through marriage by a branch of the Moncrieff family of Moncrieff, who, in 1665, sold it to William Bruce.

William was the second son of Robert Bruce of Blairhall. The date of his birth is uncertain, but by 1660 he was Clerk of Bills and some years later Surveyor to Charles II, for whom he restored and rebuilt Holyroodhouse. A zealous Royalist and supporter of the Restoration, in his youth and early manhood it seems he was more occupied with politics than with architecture. In 1663 he was King's Messenger in Scotland, yet in spite of the pressure of state business, Bruce must have studied building with enthusiasm and industry. Travelling in Italy, he absorbed Renaissance architecture with a lively intelligence, and, as Inigo Jones had done for England, brought it back to his native country with the fervour of a convert and the imagination and ability to translate rather than copy.

The long unbroken line of the south front of the house, with its tall chimneys, steepish roof of golden-lichened slates and row of semi-dormers, has been somewhat altered in appearance by the long windows and veranda running the length of the first floor, added in the 19th century. The bow window is mid-Victorian. Balustraded stone steps lead down from the wide green plateau of lawn and flagged rose-gardens before the house to the terrace on the next level, where high buttressed walls make impregnable shelter for palm trees, magnolias, New Zealand laburnum, Indian strawberry and all manner of shrubs and plants, many of them rare so far north. Grey lichened Grecian urns set on the balustrade above the wall and weathered busts of Roman emperors perched on the buttresses overlook this grand terrace with its lawns and flowerbeds. I can remember no more splendid yet peaceful garden in Scotland, with its superbly ordered view to the Firth of Forth. The walled gardens on the lower terrace were added to Bruce's design in the 19th century.

The interior has been altered somewhat since Bruce finished the house. From the hall a Victorian staircase leads up to a long gallery which was originally an open court. The drawing room, opening off the gallery, is a long, spacious room with four south-looking french windows, where a number of good paintings are well shown, among them family portraits by Reynolds, a crayon set of Georgian ancestors by John Downman (1750-1824) and

BELOW: *This painting by Jacopo Bassano, in which El Greco and his daughter were used as models, hangs in the smoking room.*

ABOVE: *The drawing room opening off the gallery, is a long spacious room with four south-looking french windows.*

LEFT: *The Globe room on the second floor has an almost medieval coved ceiling with plaster bands and a central hanging globe bearing the Signs of the Zodiac.*

an interesting portrait by Raeburn's master, Owen. In the library and dining room are landscapes by Gainsborough. The richly encrusted plasterwork ceiling has a central garland of flowers in deep relief surrounded by flatter clusters of fruit and leaves. A Savonnerie carpet, Louis XVI chairs worked in petit point and gilt console tables give the room a not very marked French aspect, for there are also handsome English and Dutch pieces of the 18th century.

In the smaller, square library, where bookcases have been built into the walls and an Adam period carved mantelpiece inserted, a bold animated ceiling dominates the room. The central painting of a Venus with cherubs

ABOVE: *The ceiling in Sir William Bruce's bedroom with his initials and those of his first wife, Mary Halkett.*

RIGHT: *The library.*

in clouds is framed by a hanging garland, the only known example by Bruce. An octagonal outer ridge is surrounded by medallions between leaves, acorns and fruit in deep relief and plump winged ladies practically in the round. The Globe room on the second floor has an almost medieval coved ceiling with plaster bands and a central hanging globe bearing the Signs of the Zodiac. In the bedroom next door, within a decorated panel, are the intertwined initials of William Bruce and his first wife, Mary Halkett.

Bruce sold Balcaskie in 1684, and in 1698 the estate was bought by Sir Robert Anstruther, ancestor of the present Laird. About the same time that the Cook family was invested in the lands of Balcaskie, the Anstruthers were established in Dreel Castle, their earlier seat, which stood above the sea at Anstruther. Possibly the first builder of the castle was William de Candela (1124-53)—"William of the Candle," a Norman baron whose name suggests he was a household officer of King David I, as were the Cooks of Balcaskie and the Chamberlains of Lundin nearby. The Anstruther family flourished and became powerful as landowners, leaders and the owners of trading ships, and intermarried with most of the old Lowland families. Their history, before they came to Balcaskie, long, eventful and spiced with traditions too entertaining to be wholly fictitious, is a great one and cannot be told here. King James VI had a particular liking for Sir James Anstruther, whom he knighted and, in 1592, made Master of the Royal Household. His son, Sir William, "the burly laird of Anster," the King called him, was a gentleman of the bedchamber, and created Knight of the Bath at the Coronation of 1603. Sir William's nephew and successor, Philip, was knighted at Scone in 1650 and next year escorted Charles II on his tour of Fife. It was on this occasion that the King, after dining at Dreel Castle, called the rugged old tower "a craw's nest" and so mortified the Laird that he there and then resolved to build a new house at Anstruther (it was destroyed in 1811).

It was Sir Philip's third son, Sir Robert—created a Baronet in 1694—who bought Balcaskie in 1698, soon after adding to it most of the Abercrombie lands. From this time to the present day the property and title have passed directly from father to son with two exceptions. General Robert Anstruther, who died in Corunna after the battle of 1809 and is buried there beside Sir John Moore, predeceased his father. The General's son, Sir Ralph, made most of the 19th century alterations and additions to Balcaskie. Perhaps, fortunately for posterity, his plans were curtailed by lack of funds.

But if the bones of the house are sacred to Bruce, it is to the Anstruther family, who have lived there for more than two and a half centuries, that the place owes its great charm and beauty today and the lively warmth of continuity. Besides the fine collection of paintings in the house, much exquisite china, old books, glass and silver, there are many treasured family relics of interest, including a gift from Queen Anne, a miniature of herself and the little Duke of Gloucester.

The present Laird, Sir Ralph Anstruther, 7th Baronet, M.C., who succeeded his grandfather in 1934, served as a Major in the Coldstream Guards and, following in the footsteps of several forefathers with court appointments, is now an Equerry and Treasurer to Queen Elizabeth, the Queen Mother. Sir Ralph's mother, Mrs. Robert Anstruther, who now lives at Balcaskie, takes a large and active part in maintaining the house and gardens as they are today—one of the loveliest, most historic and delightful homes in Scotland.

Balmanno Castle

The approach to Balmanno Castle through a narrow lane off the main Edinburgh-Perth road near the village of Glenfarg, leaves the visitor totally unprepared for his journey's end. Agricultural land and farmsteads stretch in peaceful monotony towards the slopes of the Ochil Hills, until the last sharp corner is turned and through the arched gateway the castle appears with all the dramatic force of a spectacular stage production as the curtain goes up. Very tall and sheer and dazzlingly white, the solid walls rise to crow-stepped gables and higher to the square tower and topmost turret, soaring above the steep roof-lines, with its pinnacle of a weather-cock silhouetted against the sky. Far down on the north side a gabled two-storeyed building stands humbly beneath the high glory of the castle. After the first sudden impact, as the eye begins to focus building and background, the puzzle of date and style is posed. Undoubtedly traditional, the castle has an unaccustomed splendour for its period, so that the newcomer to Balmanno is both visually bewitched and intellectually intrigued before the castle is entered.

The family of Balmanno of that ilk who owned the property in 1530 seem to have disappeared into obscurity. Soon after that date they sold the estate to George Auchinleck, a cousin and "notorious instrument" of the Regent Morton, who built the present castle, according to the Great Seal Register, in 1570-80. Although it was semi-fortified with massive walls and an outlook tower with a defensive parapet, Balmanno was, in effect, a country house and one of the earliest in Scotland. Traditional in plan, with two wings built at right-angles in the shape of an L and a staircase tower set between the two inner joints, the steep, crow-stepped gables and solid chimney-stacks are typical but tamer versions of Scottish Baronial castle detail. With three large reception rooms on the first floor and a number of good-sized bedrooms above, the Auchinlecks in 1580 could boast of a spacious, important house in which to practise the gracious living which, after the more Spartan existence enforced by the old military dwellings, was now developing in Scotland. Unfortunately, no furniture or decoration of this period survives at Balmanno to compare with such contemporary houses as Earlshall in Fife and Crathes Castle in Aberdeenshire.

Towards the end of the 17th century Balmanno was sold by George Auchinleck's great-grandson, Archibald, to Anthony Murray, an Edinburgh merchant and younger son of Sir Thomas Murray of Glendoick on the other side of the Tay. Little is known of their tenure there, but a certain laconic Sir Peter Murray of Balmanno is commemorated in verse by the eccentric minor poetess, Lady Anne Dick of Corstorphine (a grand-daughter of Sir George "Bluidy Mackenzie"), who had evidently found no favour in his eyes. She writes sadly:

Oh, wherefore did I cross the Forth,
And leave my love behind me?
Why did I venture to the north
With one that did not mind me?

Had I but visited Carin!
It would have been much better,
Than pique the prudes and make a din
For careless cold Sir Peter.

I'm sure I've seen a better limb,
And twenty better faces:
But still my mind it ran on him,
When I was at the races.

At night when we went to the ball,
Were many there discreeter:
The well-bred duke and lively Maule,
Panmure behaved much better.

They kindly showed their courtesy,
And looked on me much sweeter:
Yet easy could I never be,
For thinking on Sir Peter.

Though Powrie left me for the spleen,
My temper grew no sweeter:
I think I'm mad—what do I mean,
To follow cold Sir Peter.

In 1752 Balmanno passed with an heiress to the Belshes of Invermay, descending again in the female line, through a daughter of Sir John Stuart Forbes of Pitsligo, to Lord Clinton, who owned it at the end of the 19th century. In 1916 it was acquired by the late Mr. W. Miller, who employed Sir Robert Lorimer to make a complete restoration of the castle and gardens. When Mr. Miller bought Balmanno it was in use as a farm house, a tall, grey, gaunt building, partly surrounded by a moat, still filled with water. Deserted by the gentry, the house had escaped Victorian alterations and additions, and Lorimer was faced with the bare but original bones of a 16th century building. It was a task much to his liking and one which he fulfilled at the height of his powers. The moment has come, many years after his death, for some people to decry Lorimer's genius as an architect. The present movement away from Romanticism in building is not sympathetic to his traditional ideals. But such a perceptible swing of opinion is automatic rather than reasoned, and Lorimer will almost certainly prove to be one of the giants who can well withstand the slings and arrows of passing criticism. In his book,

LEFT: *A detail of the plasterwork frieze in the Hunter's Bedroom.*

The Works of Sir Robert Lorimer, published in 1931, Christopher Hussey says: ". . . there was no living tradition of architecture in Scotland before he (Lorimer) unearthed and assimilated it. . . ." To forget this fact, in critical detail of his work, is to make nonsense of Lorimer's main contribution to Scottish building.

The interior, also entirely planned by Lorimer, from the structural alterations to the furniture for each room, made by Messrs. Whytock and Reid, is comparable to the full scale and detailed designing carried out by Robert Adam for his clients. Lorimer's furniture is no longer at Balmanno, but little else has been substantially changed. In 1950 the castle was sold to the present owner, the Hon. James Bruce, a son of the Earl of Elgin, who lives there today with his wife and family. The original tower entrance is still used, the front door opening into the vaulted ground floor apartments which once accommodated cellars, offices, storage room and kitchens. These Lorimer converted to family living rooms—a long cool stone hall to the left of the door, and beyond, to the right, a dining room within the old kitchen. With this transformation of kitchen-into-dining room in 1921, Lorimer set a fashion which has since been followed in numbers of 16th and 17th century houses and castles. At Balmanno, where the proportions are particularly good, cream-painted vaulted walls reflect a sunny light over the room, throwing up the dark outline of naked stone round the old kitchen chimneypiece. The wood-block floor covered by a carpet in blue-green tones gives the room ease and warmth, the long refectory oak table exactly suits the dimensions, and handsome 17th century Flemish chairs upholstered in olive green velvet add a touch of grandeur. The wrought-iron chandelier was part of Lorimer's decorations.

On the first floor the two main reception rooms are connected by double doors. The drawing room, looking south, was, in the 18th century, turned into a main entrance hall approached by a flight of stone steps from the garden. Lorimer panelled the walls in oak and put in the plasterwork ceiling with its deeply

LEFT: *The top of the wheel stair with its wrought-iron balustrade modelled by the late Thomas Haddon.*

LEFT: *The dining room within the old kitchen. With this transformation of kitchen-into-dining room in 1921, Lorimer set a fashion which has been followed in numbers of 16th- and 17th-century houses and castles.*

BELOW, TOP: *The drawing room.*

BOTTOM: *A panelled bedroom on the second floor.*

recessed circular centre surrounded by decorative work in vine-leaf pattern which was hand-moulded by the late Sam Wilson. Persian rugs, modern furniture mixed with older pieces and paintings by Zoffany, Patrick Naysmith, Crome the elder and others give this room a comfortable elegance. Next door, a children's playroom replaces Lorimer's billiard-room, also with a richly ornamented ceiling. At the top of the wheel stair with its wrought-iron balustrade modelled by the late Thomas Haddon, the main bedrooms are all treated with individual interest. Panelled in a variety of woods from elm and ash to kauri pine and larch, each one has a decorated ceiling of a different design. While the living room ceilings on the first floor are somewhat heavy in feeling, the plasterwork moulding in the bedrooms is altogether charming. Reminiscent of Jacobean work, it is at the same time imaginative and lively and quite firmly 20th century. Here, as elsewhere in and outside the house, Lorimer's grasp and knowledge of traditional forms is perfectly integrated with his own boundless creative powers.

Mr. and Mrs. Bruce, while not in any way detracting from the architect's conception of the interior, have brought to Balmanno their own choice of furniture, china, pictures and furnishings. Without such renewal of personal taste and family history, a house tends to become a period museum. The present owners, who combine respect for the past with a live sense of the present, are fully appreciative of their opportunities to preserve and cherish Balmanno. The garden is also very much of interest to them and has various new and delightful aspects—as, for instance, the pale pinks and deep reds of climbing roses splashed against the shining west wall on a summer day. A last view of the house from the wide lawn on this side, confirms Lorimer's own opinion that of all his buildings and restorations, Balmanno is the one he would have chosen to live in himself. It is also, perhaps, his best and most brilliant piece of work.

BELOW: *View from the east side of the house.*

Kinross House

IN THE YEAR 1720, DANIEL DEFOE, author of *Robinson Crusoe*, after visiting Kinross, wrote: " At the West End of the Lake and the Gardens reaching down to the very Water's Edge, stands the most beautiful and regular Piece of Architecture (for a private Gentleman's Seat) in all Scotland, perhaps in all Great Britain, I mean the House of Kinross. The Town lies at a little Distance from it, so as not to annoy the House, and yet so as to make it the more sociable; and at the Town is a very good Market; and the Street is tolerably well built. The House is a picture, 'tis all Beauty, the Stone is white and fine, the Order regular, the Contrivance elegant, the Workmanship exquisite."

When Defoe saw it, Kinross was little more than a quarter of a century old, one of the first and loveliest houses of the High Renaissance in Scotland. No wonder this traveller from over the Border was impressed. In a land of grey stone fortresses, turreted castles and rugged towers, he suddenly came upon this " most beautiful and regular Piece of Architecture " standing above the shores of Loch Leven. He had found one of the few Scottish houses which could vie with the magnificent English mansions of that period.

There is no more delightful vista in Scotland than that which stretches from the east side of the house, down the long terraced garden with its rose beds, herbaceous borders and yew hedges set in sweeping lawns, to the wild shores of the Loch and beyond the waters to Loch Leven Castle on its wooded island. It is a scene long familiar with memories and associations of Mary Queen of Scots. Here, in the years 1567-68, she faced bitter humiliation of body and spirit where " in the narrow chamber of the tower on the islet she could draw breath and know herself deserted, stripped of everything, insulted and in peril of death, all for a little of dear-bought love." Of the numberless historians, writers and poets who have been fascinated by this drama, perhaps Scott in his novel *The Abbot* has left us the clearest, if not the most authentic, picture.

Loch Leven Castle, which was part of the Kinross estate for hundreds of years until it was handed over to The National Trust in 1938, was a royal fortress in the time of David II, but later became a Douglas stronghold. When Queen Mary was imprisoned there, it belonged to Lady Margaret Douglas, one-time mistress of James V, to whom she had borne a son, James Stuart, Earl of Murray. He was appointed Regent of Scotland when an abdication had been forced from the helpless Queen in favour of her infant son. Mary's enemies had reason to think she was in unsympathetic hands at Loch Leven and that she would be safe in her island prison, but they calculated without her powers of fascination. One of the younger sons, George Douglas, succumbed to the young queen's charm and in a " phantasy of love " with her eventually helped her to escape.

The castle remained in the Douglas family until 1675, when the 11th Earl of Morton sold it with the Kinross estate to Sir William Bruce, who built the present house. Bruce, who was the first Scottish architect to build in the manner of the full Renaissance, may be said to have done for Scotland what Inigo Jones and Sir Christopher Wren did for England. Although he lacked the genius and originality of his great contemporaries, he was an enterprising architect, and his influence on Scottish building was considerable.

The interior is beautifully proportioned, spacious, and richly elegant in line and detail. Bruce carried out the new form and feeling here as admirably as he did outside, and there are few relics of the old Scots Baronial style in the long light panelled rooms, the dignified staircase with its carved wood balustrade, and the finely ornamented ceilings. So abrupt and complete is this transformation at Kinross, one might almost imagine a wand had charmed away every lingering medievalism and created a new medium at one touch.

Whether it is true or not that Bruce built the house with a view to its being a royal residence, this never came about, for when James II came to the throne he lived at Holyrood when he was in Scotland, as his ancestors had done. Bruce, who, besides his architectural activities, held many public offices and was M.P. for Kinross-shire, gave up the house to his son in 1700 and retired to the old seat of the Earls of Morton close by, which has since been demolished. It is interesting to know that William Adam, Bruce's pupil and in some degree his professional successor, was born at Blair Adam, only four miles from Kinross, in 1679.

Kinross narrowly escaped forfeiture by the crown during the 1715 Rebellion, when Bruce's grandson, Sir Thomas Bruce-Hope, who had succeeded to the estate, proclaimed the Old Pretender King James VIII at the market cross of Kinross. However, his half-brother, a staunch Hanoverian, saved the situation by taking Sir Thomas prisoner and compromising with the officers of the crown.

The property remained in the Bruce family, descending through the female line, until 1777, when it was sold to George Graham, who was succeeded by his brother, Thomas Graham, an ancestor of the present owner, Sir David Montgomery whose mother lives in Kinross House. Thomas Graham's daughter, whose portrait by Raeburn now hangs in the ballroom at Kinross, married Sir James Montgomery of Stobo Castle, Peeblesshire. At this time, the house, for some years in the hands of Graham trustees, was dismantled and closed, and from 1819 to the end of the century remained unoccupied. In this state, Kinross at least escaped the possible dangers of Victorian restoration.

It was not till 1902, when Sir Basil Graham Montgomery came to live at Kinross, that the present gardens were laid out and the house redecorated and put in order. The actual buildings had fortunately not suffered from neglect, and knowledgeable and conservative treatment of the place in the early years of this century has revived rather than altered many of the original features. Defoe saw Kinross in its pristine glory, but the years have given more than they have taken away, and his judgement that " 'tis all beauty " is amply justified today.

ABOVE: *The spacious entrance hall.*

BELOW: *The ballroom, a long light panelled room.*

House of Aldie

THE HOUSE OF ALDIE IS ONE OF THOSE buildings which, like a forgotten painting, can suddenly recapture a startling image of the past. Perched on the edge of a steep bank above a wide valley at the foot of the Cleish Hills, Aldie standing tall and white and stark, has an arresting beauty, set off in Spring by surroundings fields of olive green grass and purplish-brown plough, and by the black bare branches of a clump of old beech trees. Five miles west of Kinross, in the parish of Fossoway, the house stands 500 feet above sea level, and from the top of the tower on a fine day there is a bird's eye view of the Loch Leven which, it is said, once stretched to the lands of Aldie. Today there is a neat garden of lawn, stone flags, flower beds and tubbed box trees before the entrance. From here the white-harled tower seems immense in height and strength, finished at the top with a crow-stepped gable and two fat little turrets corbelled out from the wall. Joined to the tower by a lower, later addition, the jutting south-east wing presents a more domesticated gable-end with its broad chimney and three tiny unevenly placed windows.

Inhabited up to the middle of the 19th century, Aldie, although complete as a building, began to fall into disrepair after the First World War. When the present owner, Mr. Hope Dickson, bought the house in 1947, he employed Mr. Ian G. Lindsay, the well-known architect, to make a full restoration of the place. The oldest part of the house is the tower, which was first built, it is thought, in 1464 and enlarged and altered in 1585, when it was described as "a castle of marvellous strength."

At this later date the top storey of the tower was rebuilt and the three turrets and little cap-house at the corners added. Soon after, the present low wing was extended southwards, on the lines of a higher earlier building marked today by some jagged pieces of masonry on the south wall of the tower. Subsequently the second addition was built out eastwards, and lastly a new entrance made, leading into the very small open courtyard standing between

TOP: *The House of Aldie, showing the entrance front, the 15th-century tower and later additions.*

BOTTOM: *Aldie from the back, showing an addition to the south, rebuilt circa 1600.*

RIGHT: *The original great hall on the first floor of the tower.*

the tower and the two wings. This is the present entrance, the little court having been covered in during the recent reconstruction. Over the entrance a weathered panel frames the arms of the Mercers of Aldie, under which are carved the initials I.M., probably for James Mercer, who was Gentleman Usher to King Charles II.

For nearly 600 years the lands of Aldie belonged to the Mercer family, although since the middle of the 17th century the inheritance has descended on the distaff side. There is an old saying that "The Mercers are aye aulder than auld Perth," and certainly they were given a burial vault by the king in the Cathedral Church of St. John about the year 1100. The first charter connecting the Mercers with Aldie dates from 1352 when John Mercer, Provost of Perth, acquired the lands from his brother-in-law, William Murray of Tullibardine. This John Mercer, merchant, financier, Member of the Scottish Parliament, and later ambassador to the Low Countries, was a man of character and importance. He was also "in

BELOW: *Formerly the withdrawing room now the dining room, in the south wing.*

The main bedroom is one of the most striking rooms in the house.

great favour with the King of France (Charles V), on account of his immense wealth, for he was skilful in matters relating to commerce and fertile in expedient and prudent in counsel, so that his opinion with regard to English affairs had, not without reason, great weight with the King and the Nation of France."

Returning home to Scotland from France in the year 1376, John Mercer's ship was driven on to the Northumbrian coast by stormy weather, and he was captured and imprisoned in Scarborough Castle. The matter was taken up on a high level when the Earl of Douglas and Mar sent a written complaint to Edward III, beginning "Most noble and mighty Prince, by these letters, I show to you Sire, and to your good Council, by way of Complaint, how that *John Mercer*, my vassal has for a long time been distressed and wrongfully annoyed in your Kingdom. . . !" Mercer was soon after set free by the Earl of Northumberland to the chagrin of others less generous, for "if he had been ransomed by the common rule, he might have enriched the King, and Kingdom with inestimable wealth." Mercer's ships and cargo, however, were held in England, and some months later his son Andrew, bent on revenge, swooped on Scarborough with a small fleet of French, Spanish and Scottish ships. Several English ships of merchandise were taken, but, instead of retiring in triumph, Andrew, "boasting of the exploits, continued to keep the sea, as defying the maritime power of England."

An enterprising English merchant, John Philpot, who later became Lord Mayor of London, raised ships and men, pursued Mercer, whom he took prisoner, and recaptured the booty. Philpot's independent action was not approved of in official circles, however, and Andrew was released and "sent honourably home" on January 1, 1378, with a safe conduct signed by Richard II. Sir Andrew Mercer was given various grants of land and money for his services to Scotland, and in the time of his grandson, in 1443, the Mercer lands, including Aldie, were made into a barony.

There is a legend that the early Lairds of Aldie held the castle on condition that a room was always kept prepared in which the king and his friends could dine when they were out hunting in the Caledonian Forest. It must have been either Sir Andrew's grandson and namesake or his great-grandson, Sir Laurence, who first built the tower. The next Laird, Sir Henry, who married Margaret Douglas of Lochleven, was killed at Flodden in 1513.

By the time Sir James Mercer arrived on the scene, Aldie must have looked much as it does today, the top of the tower having been rebuilt and both wings finished. Sir James, who attended Charles II at court and was made a baronet, died in 1671. Having no sons, he left his estates to his daughter Helen, with a proviso that the husbands of all future female heirs must change their name to Mercer. On the face of it, this looked very like a safeguard against the Curse which, tradition records, was laid on the house by a groom hanged on a holly tree, which still stands near the tower, for some minor offence. Infuriated by the injustice of his punishment, he swore that no son should inherit Aldie for many generations. It must have been difficult for the credulous not to believe that the Curse was at least partly operative, for during the next 200 years there were six female heirs and only two male.

These daughters of the house married into various old and noble families, including the Nairnes, the Elphinstones, and the Lansdownes. In 1817 Margaret Mercer Elphinstone, Baroness Nairne and Keith, who was Lady-in-waiting to Princess Charlotte of Wales, married the French Ambassador, Count de Flahaut. Their daughter, Emily Jane, married the Earl of Shelburne, afterwards Marquis of Lansdowne. The present and 8th Marquis, 18th in line from John Mercer, whose charter of Meikleour and Aldie dates from 1352, still owns the former property in Perthshire.

Aldie is not the first tower-house to be converted to a present-day home. With all their show of height and semi-fortified strength, these 16th and 17th century Scottish buildings make comfortable and often convenient houses today. Their simplicity, limited accommodation, small rooms and stout walls, which keep out weather and to some extent cold, are all suited to contemporary needs. Although Aldie has been restored with an expert knowledge of the original building and decoration, 20th century comfort and taste has also been studied. In early days the only entrance to the tower was a door on the first floor leading into the great hall. Today there are two doors in this cosy, charming room, one from the straight staircase to the entrance and the other to the spiral stair in the tower. Well lit by enlarged windows on three sides, the hall retains something of its old character with a beamed ceiling and the original fireplace. The white painted walls are hung with French tapestries, Eastern rugs and paintings of widely different interest, including an architectural painting by Giovanni Paolo Pannini (1692-1768).

Mr. Hope Dickson has spent many years in the Middle East, and everywhere in the house there is evidence of his travels and his love of beautiful and curious things. Among these in the hall are collections of Meissen china, blue and gold Eastern glass and Turkish church ornaments of the 17th century.

On the second floor of the tower, above the hall, the main bedroom is one of the most striking rooms in the house. Here the decorated plasterwork ceiling and coat of arms over the old fireplace, executed in 1960 in the Scottish Jacobean manner, is both robust and simple, the stout cherubs and modelled pomegranates, enclosed in panels, having every appearance of familiarity with their surroundings. Brass beds, a saxe blue carpet, white rugs and yellow patterned curtains, with some Georgian furniture, bring this delightful room into the 20th century. On the top floor there are three enchanting small bedrooms with powder closets in the turrets, transformed by rosy wallpapers and 18th century furnishings to entrancing dressing or writing rooms. In the long, narrow dining room, formerly the withdrawing room, in the south wing, with its coved timber ceiling and parquet floor, both recent additions, there are vivid Caucasian and Persian rugs, also family portraits and silhouettes, as well as many other relics and treasures, both Scottish and Eastern.

LEFT: *Culross from the south in 1693.*
RIGHT: *A view taken in 1953 showing the dereliction.*
BELOW: *The house today.*

Culross Abbey House

THE GRANDEST AND MOST COMPLETE of the 16th and 17th century houses which form the main part of the little Royal Burgh of Culross on the Firth of Forth, the so-called Palace, was built by Sir George Bruce between 1597 and 1611. Sir George, who introduced a system of draining in his coal mines so that they could extend under the Forth, one day had the honour of taking James VI on a tour of inspection there. But the King, on emerging from a dark tunnel, found himself on an artificial island surrounded by the Forth and imagined that the exercise was an attempt on his life. "Treason! Treason!" he shouted desperately. Sir George quickly reassured the King and pointed to a magnificent barge waiting to row them back to Culross where a banquet was in readiness.

Sir George's elder brother, Sir Edward Bruce, who accompanied James VI to England on his accession to the throne in 1603, began the building of Culross Abbey House on a commanding site above the Forth, adjacent to the old Cistercian Abbey from which, it is said, stones were used for the new building. Sir Edward, later created 1st Baron Kinloss, died in 1610 before the original two-storeyed house was finished. His successors in the 17th century added considerably to this fine though comparatively small country house with its formal gardens and orchards and plantations stretching down to the shore of the Forth. Most important of the building lairds was Alexander Bruce, 2nd Earl of Kincardine, who married a Dutch heiress, Veronica Van Sommelsdyke (their portraits hang in the drawing room today). He added the third storey about 1670, laid out the garden, including the charming summer-house, and finished the house as it is shown in the fascinating engraving by John Slezer, dated 1693. In view of the fact that Sir William Bruce, the great architect of the day, was Lord Kincardine's cousin and lived not far away, first at Balcaskie and then at Kinross, it is possible that he was consulted on the 1670 additions to the house.

Thus, at the turn of that century, Culross Abbey House, in all its glory, could be said to represent one of the splendid variations on a Renaissance theme which appeared at that time in Scottish building. The house stood three storeys high, the long symmetrical south front flanked by slightly projecting towers of four storeys. The bell-shaped roofs on these towers, the massed chimney-stacks, the rather stolid pediments above the first-floor windows and above them the row of dummy gargoyle-like water-spouts are all characteristic of the time.

During the following century the house passed from the Bruces to the Cochrane family. Alexander, 2nd Earl of Kincardine, was succeeded by a son who died unmarried and then by a daughter, Lady Mary Bruce, who married William Cochrane of Ochiltree. Their grandson succeeded to the Earldom of Dundonald and the family remained at Culross Abbey House till early in the 19th century. It is interesting to find that Lady Mary's sister, Lady Elizabeth Bruce, married Alexander Boswell of Auchinleck and became the grandmother of Dr. Johnson's biographer.

In the year 1775 there was born at Annesfield in Lanarkshire one of the most famous members of the Dundonald family—Thomas Cochrane, afterwards the 10th Earl, but best known as Admiral Lord Cochrane. He spent most of his early years at Culross Abbey House. There, tradition records, he first set sail on the waters of the Forth in a vessel whose speed was accelerated by hoisting his bedroom sheets. He and his brothers had a piecemeal education from a fleeting number

The staircase. The portrait of the present Earl of Elgin is by the late Oswald Birley.

of tutors. Of one of these, a Frenchman, the Admiral later wrote in his *Autobiography of a Seaman*: ". . . on one side of the church-yard was the Culross Abbey cherry garden, full of fine fruit, of which he was very fond, as were also the magpies which swarmed in the district. One Sunday whilst the people were at church, the magpies, aware no doubt, of their advantage, made a vigorous onslaught on the cherries—provoking the Frenchman who was on the watch, to open fire on the intruders from a fowling-piece. The effect of this reached further than the magpies. To fire a gun on the sabbath was an abomination . . . and neither before or after did I witness such a hubbub in the parish. . . Annoyed at the ill-feeling thus created he relinquished his engagement before we had acquired the rudiments of the French language."

In one direction, however, the brothers were constantly instructed. Their father, intensely interested in scientific study, was all his life engrossed in (sometimes financially disastrous) experiments in his collieries and salt-mines. The boys were also occasionally dispatched to other parts of the country to widen their minds. "I have just seen the young gentlemen off by the coach," writes the 9th Earl's agent. "It is true they have not had very much education, but they are strong and fine to look at and very sensible and will get on anywhere." Thomas more than fulfilled this prediction. He joined the navy in 1793 and by 1800 had done so well on the French and Spanish coasts that Napoleon had christened him "Le Loup de Mer." In 1806 he was elected Whig Member of Parliament for Honiton in Devon and began the long fight against Admiralty abuses which made him many enemies in high places but endeared him to the vast majority of his fellow countrymen. In 1814 he was falsely accused of a Stock Exchange fraud and expelled from the navy and Parliament, but was at once re-elected by his constituents who paid the £1000 fine imposed on him by penny subscriptions. In 1817 he accepted the command of the Chilean Navy and by a series of brilliant successes against the Spanish forces, obtained the independence of both Chile and Peru. Subsequently he became Admiral of the Brazilian Fleet and the Greek Navy. In 1832, a year after his succession as 10th Earl of Dundonald, he was re-instated in the British Navy—and later made Admiral of the Fleet. He died in 1860 and was buried in Westminster Abbey, one of the greatest heroes Scotland has ever produced.

In the early days of Cochrane's naval

career, his father, the 9th Earl of Dundonald, impoverished by his experiments in extracting gas and tar from coal, had been forced to sell Culross Abbey House to his cousin, Sir Robert Preston of Valleyfield. It is said that, to spite its former owners, Sir Robert took off the roof of the house, gutted the interior and left the place to become a ruin. Sir Robert set up his coat of arms above the front door on the north side of the house where it remains today, and radically reconstructed the interior.

After Sir Robert's death the house reverted to the Earl of Elgin's family. By the end of the century the building, now riddled with dry rot, was abandoned for sixty years. In 1952, the present Earl, a distinguished and indefatigable public worker, actively interested in a wide range of Scottish affairs, put in hand a complete rehabilitation of the house. Less of a restoration than a new and original design fitted into the shell of the old house, approximately reduced to its 1608 proportions, the work, carried out to the plans of Mr Robert Hurd of Edinburgh, was finished in 1956. Today a most comfortable modern house has been formed out of the stone of the twice remodelled older building which has stood there over the last three hundred and sixty years.

Like children with a box of bricks, succeeding generations have put up and pulled down this grave, grey, imposing house above the Forth. Largest and most resplendent after the additions of 1670, it is today once again diminished to a manageable size. This has been effected by removing the third storey (the dormer windows built up in the centre of the south front to light the attic rooms were constructed from stone window surrounds salvaged from the former towers), by reducing the length of the house at either end, by removing the early 19th century north wing and by decapitating the two towers at first floor level. These last, now joined to the main block by walls which screen a garage and kitchen court on the north side, have been capped with modern ogee-shaped roofs which are exceptionally fine examples of 20th century stonework. All new work has been carried out with stone from the previous houses—a light grey flecked with ochre yellow.

The interior, virtually a contemporary design within the limitations of an outside shell, with its original window-spacing and the old central wall running through the middle of the house, is both gay and elegant, comfortable and convenient. There is no sudden break with tradition and yet no actual imitation of any original detail. The straight staircase with its charming modern wrought-iron work embodying a motif of roses and tulips, which skirts the entrance hall, was suggested by a secondary stair at Caroline Park, Granton. The long, low-ceilinged drawing room with its white-painted walls, Georgian furniture, family portraits and handsome white and gold leaf curtain, hand-blocked printed on glass fibre, is, in spite of the old stone chimneypiece dated 1669, 20th century in feeling. The smaller dining room shares the magnificent panorama over the Forth. On the first floor are two main bedrooms each with dressing room and bathroom, two smaller bedrooms, another bathroom and a linen room, and above are two attic rooms.

Lady Elgin, who is a granddaughter of the 11th Earl of Dundonald (thus both she and her husband are descendants of the early owners of the house), has restored the garden to its original form and splendour. Perfect is a word to be used sparingly, but it is the right one to describe this ancient garden in summer, overlooking the grey-blue water, the brown rocks and the green banks of the Forth.

The dining room is divided from the drawing room by doors which slide out of sight.

The library. Over the chimneypiece hangs a painting of the old house by Alexander Nasmyth.

The Binns, showing the north and (left) east faces.

The Binns

The picts are said to have made their last stand against the invading Romans on the two hills rising above the Binns and overlooking the Firth of Forth in the parish of Abercorn. Tradition also tells of Pictish dwellings on the site of the present house, but the earliest records of "the lands of the Bynnis" date from 1335. Although a building is mentioned in the 15th century, so much has been put up and pulled down since then, that periods are difficult to define until 1612, when Thomas Dalyell, first of the Binns, bought the property and added to and decorated the existing house.

Thomas Dalyell, a cadet of the old Lanarkshire family of Dalzell of Dalzell, later Earls of Carnwath, was one of the first of the "hungrie Scottis" to make his fortune in London. With King James VI and the Scottish court he moved there in 1603 and became Deputy-Master of the Rolls under his father-in-law, the 1st Baron Kinloss. Returning to Scotland in 1612, a rich man, he bought the lands of the Binns and rebuilt the house, which remained in the possession of the Dalyell family until 1944. That year Mrs Eleanor Dalyell, who still lives in the house, handed it over to The National Trust for Scotland with a charter containing certain reservations, including the right to "the

The Binns, south front.

The wagon roof of the Sea Room, with its heavy pendants.

The High Hall, with its ornate plaster ceiling. The pattern is geometric, with heraldic decoration.

hidden treasure of the Binns should it be recovered . . ."

But in 1612, to the neighbouring landed families, Thomas Dalyell was still one of the "new rich," and when he was refused seating accommodation in Abercorn Kirk by these aristocratic lairds, he wrote immediately to his kinsman the Bishop of Dunkeld. Permission was granted him not merely for a seat in the Kirk, but to rebuild an aisle, thereafter called the Binns Aisle, with its own private door, having no communication with the rest of the church. This privilege holds good to the present day.

Thomas Dalyell's 17th century house has been partially concealed and altered outside by the work of William Burn, the architect, dating from about 1810. The original steep roof, the corbie steps and the pointed turrets have been replaced by "Gothick" battlements, those harbingers of the Romantic Revival and the Victorian passion for Scottish Baronial restorations. There have also been additions, including two rooms on the south side, built in the mid-18th century, and several rooms in the west wing.

Much of the interior remains characteristically 17th century, and the ornamented plaster ceilings are among the finest and the best preserved in Scotland. These are thought to have been done by the same Italian or Italian-trained Scots workmen who executed the ceilings at Linlithgow Palace which were destroyed by fire in 1746.

The two portraits of General Tam Dalyell of the Binns which hang in the house today show one of those rare faces combining alert sensibility with inflexible purpose. The son of Thomas Dalyell, he was born in 1615, and his long and active span of years coincided with troubled times in Scotland. The bitter struggle between Royalists and Covenanters in the 17th century divided Scotland even more decisively than the Reformation a century earlier. Both sides inspired great loyalties and great suffering which have not been forgotten today.

After a Grand Tour of the Continent, lasting three years, Tam Dalyell returned to Scotland and, with his father, signed the petition, drawn up in 1637 and addressed to the Privy Council, protesting against the forced use of the Prayer Book in Scottish churches. But when the extremists openly opposed Charles I, Dalyell gave his unswerving loyalty to the crown. When the king was executed in 1649 he made a solemn vow never to cut his hair or his beard till the monarchy was restored, and the immense comb, nearly a foot in length, which he was henceforth obliged to use, is still preserved in the house. Following a military career, he fought on several occasions against the Parliamentary forces, and at the Battle of Worcester in 1651 was captured and thrown into the Tower of London by Cromwell.

Escaping from the Tower, he returned to Scotland in 1654, and later joined Charles II on the Continent. The next few years were spent in the service of the Russian Czar, when Dalyell helped to reorganise the army, fought with them in several campaigns and was eventually made a general and a noble of Russia. In 1666, some years after the Restoration, he was sent for by Charles II and put in charge of His Majesty's forces in Scotland. His task now was to suppress the "Rebel Covenanters," which he did so forcefully on various occasions that he earned many hard names, among them "The Bloody Muscovite." But the fact that he resigned his commission after the Battle of Rullion Green, because certain women and children following the Covenanters (to whom he had given quarter on the field of battle) were shot in Edinburgh in abuse of his quarter, is evidence that his purpose was tempered with humanity.

More than ten years later he was recalled by the King and in 1679 succeeded the Duke of Monmouth and Buccleugh as Commander-in-Chief of the Scottish forces. In 1678, he mustered a new regiment at the Binns, the Scots Greys, so called from the stone-grey cloth imported by Dalyell for his new dragoons. General Tam died in 1685 and was buried with military honours. A contemporary account records that "Some were observing that few of our General personis in Scotland had come to their graves without some tach or note of disgrace which Dalyell had not incurred."

Legends about General Tam are legion, but one in particular would seem to have a very solid piece of evidence in the heavy carved marble table which stands in the Laigh Hall. This was said to have been hurled at the General's head by the Devil after the former had beaten him at cards. It missed its mark, however, and landed in the Sergeant's Pond below the house, where it was recovered in 1878 during a very dry summer, having apparently lain there for two hundred years.

James VII conferred a baronetcy on General Tam's eldest son, an honour which Charles II had meant for his father. Later generations of Dalyells distinguished themselves in the army and the navy, and Sir John Graham Dalyell, who succeeded in 1841, made a name for himself in literature and science, his best-known work being *The Rare and Remarkable Animals of Scotland.* Mrs Eleanor Dalyell of the Binns is the daughter of the late Sir James Bruce Wilkie Dalyell, her husband, Colonel Dalyell, having taken the family name.

The Dalyells have played a continuous part in Scottish history for more than three hundred years, and in their home are preserved not only the ancient stones of other days but also the story, the portraits and the intimate relics of such a family. There is another Tam Dalyell, who is Member of Parliament for West Lothian, to bring the story to the present day. The family's hospitality and personal interest add very greatly to the pleasure of visiting this historic house whose traditions and treasures will in future be held by The National Trust for Scotland.

Doorway with Tam Dalyell's initials above.

Lt. Gen. Tam Dalyell's portrait in the dining room.

Plastered ceiling in the King's Room, with the royal arms over the fireplace.

Hopetoun House seen from the south colonnade of William Adam's east front.

Hopetoun House

THE SETTING OF HOPETOUN HOUSE, certainly the most imposing and perhaps the finest Renaissance house in Scotland, has a calculated perfection it would be hard to improve. Yet the 18th century planners, massing horizontal grey stone against long level swards of green grass, and shaping the vista of the Firth of Forth between plantations of trees, left two dramatic details, one to the Victorians and one to the sixties. For the giant contours of the great Forth Bridges rising very often through mist and haze, carry the eye away into the far distance, as the background of a painted landscape sometimes diverts the onlooker beyond the actual picture. But Sir William Bruce, the architect, who started the house in 1699, had no such panorama in mind. His building (only the central portion remains today), which cannot be seen from the present east entrance, stands facing west.

Most of the imposing eastern facade was added by Bruce's pupil, William Adam, between 1721 and 1746, and the house finished by Adam's three sons, John, Robert and James, who are entirely responsible for the interior decoration carried out during the years 1750-1768. The whole building, therefore, is the work of three successive generations of architects bound in the same tradition—for each was either master or pupil of another. The factors of time and fashion, however, obviously prevented complete harmony in the building as a whole, and as the seams in an intricate garment are clues to its making, so these joins at Hopetoun House are interesting pointers in its evolution.

The present owner of Hopetoun, the 3rd Marquess of Linlithgow, is a descendant of John de Hope, who came to Scotland with the court of Magdalen de Valois, Queen of James V. John de Hope settled in Edinburgh, where he became a very successful merchant. During the next century the Hopes made their mark in law, and John's great-grandson, Sir Thomas, rose to be Lord Advocate under Charles I. In 1678 his son bought the barony and estate of Abercorn, but four years later

FAR RIGHT: *The West Wainscot bedroom in the old house. Flemish and English tapestries cover the walls.*

RIGHT: *Charles, Lord Hope, by Nathaniel Dance.*

was drowned in the disaster of the *Royal Gloucester*. The story goes that Hope gave his place in the lifeboat to the Duke of York and that this was remembered by Queen Anne, who, in 1703, created his son Earl of Hopetoun. This young Earl was Member of Parliament for Linlithgow at the age of twenty-one, and soon after became a Privy Councillor. A progressive of his time and an ardent supporter of the Union between Scotland and England, Hopetoun belonged to that group of wealthy and well-born leaders (which included the Duke of Argyll, the Marquess of Tweeddale and Sir John Clerk of Penicuik) who were convinced of the advantages of an Anglo-Scottish alliance.

Sir William Bruce, who began Hopetoun in 1699, was himself an English ambassador of a kind. For in bringing to Scotland a new style of building and effecting there in his lifetime an almost complete transition in the shape of houses, from the old native style of the Middle Ages to the Renaissance mode already adopted in England, he brought the two countries into line architecturally after more than four centuries of widely differing tradition. But, although the outside of the house (Italian in design) marked a new age, the inside differed less from its Scottish predecessors, despite the fact that the central octagonal staircase, decorated with rich wood carvings in the manner of Grinling Gibbons,

RIGHT: *The late 2nd Marquess of Linlithgow by Oswald Birley.*

FAR RIGHT: *The Yellow Drawing Room.*

BOTTOM RIGHT: *The Red Drawing Room.*

BELOW: *The central staircase.*

was a fashionable innovation. The main rooms in this old house are panelled in wood and the dining room in particular is a good example of the pre-Adam interior typical of the turn of the century in Scotland. However, most of the furniture in Bruce's house dates from the time of his successor, William Adam.

The 1st Earl of Hopetoun, with his prominent pro-English friends, greatly admired the grandeur and comfort of the country houses south of the Border. Such architects as Inigo Jones, Wren, Vanbrugh and Gibbs had, during the last hundred years, set English domestic architecture as high as any in Europe. And especially in her great *country* houses of the period was England glorified. So, in 1721, William Adam was called in to enlarge Hopetoun with something of the same splendour. These additions were not carried out in a single inspired exercise, but piecemeal, with much delay and change of plan (in a letter from Hopetoun's uncle, the Marquess of Annandale, to Sir John Clerk of Penicuik, dated Jan. 23, 1724, he observes: " As for Adams, he has so many Real and so many Imaginary projects that he minds nobody, nor no thing to purpose "). By 1746, however, the new facade facing east, with the great central block flanked by bays, pillared colonnades and outlying pavilions, must have been practically complete, for William Adam sent in his account for £4,443—not an excessive bill, considering the work covered twenty-five years.

A few details of the structure remained to be finished after William Adam's death in 1748, including the north (stable) pavilion. But nothing has been added or altered outside the house since 1754. This last work and the interior decoration was carried on and finished by Adam's three sons. Inside the house it is at once evident that they followed faithfully in their father's footsteps. There is no sudden change of tempo, but an ordered continuity of design and feeling from exterior to interior. It was, of course, early work for the Adam brothers. Their later, more familiar style was not yet formed although it can be traced in embryo in the richer, more solid parental style at Hopetoun. The Yellow Drawing Room, for instance, with its coved ceiling decorated at each corner by gilded spandrels and a courant frieze picked out in gold, is rich yet restrained. The walls and some of the furniture are covered with the original yellow silk brocade made, probably in France, in the 1750s. In this room with its fresh and enchanting colour scheme of yellow, white and gold, Sir Henry Raeburn was knighted by George IV in 1822. The Red Drawing Room, grander and more sumptuous, has an almost rococo ceiling of mixed French and Chinese designs, quite unlike Robert Adam's later work. Red silk brocade wall coverings, a bold marble chimneypiece by Michael Rysbrack (1694-1770) and some good furniture (including a collection of Restoration pieces) make this room a showplace.

The 1st Earl of Hopetoun died in 1742, and was succeeded by his son, John, with whom the Adam brothers were on very friendly terms. So much so, that in 1754 Robert accompanied the 2nd Earl's brother, the Hon. Charles Hope, to Italy on part of the " Grand Tour " then considered necessary for every young gentleman of rank. (Robert, who had saved up £5,000 out of the firm's profits for this enterprise, stayed abroad for four years.) Hopetoun commissioned Robert to buy furniture and pictures for the house, although little that can be traced to this period remains there today. On his own authority, Robert found it difficult to please His Lordship in the matter of paintings, for he wrote from Rome, " first of all, the price he allows is not sufficient for a Tip Top, & a Second Rate with those qualifications he wants & the Dimensions he Stipulates, it is the Divil and all to find. I have people seeking in all quarters & have now extended my search to Florence where there are some good Pictures but having Naked figures in them will not answer, & His Lordship may well know without Nakedness no pictures can be found. Italian painters are given to Nakedness as the sparks to fly upwards." But the collection of paintings at Hopetoun today forms one of the finest in Scotland. Besides family portraits by Raeburn, Allan Ramsay, David Allan, Nathanial Dance and Gainsborough, there are works by Rubens, Van Dyck, Canaletto, Teniers, Mytens and Cuyp. Some of the best of these were bought in Genoa in 1827. On his return to England, Robert continued his search for furniture with more success, for many of the pieces at Hopetoun today were ordered by him in London, most of them from the cabinetmaker, James Cullen, who supplied much of the furniture at Blair Castle in Perthshire.

The Hopetoun family have always been excellent public servants, besides distinguishing themselves in various other directions, notably the army, law and politics. The 4th Earl (as General Sir John Hope) carried out the embarkation of the British Army at Corunna after the death of Sir John Moore in 1809. He it was who later entertained George IV at Hopetoun, and his statue stands in St. Andrew's Square, Edinburgh. The late Marquess of Linlithgow, who died in 1952, was Viceroy and Governor-General of India from 1936-43. The present Marquess, who takes an active part in the House of Lords, still lives at Hopetoun for part of the year with his wife and family. His twin brother, Baron Glendevon created in 1964, was Member of Parliament for the Pentlands Division of Edinburgh and Joint Under-Secretary of State for Foreign Affairs.

The imposing east front of Hopetoun House.

Newliston

TEN MILES FROM THE CENTRE OF Edinburgh, Newliston stands surrounded by wide lawns, parklands, fields and woods, apparently as pastoral and serene as when the grounds were laid out nearly 250 years ago. The estate lies in West Lothian between two main westward roads and only a few miles from Turnhouse airport. Railway lines, shale bings, new factories and house building have steadily encroached on its borders. Yet from the house, the rural landscape is miraculously complete.

For nearly three centuries the property of Newliston was owned by a cadet branch of the Dundas family of Dundas. Duncan, 1st Dundas of Newliston, held the office of Lord Lyon, King of Arms from 1452-71. In 1669, Elisabeth Dundas, heiress of Newliston, married Sir John Dalrymple, who, after succeeding his father as Viscount, was in 1703 created Earl of Stair. It was their son, Field Marshal the 2nd Earl of Stair, who laid out the present grounds as the setting for a very grand neo-Palladian house, designed by William Adam, which was never built.

After a long and distinguished career both as soldier and diplomat, in 1701 Stair became A.D.C. to Marlborough and fought at the Battles of Ramillies and Malplaquet. On his return from a post at the Embassy in Paris in 1720, of which he had been relieved under some political cloud, he "lived in comparative seclusion . . . from 1722-42 . . . during the greater part of each year at the house of Newliston." Lord Stair, who was one of the first and most energetic members of the Honourable Society for the Improvement of Agriculture, spent these twenty years to good effect, laying out the grounds at Newliston and at the same time developing his old family property, Castle Kennedy in Wigtownshire.

During the 18th century English experts on agriculture and landscape gardening were in demand north of the Border, among them Switzer, Laurence and Langley. Newliston is one of the houses the ground plan of which has been attributed to Switzer. It is probable, however, that Lord Stair himself, widely travelled in Europe and familiar with Versailles and the châteaux of France, was mainly responsible for the formal French style of the lay-out at Newliston, such as the sunk fences with high walls and bastions, artificial ponds and avenues of trees. The eight avenues of pollarded lime trees forming a Union Jack were all felled and replanted in 1964. But in all probability they were planned, if not actually planted, along with the other planting activities, some time before the Battle of Dettingen which they have sometimes been said to commemorate, at least in retrospect. The original project was carried out mainly by farm and estate workers with the help, it is said, of troopers of the Scots Greys who were stationed at Newliston as a bodyguard to Lord Stair.

In 1742 Stair had been recalled to command an expeditionary force at Dettingen. After winning the battle he resigned as a protest against the King's preference for Hanoverian generals, but returned once more as Commander-in-Chief, South Britain, before the '45 Rising. He died in 1747 at his town residence, Queensberry House in the Canongate. The old Scottish Baronial house still stood, and presumably through lack of funds, William Adam's imposing building which was to have been the centrepiece of the new setting, never materialised.

About 1750 Newliston was sold by Lord Stair's executors to Roger, Hog who came of a

The wrought-iron balustrade follows the straight flights of stone steps with a curving flourish.

Part of the ballroom in the mid-19th-century addition.

Berwickshire family and had been a merchant in London. Roger Hog, a direct ancestor of the present owner, lived on in the old house till his death in 1789. His son Thomas, with his wife, a daughter of the Earl of Lauderdale, at once revived the long deferred plan to build a new house in keeping with the grounds and gardens. Robert Adam, William's more famous son, was employed to design the house which, at his death in 1792 was scarcely complete.

His last and smallest country house, Newliston is in several ways unique. In general outline the building follows the Adam style, but in a greatly simplified form. The wings and forecourt were added by David Bryce in 1845, so that Robert Adam's original house stood, tall, three-storeyed and perfectly proportioned, four-square to the grand southward vista. Only the central facade on the entrance front is ornamented, four columns supporting a pediment, and on the north side the middle feature is apsidal, the bow gently breaking the straight lines and the height of the walls. For all its comparative simplicity, the house has a dignified hauteur well suited to its setting.

Compared to the palatial scale of his other country houses, one might almost say that the interior of Newliston is a Robert Adam miniature. Only the square, stone-flagged entrance hall with its colonnade of pillars and handsome frieze strikes a note of classical grandeur. The Signs of the Zodiac, a motif found throughout the house, are here shown in the carving of Taurus the Bull on the unusual sandstone chimneypiece. The frieze has recently been picked out in terra-cotta on a grey background. It is probable that Robert Adam died before the decoration of the house was completed. In the small panelled drawing room the walls have been painted pale green, the delicate frieze enrichment left white. Of special interest are the gilt pelmets designed by Adam, the white marble mantelpiece with carved decoration, including the favourite pattern, used elsewhere, of a Roman catkin chain (*garrya elliptica*) which may have impressed him during his stay in Rome many years before. Formerly all the panels were filled with appliqué needlework, designed by Adam and carried out by Lady Mary Hog. Two unfinished pieces remain in the house; the rest, having deteriorated beyond repair, were disposed of in 1928.

The original dining room, with its great curve of windows overlooking green lawns and woods to the north and a pond where elegant, unhurrying swans seem part of the ordered view, has now been replaced by the smaller south room. Over the carved wood chimneypiece here hangs one of the superbly graceful gilt mirrors designed for the house by Adam. The wrought-iron balustrade of unusual height, it has been suggested for a predominantly tall family, describes a restrained upward movement, following the straight flights of stone steps with a curving flourish. Among other paintings above the stairs are portraits of Elizabeth Wood, daughter of Robert Wood, explorer, author and politician, who is an ancestor of Mrs. Hog's, and a copy of the

enchanting picture of Harriet Maconachie Welwood as a child, by William Dyce.

In one of the bedrooms upstairs is a gold and white painted four-poster, thought to be of Adam's design, with furnishings and bed-cover ornamented with appliqué work by the Lady Mary. In the library is a set of twelve plaster casts of the Stirling Heads. The original 15th century oak carvings, now in the Smith Institute, Stirling, once decorated the ceiling of the King's Presence Chamber in Stirling Castle. These were rescued, according to tradition, on their way to a local baker to be used as fuel, by the Judge, Lord Cockburn, who made three sets of casts and presented one to the Laird of Newliston.

FAR LEFT: *The pillared entrance hall.*

LEFT: *One of a pair of gilt mirrors, designed by Adam, now in the drawing room.*

BELOW: *The small panelled drawing room.*

When Thomas Hog's son died unmarried in 1833, the estate went to his half-brother, James Maitland Hog, and much of the original furniture to his sister, the wife of Sir John Buchan Hepburn of Smeaton. In 1845 the wings and balustrade were added to the house by Bryce, in the time of Major Hog's great-grandfather, James Maitland Hog. To this period belongs the large, L-shaped ballroom opening out of Adam's drawing room. Spacious and light with its three tall windows, high coved ceiling, white painted walls and long gilt mirrors, this room provides contrast to rather than imitation of the rest of the house. The charming white and gilt Regency furniture—settees, barrel chairs and smaller chairs—were made by Richard Clark and Son in Leith in 1826.

Major and Mrs. Hog, who live in the house today, have not only brought back to Newliston many aspects of its former character, but are equally interested and skilled in the preservation of the gardens and grounds.

LEFT: *In one of the bedrooms upstairs is a gold and white painted four-poster, thought to be of Adam's design, with furnishings and bed-cover ornamented with appliqué work by the Lady Mary.*

BOTTOM LEFT: *The south dining room. Over the carved chimneypiece hangs one of the superbly graceful gilt mirrors designed for the house by Adam.*

BOTTOM RIGHT: *Portrait of Thomas Hog (1742-1827), in the entrance hall.*

Pinkie from the south-east.

Pinkie House

"The village of Inveresk enjoys so good an Air, that the eminent Dr. Pitcairn called it the Montpelier of Scotland," said Daniel Defoe after his visit there in the early 18th century. "It is full of People and there are several very Handsome Houses and Gardens in it, which invite the Citizens of Edinburgh to take Lodgings here in the Summer... But the Glory and Beauty of this Parish is Pinkey..." An inscription (now obscured by additions) on the outside wall of the house recorded that "Alexander Lord Seton built this house in 1613, not as he would have wished but according to his means." Perhaps Pinkie might have been larger and grander if Lord Seton's means had equalled his wishes, but I doubt whether more money could have improved on its particular splendours.

Alexander Seton, who was made Earl of Dunfermline in 1605, had already enlarged and altered Fyvie Castle in Aberdeenshire when he started to build Pinkie—or rather to reconstruct and elaborate the old house which then stood on the site. This 16th century building, which included the present square tower, originally belonged to the Abbey of Dunfermline. Seton obviously had taste and imagination as well as great talent for design, and laid out the new house round a courtyard which was enclosed on two sides by the south and east wings. Whether the ornamental walls forming the rest of the square were ever completed is doubtful, but the Renaissance well-head, resplendent under a "crown" spire, remains intact today.

The main part of the house, facing east, with its seven tall chimney-stacks, steep crow-stepped gables and lovely oriel window—this last an English innovation—has all the grave dignity of an accomplished set piece. But the south range, a storey lower and altogether more homely in appearance, gives Pinkie that element of pleasant irregularity typical of Jacobean times. "There is no excellent beauty," said Francis Bacon, "that hath not some strangeness in the proportion." The south wing too, carries most of the later additions to the exterior—the 18th century round tower built out to make bow windows on two floors, the modern entrance (re-opened where the original gateway led into the court-yard) and a recently put up tail-piece at the west end.

Alexander Seton, a godson of Mary Queen of Scots, belonged to a family consistently loyal to the Stuarts—his father had been exiled to Flanders after the Queen's defeat at Langside in 1568. Alexander, who became successively a judge, Lord President of the Council and Lord High Chancellor of Scotland, was a favourite and friend of James VI and I, and was entrusted with the care of his infant son (later Charles I), who "he keeped... in his house three years, and carried... into Englande himselfe, by land, to the King and Queen's Majesties, well and in health; for which faithful service the King's Majestie was thankful to him." The Prince's temporary home, however, was not Pinkie, as some records maintain, but Fyvie Castle.

It seems likely, though, that Prince Charles Edward Stuart did, as the story goes, sleep in the King's Room at Pinkie (which has one of the most splendid and elaborate plasterwork ceilings in Scotland) after the Battle of Preston-pans in 1745. By that time Pinkie was in the possession of the Marquis of Tweeddale, and the Setons had in 1690 forfeited the Dunfermline title for adherence to the cause of James VII. In 1788 the property was acquired by the Hope family, who remained there till the middle of this century.

The Governors of Loretto School bought the house and grounds of Pinkie in 1950. Only a few minutes' walk from the rest of the school buildings, it was the ideal place for a necessary expansion of accommodation and playing fields. The grounds now contain two boarding houses, situated to the west and south-west of Pinkie House and an extension has been added to the old manor itself. A fairly extensive reconstruction had to be planned for this purpose, but so admirably have these alterations been carried out that the best of the old interior has not only been preserved but (with financial help from the Pilgrim Trust) in many cases restored to much of its original beauty.

The long gallery, with its gay and immensely interesting painted ceilings and oriel window, is now a large dormitory with a new hardwood floor. Perhaps the greatest tribute to the architects here is the fact that there is nothing incongruous in this transformation. Nor are the magnificent plasterwork ceilings out of place over the pulsing life of a school. Rather one feels that Loretto may indeed inherit the future once possible to the owners of a family home, as well as the pride and appreciation to cherish such " excellent beauties."

The housemaster's accommodation at the north end of the main block forms a compact unit of the least altered part of the house, including the best of the plasterwork ceilings. The rest of this range, much of which had been altered in the 19th century, is taken up with dormitories and sitting rooms for sixty boys, and here new wash-rooms and other facilities have been added as well as an oil-fed hot water and central heating system.

The Renaissance well-head set in the courtyard.

The south wing has been charmingly adapted to its new use as the headmaster's house. Especially delightful is the small vaulted dining room with a door through the massive breadth of the wall into a similarly vaulted but now immaculately up-to-date kitchen. This sunny range, overlooking wide lawns and gardens, with its 17th century outline, Georgian refinements and most skilfully blended present-day comforts and colours, seems to have the best of all worlds.

" For his own benefit, for the benefit of his descendants, and for the benefit of all good, humane and cultured men, Alexander Seton, a devout lover of all culture and humanity, founded, erected and adorned his country seat, the gardens and these suburban buildings," began the inscription carved in Latin on one of the dedication stones at Pinkie, ". . . for the gracious welcome and hospitable entertainment of guests a fountain of pure water, lawns, ponds and aviaries. In ways of pleasantness he has laid out all these for the honourable delight of body and soul."

It seems likely that these " ways of pleasantness " will now delight even more " good, humane and cultured men " than their founder imagined possible.

The 78-foot-long Painted Gallery is now used as a dormitory.

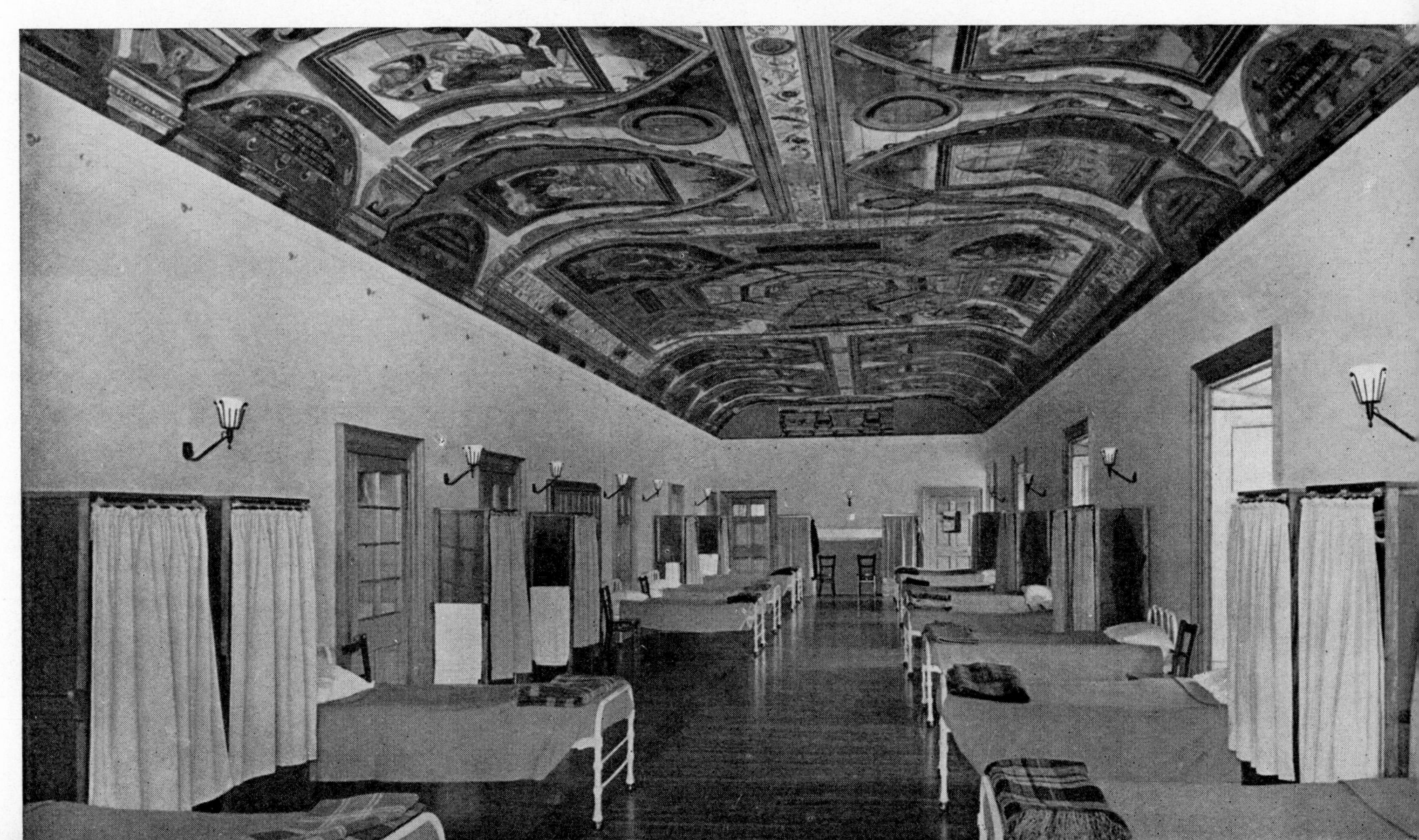

Penicuik House, seen from the steps of the old house, which was destroyed by fire in 1899.

Penicuik House

SIR JOHN CLERK OF PENICUIK (1676-1755) was a man of his time in the best sense of the word. Reading his memoirs, it is impossible not to admire and regret such Scotsmen, a type, it seems, wholly the product of the 18th century. Judge, politician, public figure, scholar, antiquarian, artist, musician and country laird, the self-portrait which emerges from Clerk's leisurely but careful jottings reveals not only a man of great ability and wide culture, but one good, wise and humble. Today, few are expected to excel in such various spheres—and few achieve it. We have replaced the man of parts by the specialist.

Born a landed gentleman of moderate fortune, Sir John was the 3rd Laird of Penicuik, his grandfather having acquired the barony in 1654. His father, a Member of Parliament for Edinburgh and created a Baronet by Charles II, married a granddaughter of William Drummond of Hawthornden, the poet. Brought up in the charming old House of Penicuik (formerly called Newbigging House), Clerk was sent to the parish school, Glasgow University, and later to study law at Leyden in Holland. Here he applied himself not only to the law but with passionate interest to Roman anti-

Converted from the stables by the present Sir John Clerk's grandmother, the late Aymée, Lady Clerk, the house, set around a courtyard, is Italian in arrangement and atmosphere, and must be unique in Scotland.

quities, music and art. Against his father's wishes and with very little money, he pursued his way to Italy, determined to see a country "so replenished with antiquities of all kinds, and so much excelling all other countries in painting and music." He also visited Vienna and Germany, and on returning to Scotland found that he "understood pictures better than became his purse, and as to musick I performed rather better than became a gentleman."

But he was no dilettante. In 1700 he was admitted a member of the Scottish bar, and hard work, together with a sound judgment, launched the young John Clerk on one of the most successful and rewarding careers of his time. His marriage to Lady Margaret Stuart, the Earl of Galloway's daughter, introduced him to her cousin, the "Union" Duke of Queensberry, who became Clerk's loyal friend and patron for the rest of his life. Through Queensberry, he was appointed to various councils to enquire into national finance and trade, and when he was barely thirty he was made one of the commissioners for the Parliamentary Union of Scotland and England in 1707. Finally, when, after the Act had been passed, the Scottish Court of Exchequer was founded, he became one of the five barons, an office which he held till his death in 1755.

Clerk's accounts of the negotiations for the Union have all the freshness and clarity of day-to-day impressions. Twice interviewed by Queen Anne, he once found her "labouring under a fit of the Gout," when "her face which was red and spotted, was rendered something frightful by her negligent dress and the foot affected was tied up with a poultice and some nasty bandages." His record of the two Stuart risings of 1715 and 1745 is written in the same informal yet considered way. Although Sir John was a Whig and a Government supporter, there is no bitterness in his comments on the Jacobites in spite of the fact that "some Savage Highlanders" took £200 worth of hay, corn and oats off Penicuik estate, and his family "was oblidged to entertain some of their Chiefs, three several times, and frequently 16 or 20 at a time."

In the early years of the 18th century, Penicuik estate was little developed—a high barren moor standing 800 feet above sea level. Clerk was one of the pioneers of tree-planting in Scotland, making a start as early as 1703, and much of the ordered beauty of the woods and the general layout of the place today is due to his foresight and skill. He also greatly improved the farm lands, the gardens and (with the eye of an artist) the arrangement of the extensive grounds. He was no less interested or active in his other properties, which included Cammo and Mavisbank near Edinburgh and Dumcrieff in Dumfriesshire.

A man of affairs with many friends and interests beyond his home, he was perhaps happiest in the country—with his family, his books and the sport of river, loch and moor. As he grew frailer, he spent more time among books, reading with most pleasure the classics in Greek and Latin. To his great grief, his first wife died in childbirth barely a year after their marriage. An interval of eight years elapsed before he "settled his thoughts on Mrs. Jennet Inglis of Cramond," a widow, and "a most religeous verteous woman, and one who in all respects might suit my humure and circumstances to rub through the world in a sober and privat state of Life." By her he had fifteen children, to whom he was a devoted and discerning father.

Baron Clerk was succeeded in 1755 by his son, Sir James. It must have been about this time that the old house was demolished, for, in 1762, the vast classical mansion, now roofless and ghostly in grandeur, was finished. It was seriously damaged by fire in 1899, and for the last fifty years the Clerk family have lived in

The sitting room of the ground floor was once the old coachhouse.

A portion of the dining room which looks out into the courtyard.

what was once the stables, a low square building, contemporary with the 18th century house, standing round four sides of a courtyard with an imposing portico at the entrance, topped by a spire originally designed by Baron Clerk for Penicuik Church.

The courtyard, with its central fountain, shaped lawns, clipped hedge and cypress trees, is Italian in atmosphere and arrangement, unique in Scotland. Ranging round the square, the coachhouse, malt house, stalls, loose boxes, hay loft and other features of the old stables have been transformed into a series of delightful, large, light, rather low-ceilinged rooms. Such fittings as the beautifully carved doors, the wainscoting and the mantelpieces have been transferred from the old house, as well as much of the 17th and 18th century furniture, a collection of family portraits and other relics and treasures. Converted by the present Laird's grandmother, the late Aymée, Lady Clerk, with remarkable skill and taste, a house of great character and charm has been contrived in which simplicity and sophistication are well blended. Commodore Sir John Dutton Clerk, R.N.R., the 10th Baronet, who has inherited his ancestor's interest in the property and farms part of the land himself, now lives at Penicuik House with his wife and family.

Borthwick Castle from the west, with the Romanesque church near the gateway.

BELOW: *The tower.*

Borthwick Castle

THE CASTLE STANDS ON HIGH GROUND above the meeting of the Gore Water and the Middleton North Burn, dominating the gently rolling lower slopes of the Moorfoot Hills and the scattered village of Borthwick, and only just over-topped by the spire of the Romanesque church near by. The great unblinking walls of the tower, heavy with 30,000 tons of masonry and pierced by midget windows, climb starkly to a height of nearly 100 feet, crowned by chimneys and little cap-houses on the roof. Originally the castle was surrounded by curtain walls, strengthened by round towers (one remains in part) and a parapet walk. Equally important from a military point of view was the defensive site, the ground dropping steeply to the river bed on three sides of the building.

Here, in 1430, Sir William Borthwick began to build the present castle on what was then called the Mote of Lochonwart. An earlier " motte " castle of timber and earthworks once stood on the site, owned by the Hays of Lochonwart, and it was not till 1438 that Sir William's mighty new tower was re-named Borthwick Castle. It is thought that the family originally sprang from Arbroath on the Borthwick Water in Angus, whence their name derives. Departing into mythology, the Borthwicks are said to have journeyed to Norway, taken part in an early invasion of Russia and settled on the shores of the Baltic. The 10th century Swedish invasion then pushed them inland and they took up a more permanent residence on the southern shores of Lake Peipus where the name flourishes as Borg, Borth, Burtick and other variations. A younger son was educated in Prague with Edgar the Atheling's children, Edmund, Margaret and Christine, whom he rescued from the English after their father had been poisoned. They then all set out for Hungary but were blown off course and had to seek refuge in the Firth of Forth where Malcolm Canmore fell in love with Margaret while the ship was being repaired. After the marriage of Malcolm and Margaret, Borthwick was given lands in the south of the kingdom " to keep the English quiet by checking the raids into Scotland from the south." These would be the lands in Roxburghshire which are now referred to as Borthwick Water.

Returning to more documented times, Thomas de Borthwick, great-grandfather of the builder of the castle, received a charter of the lands of Ligertwood near Lauder in 1357. Sir William's father, who was sent on diplomatic missions to England between the years 1398-1413, possessed the property of Catcune in Midlothian and acquired other lands in Selkirkshire. Sir William himself, who was Captain of Edinburgh Castle in 1420 and held an official appointment as Collector of Customs, spent two years in England as one of the hostages for James I, where he was kept under close guard in York Castle. Three years after his return to Scotland in 1430, he was granted, by a no doubt grateful sovereign, a letter of licence to build and fortify his castle.

During the 15th century, when baronial power and pomp were at their height in Scotland, the nobles and gentry aimed to make their castles something more than the military strongholds of earlier times. The vertical stone tower house with its massive walls and roof parapet (used for both observation and defensive operations) still served as a necessary citadel against attack, but the interior now became grander and more spacious and convenient. Borthwick was conceived with immense skill, cunning and imagination and when it was finished must have been the most advanced and up-to-date castle in the country. The building consists of a high rectangular tower, rising sheerly to the machicolated parapet encircling the roof, upon which the two cap-houses (terminating the wheel stairs) squat among the chimneys like miniature cottages borne aloft by some freak whirlwind. Two uniform wings extend from the west side of the tower, leaving a grim, narrow void between. There is a legend that prisoners challenged to leap the horrific gap, if successful, were rewarded by freedom.

BELOW: *A 14th-century breviary belonging to the Borthwicks of Crookston.*

The main entrance at first floor level on the north side of the castle was formerly reached by a bridge from the curtain wall, now replaced by a stone stairway. Stepping across a small lobby flanked by the guard room inside the entrance, the visitor immediately enters the great hall, a huge, vaulted apartment filling the entire first floor of the main block. " It is so large and high in the roof," said Alexander Nisbet, the 17th century writer on heraldry, " that a man on horseback could turn a spear in it with all imaginable ease." It is a giant's room, people and furniture dwarfed by the soaring barrel-vault, the tall arched windows with deep embrasures and the huge, hooded chimneypiece. On the north wall, opposite the fireplace, the original minstrels' gallery and screens (enclosing the service quarters) have been replaced by a modern loft and long velvet curtains, but the general effect has been preserved. What has faded, however, is the original colour scheme which must have been gay and vivid when the walls were covered in hanging tapestries and the vault plastered and painted with allegorical scenes and inscriptions. On one side of the dome were the words in Gothic letters (now almost obliterated) " ye tempil of honour," and on the other (now effaced) " ye tempil of religion." Close to one of the six doorways out of the hall, a beautifully carved wash-basin is corbelled out from the west wall in the form of a church piscina. In fact, an almost exact replica of the design exists in the church of Semur-en-Auxois in France.

Opening out of the great hall on the first floor (but originally divided by a passage) are the kitchen and the Laird's private room in the wings—an extremely convenient and modern arrangement for ensuring hot meals and labour-saving service. Above the first floor, however, the main block and the wings do not connect on the flat, there being six, seven and eight respective storeys in each. Dark winding stairs ascend mysteriously in dizzy whorls to the roof, punctuated by doorways at every level—a device calculated to baffle anyone, friend or enemy, not acquainted with the castle. Over the great hall are three similar apartments, the one on the second floor, in recent times used as a drawing room, having an oratory in a window embrasure. The main bedrooms are situated on the second floor of the wings, with servants' quarters at different levels and a maze of small rooms tucked into the thickness of the walls. The vaulted basement, designed for storage, cellars and dungeons, has a separate entrance under the main doorway on the north side.

Portrait at Crookston of James, 7th Lord Borthwick.

Ou the north wall of the great hall the original minstrels' gallery and screens (enclosing the service quarters) have been replaced by a modern loft and long velvet curtains.

Sir William Borthwick died some 20 years after his castle was built and his son, another William of many to follow, succeeded him. This 2nd Sir William had travelled to Rome in 1425 as an ambassador from Scotland, with a deputy including the Bishops of Aberdeen and Dunblane, and five years later received a knighthood. It is said that this ceremony took place at the christening of the twin sons of James I. Later, Sir William was created Lord Borthwick. The 4th Lord, who is said to have been killed at the Battle of Flodden, and his wife are probably the subjects of the marble effigies which lie in the old part of Borthwick church today. John, the 6th Lord, who married a daughter of the Earl of Crawford, supported the Earl of Arran against the Queen Mother, Mary of Lorraine, in his bid for the regency. For this he was seized by Sir George Douglas and imprisoned in Dalkeith Castle, but Lady Borthwick soon found an opportunity to retaliate and detained Patrick, Earl of Bothwell, at Borthwick Castle. " Bicause the Lady Borthyke was faire," wrote a contemporary witness, " he came to hir for love, but she made hyme to be handled and kepte."

Lord Borthwick was later a devoted supporter of Mary, Queen of Scots, who made two visits to the castle in his lifetime. His son, William, was host to the Queen and her husband, the Earl of Bothwell, on a more momentous occasion in 1567 when the castle was suddenly surrounded one evening by the insurgent Lords and a thousand men, hoping to capture the royal couple. But Bothwell, warned of the impending invasion had ridden off the night before, leaving Mary with several attendants. The Lords then withdrew, afterwards giving this as proof that they had no designs upon the Queen herself " it being maist easy to have been taken." Mary " in mennes claithes, butit and spurrit, departit the samin night of Borthwick to Dunbar."

Lord Borthwick remained a loyal friend to the Queen, meeting her at Hamilton after her escape from Loch Leven and fighting with her forces at Langside. But as a husband he fell short of grace and his wife, Grissel, a daughter of Sir Walter Scott of Branxholme, complained in 1578 to the Privy Council that " scho, being lauchfullie with Williame Lord Borthuik hir spous, continewit with him in mutuall societie and band of matrimony this lang tyme bipast, having borne unto him in the menetyme sevin bairnis yit on life. Nochtwithstanding, he, being instigat be Sathan, not onlie abstractit his cumpany and societie fra hir, bot als delt verray unkyndlie with hir, in geving hir mony injurious wordis, stryking and dinging of her to the effusioun of hir blude in greit quantitie, without feir of God, petie or compassioun of her estait, being then greit with chyld." The Privy Council did their best to prevail on the couple to settle their differences from time to time, but without much success. Lord Borthwick died in 1582 in the Canongate of Edinburgh.

In 1650 the 10th Lord Borthwick held the castle against Cromwell and in November of that year General Lambert was sent out from Edinburgh with " two mortar-pieces " and " two great guns," followed by a threatening letter in the following terms:

TO THE GOVERNOR OF BORTHWICK CASTLE: THESE

Sir,—I thought fitt to send this trumpet to you, to lett you to carry off your armes and goods, and such other necessaries as you have. You have harboured such parties in your house as have basely (and) unhumanely murdered our men; if you necessitate me to bend my cannon against you, you must expect what I doubt you will not be pleased with. I expect your present answer,

and rest your servant,

O. CROMWELL.

The east wall of the castle today bears the marks of General Lambert's artillery, but Lord Borthwick eventually took Cromwell's advice and saved further destruction of the castle. According to Carlyle, he " walked away in surrender, having been allowed 15 days to pack."

On the death of this 10th Lord Borthwick, without issue, both the succession and the property wandered from the hitherto direct descent. The castle was sold to the Dalrymples and from them passed through various hands till in 1812 it was bought by John Borthwick of Crookston, of a collateral branch of the family, with whom it remains today. His descendant, the present owner, Major Henry Borthwick of Borthwick and Crookston, was in 1944 recognised as the Chief of Borthwick by the Lord Lyon, and is the 24th *de jure* Lord, the title having been in abeyance since 1910. Major Borthwick, who served with the Allied Government Staffs in the Second World War and is a D.L. and J.P. for Midlothian, lives with his wife and family at Crookston, near Heriot, having leased Borthwick Castle to Mr. Peter Daniel, the architect.

LEFT: *The south end of the vaulted great hall showing the hooded chimneypiece. This is a giant's room, with people and furniture dwarfed by the soaring barrel-vault and the tall arched windows with deep embrasures.*

Hamilton House, Prestonpans, built in 1628. On the left stands Preston Tower, dating from the 15th century.

Hamilton House

WITHIN A FEW HUNDRED YARDS OF each other, on the outskirts of Prestonpans, among streets of Victorian houses and modern housing estates, stand three remarkable old buildings, like curious sentinels of another age. The tallest and most northerly of these, Preston Tower, dates from the 15th century, although the ruinous top-piece was a later addition. Uninhabited and roofless, this strangely shaped keep, which looks like the toppling remains of a child's play with a box of bricks, was once the home of Sir John and Dame Katherine Hamilton. A stone's throw away, to the south of the main road, within a large garden enclosed by high walls, rise the picturesque turrets and gables of Northfield House, built in the early 17th century by Joseph Marjoribanks, an Edinburgh merchant. And lastly, just across the road between Northfield and Preston Tower, stands Hamilton House, smaller and squatter than either and set back from the pavement in a little sunken flagged courtyard, the walls a dazzling white against the steep dove-grey roof.

Hamilton House has been described as the prettiest house in the Lothians, and although this might be disputed in three counties so rich in old houses, in the sense that a small English country house of the period or a little French manor may be pretty rather than imposing, this Scottish Jacobean merchant's house is charmingly and unusually so. For it has nothing of the rugged grandeur or the baroque fantasy characteristic of many larger Scottish Baronial buildings. It was finished in 1628 for John Hamilton, a merchant burgess of Edinburth, who, contrary to popular belief, claimed no direct relation to the Hamiltons of Preston Tower. Indeed, the two families may not have been related at all, for the name was a common one in the district. But the myth that Hamilton House was the dower house of the Tower dies hard. With Northfield House, however, there were strong family ties, for Joseph Marjoribanks and John Hamilton married two sisters, Katherine and Marion Symesoune.

John Hamilton, who had evidently prospered as a merchant in Edinburgh, built his house two storeys and an attic in height, with a main block running north and south, and two wings jutting out westwards to form three sides of a square enclosing the courtyard. Here, overlooking the paved courtyard, are crowded many typical architectural features of the time—the great white crow-stepped gable-end with its broad chimneystack, the two dormer windows breaking the steep roof-line, the fat little turret squeezed into the north-west corner and the elegant front door with its inscribed pediment under the decorated window in the angled stair turret. Although the house has undergone various alterations since it was built, the general appearance has not been disturbed. The effect is still one of robust and sprightly charm. On the east side, which faces the original garden, a massive central chimneystack, flanked by two solid gables and decorated dormer windows, diminishes the roof-line to

The east side facing the original garden.

a mere background almost in the manner of an English Elizabethan manor.

In the pediment above the front door, freshly painted in red, blue and gold, are set the impaled arms of Hamilton and Symesoune and the date 1628. And under a chubby angel carved in stone above the stair window are the words, "PRAISED BE THE LORD MY STRENGYTH AND MY REDEIMER." Texts of this sort to commemorate the building of a house were not uncommon in Scotland in the 17th century. Over the entrance to Northfield House is written, "EXCEP THE LORD BULD INWAE (in vain) BULDS MAN."

The Hamilton family had evidently been settled in Prestonpans for some time before the house was built. There are records concerning the builder's grandfather, Jerome Hamilton, who owned land in Salt Preston in 1544 and a dwelling house in the Canongate, Edinburgh (then the aristocratic end of the High Street) in 1563. Before his grandson John built the house, he was designated "of Little Fawsyde." Apprenticed to an Edinburgh merchant, one Hector Ray, in 1599, he was admitted a merchant burgess in 1615 and a guild brother five years later. He married Katherine Symesoune and they had four sons, the eldest, John, succeeding his father at Hamilton House in 1634. John the second, who was on the Committee of War for Haddingtonshire in 1649 and ten years later was made a burgess and guild brother of Edinburgh in place of his father, married a Helen Cockburn, and they had a family of four, two sons and two daughters. After the death of both sons, a grandson, William Russell, was served heir to his grandfather at some time in the 1740s.

Possibly they were still the owners of the house when, in September, 1745, Prince Charles Edward billeted some of his victorious Highland army there after the Battle of Prestonpans. The episode, however, is traditional rather than documentary, the only evidence, if it will pass as such, being the marks left on a stone window surround and a chimneypiece which were used by the soldiers, it is said, as knife-sharpeners. As is well known, the battle, which was fought between Cockenzie and Prestonpans against Sir John Cope and his English dragoons, resulted in an overwhelming victory for the Jacobites, mainly owing to surprise tactics and unorthodox methods of warfare. ". . . The Highlanders, having discharged their muskets," records the *Scots Magazine* for September, 1745, "threw them down, then drew their swords, and carried all before them like a torrent, so that in seven or eight minutes both horse and foot were totally routed, and drove them from the field of battle, though it must be owned that the enemy fought very gallantly; but they could not withstand the impetuosity or rather fury of the Highlanders, and were forced to *run* when they could no longer resist."

In 1937, nearly two hundred years later. Hamilton House was scheduled for demolition so that the main road could be widened. By this time it was used as a tenement to house four families. Extra doors had been knocked through the walls, an outside staircase erected for the top flat, the interior completely altered to suit its new purpose, and the harling was flaking off the old stone. At the eleventh hour the house was saved from destruction by The National Trust for Scotland. Although the old stables, a continuation of the south-west wing, were lopped off to make space for a wider road, The Trust bought the building otherwise intact, and restored it.

In the long living room, which runs the breadth of the house with windows to the east and west, a huge stone chimneypiece bearing the arms and initials of the original owners was discovered. Also the oak beams of the ceiling were uncovered—a delightful feature more usual in a town house of the period. Except for the window-surrounds, the stone walls have been plastered and whitewashed. Four doors, painted primrose yellow, open out of this room, one leading to the spiral stair in the north-west angle of the house. Persian rugs, some pieces of period furniture, a grand piano and old prints and portraits on the walls, make this ancient "great hall" a charming room today. A small sitting room beyond, where the rafter ceiling has been replaced and painted pale green, as are the doors, has wooden shutters with painted ornamentation in the manner of 17th century interior decoration. The rooms on the upper floor have been entirely reconstructed and only two old stone fireplaces remain.

One of the first tenants to live in Hamilton House after it had been restored was Mr. Jo Grimond, who was then Liberal leader and Secretary of The National Trust for Scotland. In 1963 a bad outbreak of dry rot, wet rot and rising damp necessitated the installation of an "electro-osmotic" damp course and also a form of internal background heating.

Hamilton House may have mellowed, but its inherent Scots simplicity of style still remains to delight the eye.

The restored "great hall" on the ground floor.

Lennoxlove, from the south-west, showing the massive 15th-century tower and later additions.

Lennoxlove

LITTLE MORE THAN A MILE SOUTH OF Haddington, a long straight drive leads up to Lennoxlove. A fully grown castle-into-house, with its massive old tower, 17th century extension and later additions, it stands among old trees, facing the rough grasslands of the park which stretch away towards denser patches of wood climbing the slopes of the Lammermuir Hills. The warm pinkish sand-colour of the stones, as well as its five centuries, give Lennoxlove a mellow completeness, as if repose had come only after a long and active life. An old garden with a square lawn surrounded by paved paths and herbaceous borders lies to the east of the house, but only a low yew hedge divides the entrance front from the park, where white clouds of seagulls swoop now and then over the trees to join the company of pedestrian crows in search of food.

At close quarters, the 14th century keep, so gracious in the distance, is almost overpowering in bulk and strength, dwarfing everything in its shadow and asserting, as it were, its one-time defensive powers. The little cap-house and parapet walk on the top are later additions.

"*Thy tour and fortres lairge and lang*
Thy nychtbouris dois excell,
And for thy wallis thik and strang
Thow justlie beirs the bell.
Thy groundis deep and toppis hie
Uprysing in the air;
Thy voltis plesand ar to sie
They ar so greit and fair."

So wrote Sir Richard Maitland (1496-1586) of the tower, which was then called Lethington and had belonged to the Maitlands since 1345. Probably the earlier keep which once stood on the site was built by the original owners, the Giffords of Yester.

It was during the 16th century that Lennoxlove moved up-stage in history. Several times it was stormed by invading English forces, although state rather than military matters eventually brought the family fame. Sir Richard Maitland, poet, collector of Scottish ballads and distinguished judge, had two sons who are even better remembered than himself. John, the younger (1545-1595), became Lord Chancellor of Scotland, and in 1590 was created Lord Thirlstane. But the elder son, William (1525-1573), better known as Secretary Lethington, is perhaps the most celebrated of all the Maitlands. Queen Elizabeth called him " The Flower of the Wits of Scotland." When Mary, Queen of Scots, returned from France in 1561, Lethington was made Secretary of State (he had held the post for her mother, Mary of Lorraine, three years earlier), and through all her turbulent reign he remained a loyal and trusted servant. He married one of the Queen's Maries—Mary Fleming—who must often have seen him pacing what is now known as " The Politician's Walk," not far from the house, while he pondered the unruly affairs of state. William Maitland died in 1573 in a Leith prison, forestalling the sentence which, after the Queen's defeat, would surely have ended his life.

Above the main entrance to the tower is carved the following inscription in Latin—" Who of the race of Maitland laid the foundations, who raised the Tower, envious antiquity has concealed. John Maitland, Earl of Lauderdale, enlarged the windows, provided an easier stairway and embellished it in the year of the Christian Era 1626." This Earl's son, a third successive John, became the first and only Duke of Lauderdale and one of the most powerful figures of the day both in Scotland (where for a time he was virtually a dictator) and in London as Secretary of State and Privy Councillor after the Restoration. An entry in Samuel Pepys's Diary gives us an informal glimpse of the great man's town life—". . . went to my Lord Lauderdale's house to speak with him. We find (him) and his lady and some Scotch people at supper. Pretty odd company. But at supper there played one of the servants upon the viallin some Scotch tunes only; several and the best

An old doorway leads from the banqueting hall to the spiral staircase.

The Yellow Room. The set of William and Mary chairs have been moved into the banqueting hall.

The Petit Point Room, looking into the drawing room beyond, is hung with 17th-century embroidery appliquéd to brocade.

of their country, as they seemed to esteem them, but Lord! the strangest ayres that ever I heard in my life, and all of one cast. But strange to hear my Lord Lauderdale say himselfe, that he had rather hear a cat mew than the best musique in the world, and the better the musique the more sicke it makes him; and that of all instruments he hates the lute most, and next to that the baggpipe."

The Duke found time to carry on his father's work of restoration at Lennoxlove (although he was much more occupied with additions to Thirlestane Castle in Berwickshire) and to build the 17th century house adjoining the old tower. In 1674, he also enclosed the park—said to be the first in Scotland thus treated. Lauderdale was persuaded by his wife to leave the estate to his step-son, Lord Huntingtower, who soon after sold it to Thomas, Viscount Teviot.

In 1703 Lennoxlove was bought by the trustees of Francis Teresa, Duchess of Lennox and Richmond, better known as La Belle Stewart, a famous beauty of the court of Charles II. The king pursued her with admiration and many fine gifts, including the lovely silver-gilt toilet set recently acquired by the Royal Scottish Museum; but to escape his attentions she eloped with the Duke of Lennox and Richmond. In her will she left instructions to purchase a property in Scotland for her cousin's son, the Master of Blantyre—". . . and I appoint it to be called Lennoxlove." Thus Lethington became Lennoxlove, for the childless Duchess hoped the name would have some sort of immortality. She never visited the house, but a portrait of La Belle Stewart by Lely hangs in the White Room today.

The Blantyres remained at Lennoxlove for two hundred years. During this time various additions and alterations were carried out, notably in the early 19th century, when an attic on the 17th century front was replaced by a full storey and the present eastern tower was built. With the extinction of the title in 1900, Lennoxlove went to a grandson, through his daughter, of the last Lord Blantyre,

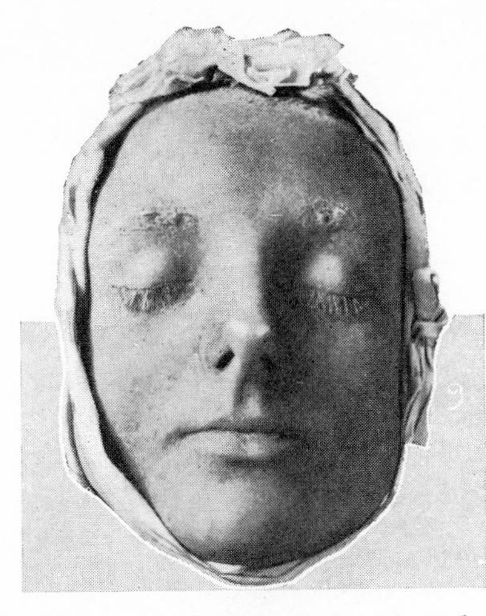

A death mask presumed to be that of Mary, Queen of Scots.

The banqueting hall.

the late Major W. A. Baird, who was responsible for the extensive 20th century restorations, including the present state of the banqueting hall. The new chimneypiece here was designed by the late Sir Robert Lorimer. Major Baird died in 1933, and in 1947 his younger son, Mr Robert Baird, sold Lennoxlove to the Duke of Hamilton, who, with his family, lives there today.

The interior of the old tower—and particularly the great hall with its ten-foot-thick walls and barrel-vaulted ceiling—is impressive and has been well preserved. The rooms in the 17th century house have been much altered and modernised, but the very fine array of furniture (mainly from English 17th and 18th century, with some good French and Dutch pieces), the paintings by Van Dyck, Raeburn, Cornelius Janssen, Lely, Kneller, Canaletto, Guardi, Augustus John and others, and the very complete and lovely old sets of china and porcelain, must be one of the most interesting collections in Scotland. These were brought mainly from Hamilton Palace, which was demolished some thirty years ago, but there are one or two portraits and three pieces presented to La Belle Stewart by Charles II which were bought with the house. Lennoxlove has so much to recommend it that everyone may find his own pleasure there.

The famous silver casket which once held "The Casket Letters" which incriminated Mary, Queen of Scots, and led to her death,

ABOVE: *The north front of Yester House.*

LEFT: *Yester House from a print dated 1821.*

Yester House

OLD YESTER CASTLE, SAID TO HAVE been built in the year 1267, is certainly one of the earliest stone castles in Scotland. So strange and fantastic did it appear to the people of the time that the builder, Sir Hugo de Gifford, was commonly supposed to be a wizard of supernatural powers. Mainly ruinous today, part of the huge underground apartment, known as Goblin Hall, is still intact—unique in Great Britain but resembling certain French contemporary castles. Sir Walter Scott describing Goblin Hall in *Marmion* says:

"*Of lofty roof and ample size,*
Beneath the castle deep it lies:
To hew the living rock profound,
The floor to pave, the arch to round,
There never toiled a mortal arm—
It all was wrought by word and charm."

Some way down Hopes Water, the present house stands surrounded by "noble Walks and Forests of Trees" originally planted and laid out by the 1st Marquess of Tweeddale in imitation of those at Greenwich and St. James's Park, London. It was his son who built the house early in the 18th century on the site of the old village of Bothans which was cleared away to make place for it. At the same time, the new village of Gifford was built outside the gates of Yester—two wide, tree-lined streets of houses, many of them feued on condition that the inhabitants shall, when desired, "attend the Marquess the space of two days yearly, sufficiently mounted with horse and arms" and shall further "perform a day's work yearly for winning of hay in the parks of Yester." These simple, harled houses with the mercat cross, tolbooth and well designed church built in 1710, form one of the most charming villages in Scotland.

The Giffords, a Norman family welcomed by David I, acquired Yester in the 12th century. Two hundred years later Sir John Gifford's daughter and heiress married Sir William Hay, said to be descended from William de Haya, royal butler to Malcolm IV and William the Lion. When Haddington was occupied by the English in 1548 "The Lord of Yester's house" (the Hay family were raised to the peerage in 1488) was alternately garrisoned by the Scots and English forces—the latter consisting mainly of Spanish mercenaries. But by 1550 Lord Hay was safely ensconced once more in his castle.

During the 17th century an earldom and later a marquisate was bestowed on the family. The 2nd Marquess who followed his father in the office of Lord Chancellor of Scotland, and became one of the main supporters of the Parliamentary Union of 1707, was an enterprising "improver" of agriculture in Scotland and an enthusiastic promoter of trade. He was no less progressive in another direction, and his new house describes that particular good taste and wide vision which is characteristic of the time. This house was built for Lord Tweeddale by William Adam, and all his plans for it are in *Vitruvius Scoticus.*

A finely balanced two-storeyed building of strawberry pink sandstone, Yester is given character and grandeur by the great classical facade in the centre of the north face (altered by William Adam's son Robert after his father's death) and the two little pavilions with bell-shaped roofs (only one remains today) which, almost alone, uphold an old Scottish traditional feature. For Yester was one of the first strictly classical houses in Scotland. It seems that the house, although not fully completed till 1789, was partly occupied as early as 1704. The story goes that the workmen finishing the roof, threw some of the slates at dragoons fleeing from the Battle of Prestonpans in 1745. After William Adam's death in 1748, he was succeeded by his son Robert, so

The dining room, which was originally the hall.

that the building and interior decoration are entirely the work of Adam, father and son.

The contrast and resemblances in the respective work of these two great artists is one of the most fascinating features of Yester. The work covers William Adam's last and best period, while Robert is often feeling his way towards his later more delicate and precise style. The dining room for instance (formerly the hall opening off the original north entrance) with its light, slender plasterwork ceiling and beautiful, subdued frieze, is, I think, one of Adam Senior's most lovely rooms, while the ballroom, completed by his son about 1760, is, although one of his earliest interiors, perhaps the finest room of its kind in Scotland. With its untypically bold, rich plasterwork ceiling, and more familiar chimneypiece and decoration in relief above the doorway, the room is so well proportioned that the effect is splendid without being overpowering. The delightful wall panels were painted (in imitation of tapestry) by the French artist William Delacour, who was for some years Director of the Edinburgh Academy of Fine Arts. Various alterations made to the house in the 19th century include the addition of the present entrance porch on the west side.

There are many interesting and descriptive family portraits at Yester, including Medina's painting of the 1st Marquess (finished in 1796) with his wife, who had died eleven years earlier, holding a wreath, his fourteen living children, and two long dead, portrayed as angels looking down from heaven. There are also portraits by Van Dyck and his pupil Soest and among

RIGHT: *Part of the ballroom, completed by William Adam's son Robert about 1760 is, although one of his earliest interiors, perhaps the finest room of its kind in Scotland.*

BELOW: *A portrait by Sir John Medina in 1796 of the 1st Marquess of Tweeddale, with his wife and children.*

several by Allan Ramsay is one of Lord Charles Hay, a hero of the Battle of Fontenoy (1745). He wrote to his brother afterwards telling him of the advance of his Regiment to within twenty paces of the French Guards. "I . . . drank to them and told them we were the English Guards and hoped they would stand until we came quite up to them . . . I immediately turned about to our own Regiment, speeched them and made them huzzah." The French commanding officer ". . . tried to make his men huzzah but not above three or four in their Brigade did." Hay did not know who began the firing but he and many of the King's Company were badly wounded.

The 7th Marquess died in the Fort of Verdun in 1804 where Napoleon had imprisoned him and his wife. His son, later a Field-Marshal, served as aide-de-camp under Wellington in the Peninsular Wars. This able and distinguished family, who have been Lairds of Yester for more than six hundred years, number many eminent men in Scottish history, particularly in the army, the law and in politics. The present and 11th Marquess who is Lord-Lieutenant of East Lothian, lives with his wife today in this most magnificent house.

LEFT: *The grand staircase and domed skylight are the work of Robert Adam, while the decoration and figures are that of Adam Senior.*

BELOW: *The double drawing room.*

Like a chopin valse which evokes others in different keys without losing any of its own character, Paxton is reminiscent of other Adam houses and is yet quite individual. Built in pink sandstone on the traditional, formal plan of a solid, central block connected by curving, balustraded walls to two low, sedate wings enclosing a spacious courtyard, Paxton is entered by an imposing, pillared portico. From here the view stretches across quiet, wooded parkland where grazing sheep wander, and on the south side, the garden, overlooking rolling Northumbrian countryside, is bounded by a lazy curve of the River Tweed. So far, there is little documentary evidence that the Adam brothers designed the house, but from the general plan, the quality of interior decoration and the fact that Patrick Home, the builder, was an old friend of the Adam family, it is assumed that John Adam was the architect, with probable co-operation inside from the more famous Robert.

Perhaps it is this rather unexpected progress from the vast, solemn exterior to the rare and exciting splendours inside, which imbues the house with a strangely dramatic flavour. Drama, however, is a determined factor at Paxton—not only in the making and furnishing of the house but also in its family history. Patrick Home was studying at Leipzig University in Germany in the year 1751 when he heard that his mother had been murdered with "a table knife" in her Berwickshire house by a servant, intent on robbery, while she sat at her desk paying out wages. Through this unfortunate lady, Patrick inherited the large fortune left by his father and eventually the castle and lands of Wedderburn.

The Homes of Wedderburn are the oldest cadets of this great and numerous Berwickshire family of whom the Earl of Home is head. Their lands, granted to David de Hum in 1413 by the Earl of Douglas, in return for faithful service, lay on the borderland between England and Scotland, and the family's main concern in early days was to guard that border against the enemy. This hazardous duty, undertaken with great courage and resource, was so costly in life that until 1574 every single Laird of Wedderburn was killed in battle. Sir David Home and his seven sons (famous as "The Seven Spears of Wedderburn" as recounted by Sir Walter Scott) fought at Flodden where the Laird and his heir fell. The banner which returned, draped round their bodies, is still preserved at Paxton today. Later on, the 1715 Rising was supported by Sir George Home of Wedderburn and his eldest son, both of whom were taken prisoner at Preston. Through Lady Grizel Hume of Marchmont a pardon was obtained for Sir George. His son was sentenced to be transported to Virginia and sold as a slave, but on arrival there found his freedom had been purchased for him by a kinsman. Young George, however, decided to settle in Virginia where he was employed by the Government as a land surveyor.

None of George's brothers left any

Paxton House from the north. The architecture is attributed to John Adam.

Paxton House

The Adam drawing room ceiling is one of the loveliest in Scotland.

The rather narrow oval staircase.

LEFT: *One of the main bedrooms showing the Chippendale furniture.*

RIGHT: *The dining room.*

children, and thus, at the age of twenty, Patrick, the eldest surviving son of his sister, Margaret Home, found himself possessed of a huge fortune and heir to the ancient estate of Wedderburn. His portrait by Reynolds (painted many years later) which hangs at Paxton today, shows a forceful, intelligent face with a touch of arrogance. At twenty, he certainly did not lack confidence. Leaving Leipzig he made his way to Berlin, where several exiled Jacobite friends of his grandfather warmly welcomed him at the Prussian Court. Shortly after his arrival there, Patrick proposed to Miss de Brandt, the illegitimate daughter of Frederick the Great. The conditions of acceptance (dictated by the king) were the transportation of Patrick's fortune to Prussia and that the young man take a commission in the Prussian Guards. This he refused to do, and on being urgently requested to leave Berlin by his outraged uncle at Wedderburn, he made his farewells to Frederick the Great and his daughter, rashly promising her that he would never marry anyone else without her written consent. Before returning to Scotland, Patrick travelled in Italy where he bought many of the pictures now at Paxton today.

But Patrick must surely have been in love with Miss de Brandt. When he got back to Berwickshire he had not abandoned the idea of marrying her, for he decided to build a house "worthy of a King's daughter." The lands of Paxton had long been the property of the Wedderburn Homes but not even a military castle could have survived on the littoral border between England and Scotland much before the 18th century. The house, therefore, unlike so many of that period, is not a replacement of an older building, nor an addition—it is completely the creation of its own age. The square, high-ceilinged hall with its rich rococo plasterwork over the chimneypiece is a delightful if somewhat puzzling introduction to the interior. Opening off the hall, the long dining room overlooking the Tweed suggests a much later date. Well proportioned, classical, Adamesque in every detail from the beautiful ceiling and the narrow panels decorated with an acorn design painted in olive green, pale blue and yellow, on cinnamon walls, to the chairs, sideboard, mahogany urns and wine-coolers, surely this room is proof of Robert Adam's guiding hand. Certainly craftsmen (English and Italian) came from London.

But where the dining room, cool and classical, wakens a gradual, measured admiration, the drawing room immediately dazzles with its many painted glories. I have never seen a lovelier Adam ceiling in Scotland. Especially beautiful is the central circlet of flower-like petals within a wider circle of the familiar fans and plaques of Greek figures painted in pale pink, cream and gold.

About 1770, before Paxton was finished, Patrick Home received news of Miss de Brandt's death. However romantic the attachment, nearly twenty years had passed since they met. Released from his promise and now Laird of Wedderburn, he next year married a Miss Graham. Wedderburn Castle was rebuilt in the fashionable mock-Gothic style of the time and Paxton sold (for £15,000) to Patrick's first cousin, Ninian Home, a planter in the West Indies. He it was, on a visit to Scotland in 1772, who commissioned Thomas Chippendale to furnish the entire house. Most of this magnificent furniture remains in the house today and is, in itself, a unique exhibition. The original receipted accounts show that the order included such items as mattresses, bolsters, dozens of yards of material and even hearth brushes! Ninian Home, however, never retired to Paxton, for in 1795, when he was Governor of Grenada, he was murdered by slaves who had been incited to rebellion by the spirit of the French Revolution.

Ninian's brother George, a legal colleague of Sir Walter Scott, next succeeded to Paxton (Raeburn painted this Laird), and in 1812, the year he inherited Wedderburn, added the Library and Picture Gallery (the latter has recently been converted to a chapel), ordering the furniture from William Trotter of Edinburgh whose shop stood on the site now occupied by the North British Hotel. Comparatively unknown, although he must have furnished much of Edinburgh's New Town, Trotter was a superlative craftsman as well as a good business man. Undoubtedly, the finest and most comprehensive collection of his Regency furniture in Scotland is housed at Paxton.

George Home, a bachelor, died in 1820, when Paxton and Wedderburn were inherited by a cousin, William Forman, whose eldest daughter and heiress, Jean, married the son of a near neighbour, Admiral Sir David Milne. Their son, the late Colonel David Milne-Home followed in succession and his granddaughter, Mrs Home Robertson, the present owner, lives there today with her husband and family.

The drawing room.

ABOVE: *Patrick Home by Reynolds.* RIGHT: *The daughters of William Forman-Home.*

BELOW: *The Regency library. The full-length portrait by Raeburn is of Sir David Milne.*

The Hirsel, Coldstream, from the north-west.

The Hirsel

THE APPROACH TO HIRSEL IS BESET BY so many distractions to the eye and to the historic sense that the house itself is arrived at all too suddenly and one realises that the long view has been missed. There can be no grander meeting point between Scotland and England on all the Border than this stretch of country where the Tweed at Coldstream has become a wide, majestic water, matched in splendour by the lofty peaks of the Cheviots to the south. The drive up to the house winds between woods, rolling fields of grass and plough and a lake, fringed in Spring by blazing orange red willow, and so through sweeping lawns, old trees, shrubs and gardens at different levels.

A long terrace on the east entrance side of the house overlooks a steep drop to the little river Leet flowing through the grounds. High grey walls rise above the terrace in an almost straight line and it is only from the west garden side that the buildings take shape and describe their age and position. An outpost of a square tower, the oldest part of the building, stands at the south end, joined to a 17th to early 18th century house of three storeys with a main block flanked by two projecting wings. The long, slightly higher building running northwards dates mainly from the early 19th century with later additions. Against this Regency facade, wrought-iron balconies outside the tall first-floor windows are painted blue. Although no attempt has been made to knit the two houses together in one design, the whole building is, to some extent, welded by the warm brownish-grey freestone, patched with shades of gold, black and bronze.

No family has deeper roots in the Borders than the Douglas-Homes. Sir Alec Douglas-Home is the present representative of the main branch of the Home clan who took their name from territory in Berwickshire and were first mentioned in a charter of 1138. Traditionally, the ancestor of the family was a grandson of the 3rd Earl of Dunbar who acquired the lands of Home by marriage in the 13th century, and the more documentary pedigree begins with Sir John Home, whose son, Sir Thomas, became the owner of the Barony of Dunglas in East Lothian towards the end of the 14th century by marrying a lady with the captivating name of Nichola Pepdie. He also held lands on both sides of the Tweed. Hume Castle, near Stichill, now a ruin, was then the family stronghold, and in 1453, when the Earls of Northumberland and Douglas threatened to invade Scotland, Sir Alexander Home received £20 by order of James II for "wines, victuals, spears and lances for the defence of his House of Home." The king granted Sir Alexander's son a crown charter of his lands and in 1473 created him Lord Home.

The 2nd Lord Home was a personage of importance in Scottish affairs and a staunch friend of James IV, who made him Warden of the East Marches and Great Chamberlain of Scotland for life. In 1496 the King paid a visit to Hume Castle. The next Lord Home with Lord Huntly commanded a division of the Scottish army at Flodden and defeated the right wing of the English forces under Lord Howard. Many of his kin were killed in the general slaughter, but Home himself survived, a remarkable feat in this most disastrous of battles for the Scots which inevitably stirred up suspicion afterwards as to his not having followed up his lone victory. It seems likely that only the multitude of dead at Flodden were immune from post-war criticism. Home was foremost among the nobles who invited the Duke of Albany (direct heir, through Robert the Bruce, to the baby King James V) from France to oppose the English influence of the Queen Mother, Margaret Tudor, sister of Henry VIII. In 1516 Home and his brother were both executed for treason and their heads hung high on Edinburgh Tolbooth for four years until their supporters gained control, when the remains were decently buried in Black Friars Kirk. Later, the forfeited estates were restored to the family.

Hume Castle took the brunt of the English invasions sent by Henry VIII to scourge the Scots. In 1545, after the first of these, the 4th Lord Home was granted £300 for the defence of the castle, "he having no guidis left undestroyit to furniss it." The same month the second English attack destroyed all Home's lands in Berwickshire and Roxburghshire. His son, a loyal Queen's man, entertained Mary Stuart at the castle in 1566 after her visit to Jedburgh, but three years later the English again took the castle and Home fled to join the nobles who were holding out for the Queen in Edinburgh Castle. There, he was eventually taken prisoner by English troops, but in 1575 "relivit out of the Castell of Edinburgh and wardit in his awne lugeing in the heid of the (Black) Friar's Wynd." In fact, he was carried there in his bed and died a few months later. Hume Castle was finally demolished in 1650 by Cromwell's men, after a brave stand and a spirited answer to the summons to surrender:

" I Willie Wastle,
Stand firm in my castle,
And a' the dogs o' your toon
Will no pull Willie Wastle doon."

But the English artillery won the day. Some 50 years later, when the estate was owned by the Earl of March, of a junior branch of the family, the mock fortress which stands on the site today was built as a memorial.

It is not known exactly when the lands of Hirsel were acquired by the Home family, but, as the name implies, the place was first a small croft or farm with shelter for sheep. The earliest part of the present building, the square, south-east tower, with the south-west wing of the old house, possibly first stood as an entity. The rest of the old house was begun in the time of the 6th Baron, created Earl of Home in 1605 by James VI, or in the time of his son who died in 1633. Later work was added at different periods. In the central portion there is a handsome stone staircase leading up from a hall and the present entrance on the north side of the house. On the squared ceiling of the stair-well, which is decorated with plasterwork friezes and garlands, there is an interior weather vane, rare if not unique in Scotland, painted gilt and black. The rest of the old house is not in everyday use at the moment.

The fine stone staircase leading from the entrance hall, in the old house.

William, 8th Earl of Home, by Allan Ramsay.

In the 17th century, Hirsel was only one of the Home properties and Hume Castle remained the chief family residence while it was still habitable. Perhaps Cromwell's pounding of the castle in 1650 hastened the move to Hirsel, for James, the 5th Earl, died there in 1687. It was his granddaughter, Lady Jean, who married the elderly Lord Polwarth (afterwards Earl of Marchmont) as his second wife, and is the subject of an old ballad. She was young and beautiful and it was thought, at the time, to be a curious marriage for her.

It must have been Alexander, the 10th Earl of Home, who built the Regency part of the 19th century house. He married a daughter of the 3rd Duke of Buccleuch, who is shown in a family group, painted by Mercier, now in the drawing room at Hirsel. His son's marriage to a granddaughter of the last Lord Douglas joined these two great Border families, and in 1889, on the death of her mother, Lady Home

ABOVE: *The drawing room.*

BELOW: *Lady Home's bedroom.*

inherited the considerable Douglas estates. Among the Douglas portraits at Hirsel today are a full-length painting in the upper hall of the first and only Duchess of Douglas, attributed to Reynolds, with Raeburn's well-known picture of her nephew, Archibald, Baron Douglas, and in the drawing room a portrait of his daughter and co-heiress, Lady Montague, by Chandler, and an enchanting head of his son, the Hon. George Douglas, as a child.

Over the chimneypiece in the smoking room at the north end of the house, hangs a portrait by James Gunn of Sir Alec Douglas-Home's father, the 13th Earl of Home, who died in 1951, greatly mourned and, as one of the national newspapers reported the day after his death, " universally loved." Lord Home is remembered as one of the architects of the League of Nations and gave his services to many other good causes and to public work of various kinds. Sir Alec, until 1963 the 14th Earl of Home, is the present Laird of Hirsel, and has a proud inheritance of service to the

TOP: *The smoking room. The portrait of the 13th Earl of Home by James Gunn.*

country extending back more than 500 years. He is, however, the first of the family to have held the highest office of Prime Minister (1963-4). Elected to Parliament in 1931, he has held many other appointments, including Minister of State for Scotland and Foreign Secretary. Active service with the Lanarkshire Yeomanry between the wars was followed by two years of crippling illness and convalescence which might have deterred many from shouldering the heaviest burdens of state. He and Lady Home have a son and three daughters and a granddaughter who made history by enlivening Number 10 Downing Street with her christening.

In recent years, various Victorian buildings on the north and east sides of the house have been removed and the Regency wing of Hirsel re-planned and decorated by Lady Home to meet the needs of the family and official duties. The long drawing room, with its four tall windows overlooking the gardens, has been formed from three original rooms. A polished timber floor not entirely covered by Spanish rugs gives the room a spacious, uncluttered look, and an original chimneypiece with white painted wainscoting is well set against very pale turquoise walls. Among many fine pieces of Georgian furniture is an unusual wagon-seat settee with four adjoining Sheraton chair designs forming the back and a cane seat. The dining room on the north side of the house has a high coved ceiling with a plasterwork frieze painted white. Tuscan red boldly patterned wallpaper adds warmth and importance to the room, contrasting with peacock blue and gold velvet curtains. Family china is shown in two narrow, upright cabinets of black enamel and gilt.

RIGHT: *The dining room on the north side of the house has a high coved ceiling with a plasterwork frieze painted white. Family china is shown in two narrow, upright cabinets of black enamel and gilt.*

The curving Regency staircase to the second floor with its plain white-painted staples and mahogany hand-rail has been much enhanced by the Adam green and white wallpaper above and below, recently designed for the house in a pattern of Greek vases, garlands and other classical symbols. Bedrooms looking east and west lead off the corridors on the second floor. In Lady Home's room with its triple window, overlooking the magnificent south-west view, the curtains and bed upholstery are of chintz with a large design of lilies of the valley, roses and leaves in pink, pale blue and green on a white background. The pale green striped wallpaper is particularly well shown by an expansive white rug covering the floor. On the walls hang an interesting set of prints by Paul Sandby illustrating his tour of Wales. The flower decoration at Hirsel where the rooms are large and high is strikingly successful in colour and arrangement, but above all in the bold presentation of tall branches and massed flowers in giant vases and bowls.

One of the chief glories of Hirsel garden is the splendid May and June display of rhododendrons and azaleas, and there are individual trees of great beauty, including a tulip tree planted in 1742 which shows its white blossoms in July. Hirsel is also famous for its variety of birds and Sir Alec's brother, Major Henry Douglas Home, the ornithologist has listed 90 different species breeding on the estate.

RIGHT: *The curving Regency staircase to the second floor has plain white-painted staples and a mahogany hand-rail.*

The east wing built in 1725.

Mellerstain

Looking south over the garden to the Cheviots.

MELLERSTAIN, ON THE BORDERS OF Berwickshire and Roxburgh, has a very special place among the great Georgian houses of Scotland. While there are others more complete as a picture of one period or another, Mellerstain spans practically the whole century. Its immense charm, however, lies not so much in the development of the house and grounds as in the beauty of various different aspects. The Georgian concept of natural beauty moulded by architect and landscape-gardener, too, is perfectly fulfilled at Mellerstain, where even the serenity and silence have been preserved. The north entrance front, facing lawns and green swards of grass, is built round a courtyard, the low, square wings dating from 1725 and the huge, honey-coloured central block added forty years later. From the south garden front with its descending terraces and rose-beds, there is a superb vista over the lake and beyond massed woods to the high peak of the Cheviot.

The estate is first mentioned in 1451 when James II gave the lands to Lord Haliburton's son, Patrick. Other families came into possession of Mellerstain in the 15th and 16th centuries, until in 1642 it was acquired by George Baillie of Jerviswood, the son of a flourishing merchant and an ancestor of the present owner, the 12th Earl of Haddington. Baillie lived and died in "ane old melancholic hous that had great buildings about it" which probably stood near the site of the present main block. He was succeeded in 1646 by his son, Robert, a zealous Covenanter who soon came into conflict with the authorities. For protesting against the illegal arrest of a relative he was fined £500 and thrown into Edinburgh Tolbooth. During his imprisonment there, a letter was secretly delivered to him from his old friend Sir Patrick Hume of Polwarth, by

The south front of Mellerstain.

his twelve-year-old daughter, Grisell. Characteristically her first appearance in the story of Mellerstain is one of courage and resource. For in all the family history, there is no greater or more lovable figure than that of Lady Grisell Baillie.

Born in 1665 at Redbraes in Berwickshire, Grisell was the eldest of 17 children. From her earliest years political troubles had gathered round the family, who were strong supporters of the Covenanting Party. On her dangerous expedition to Edinburgh Tolbooth, Grisell met for the first time her future husband, the prisoner's son, George, whose admiration for her dated from this encounter. Meanwhile, Sir Patrick, already in trouble with the Government, was arrested and imprisoned in Dumbarton Jail. When he was released after 15 months it was only to find that soldiers were on their way to capture him on a new charge of complicity in the Rye House Plot. With the help of his wife, Grisell and an old servant, he ensconced himself in the family vault of Polwarth Kirk. By day Grisell went about her usual duties in the house, creeping out after midnight with provisions for her father. The first night the minister's dogs set up such a pandemonium of barking that Lady Hume, inventing the story of a mad dog in the neighbourhood, persuaded him to have them all hanged.

After the news of Robert Baillie's execution as a traitor, Sir Patrick realised his only safety lay in escape from Scotland and, disguising himself as a travelling apothecary, set out for Utrecht in Holland. His family joined him in due course, and there they all lived in exile and extreme poverty for three years. Grisell managed the humble establishment—cooking, cleaning, washing, mending, looking after her younger brothers and sisters and still finding time to take lessons on the harpsichord and to write snatches of poetry which have since become part of the Border Minstrelsy. It was during this time that she wrote the ballad "Were'na my heart licht I wad dee."

When William of Orange and Mary came to the throne of the United Kingdom, the Hume family accompanied them from Holland and were soon re-established in the Borders. In 1690 Sir Patrick became a Privy Councillor and seven years later was created Earl of Marchmont. Grisell refused an invitation to become Maid of Honour at court, for she wanted nothing more than to return home and marry George Baillie, who was later made a Lord of the Treasury. The marriage was an

From the inner hall the double flight of stairs leads to the first floor.

Lady Grisell Baillie, painted in 1725 by Maria Varelst.

The library is the finest Adam room in Scotland.

exceptionally happy one, and, we are told, "they never had the shadow of a quarrel or misunderstanding or dryness betwixt them, not for a moment. . . . He never went abroad but she went to the window to look after him, and so she did that very day he fell ill the last time he went abroad, never taking her eyes from him as long as he was in sight." The most beloved of wives and mothers and an excellent housekeeper, Lady Grisell kept a Day Book which has become a classic of its kind. She died at Mellerstain in 1746, mourned by all who had known her during her long and eventful life.

Part of the lengthy epitaph above her tomb reminds us that " . . .
love of her country,
Zeal for her friends, compassion for her enemies,
Cheerfulness of spirit, pleasantness of conversation,
Dignity of mind,
Good breeding, good humour, good sense,
Were the daily ornaments of an useful life."

It was for George and Grisell Baillie that the wings of the present house were built in 1725. They were intended to accompany a charming centre-piece, designed by William Adam in the Dutch Palladian style, which was never built. Lady Grisell and her family lived in the east wing which is, in itself, a delightful example of a small Scottish house of early Georgian times. The west wing then housed the stables. Whether there was anything left at that time of the "old melancholic hous" between the wings is not known. Trees were planted and the grounds laid out with marked Dutch influence (which has since been modified) as a setting for the planned house. An only son of the marriage died in infancy and the younger daughter, Racheal, married in 1717 Charles, Lord Binning, eldest son of the Earl of Haddington. Their elder son eventually succeeded as the 7th Earl, but it was the younger son, George, who in 1759 inherited Mellerstain and took the name of Baillie.

This second George Baillie was a man of cultivated tastes, and during his travels on the Continent had been imbued with the prevailing passion for classical art. When he succeeded to Mellerstain he employed the most fashionable architect of the day, William Adam's son, Robert, to design the long delayed central block of the house. By the time work began, about 1770, the Romantic Movement was abroad. Ruined medieval castles and towers had begun to appeal to their owners and builders were starting to imitate Gothic outlines and decoration. Whether it was George Baillie or Robert Adam who decided on the castellated exterior of the new house is uncer-

ABOVE: *The small drawing room has a spiders' web ceiling. The portrait is of the Countess of Haddington by Oswald Birley.*

LEFT: *The front hall with its apsidal ends, richly embellished ceiling and bold frieze. In this hall hangs the portrait of Lady Grisell Baillie by Maria Varelst.*

tain, but the building with its massive, rather sombre aplomb, is not altogether typical of Adam or in keeping with the earlier wings. Nor is the interior planning of the house characteristic of Adam's precision and perspective. In the brilliance and finesses of the interior decoration and the excellence of the craftmanship, however, his genius dispels any criticism of the setting.

In the front hall, with its apsidal ends, richly embellished ceiling and bold frieze, hangs a portrait of Lady Grisell Baillie by Maria Varelst. From the narrow inner hall a rippling double flight of stairs ascends to the first floor. Here, below, one is first aware of the colours which are such a delight throughout the house—walls of pale green, pale blue and cinnamon, plasterwork decoration painted shell pink, ivory, smoke grey, warm apricot, crimson, gold and Tuscan red, and white painted woodwork.

The library, the first room to be completed, is the most beautiful in the house and in Scotland. Five long windows light up the subdued colour scheme of smoke grey and white, the delicate tracery of the frieze and the bold plaques above the book-cases, showing Roman and other antique scenes in high relief. The pastoral landscape in the panel over the green and white marble chimneypiece and the ceiling decoration, more widely spaced and deliberate than others in the house, add a cool elegance to this serenely classical room.

The music room has a lighter, more feminine grace and an enchanting ceiling ornamented with eagles, sphinxes and garlands. The white marble mantelpiece is flanked by the carved female figures of War and Peace and on the central panel a man is ploughing with oxen. Above this hangs a portrait of Sir Patrick Hume by the Scottish painter, Aikman. The long barrel-vaulted gallery on the upper floor was evidently left unfinished as the ceiling is not ornamented. The room is now used as a museum for family portraits, china, books, period clothing and other treasures. There is much good furniture in the house, mainly of the 18th century, interesting collections of portraits and china and some old and valuable books.

The house, inside and out, has been little altered since it was finished, although the Adam colours have been carefully renewed and some of the rooms re-arranged. In 1909, the terrace and loggia on the south side of the house were added by Sir Reginald Blomfield who also enlarged the lake, connecting it to the terraces by the long sloping span of grass. Of particular interest among other flowers on the terraced gardens in summer are the many species of old roses, planted recently by Lady Haddington and now growing in profusion. These include the ancient Centifolias, Gallicas, Hybrid Musks, Damascena and Bourbons. Lord and Lady Haddington now live mainly at Tyninghame, East Lothian, another family home. Lord Haddington, a past President of the Royal Society of Antiquaries (Scotland) and President of the Scottish Georgian Society, cherishes the history and architecture of Mellerstain with knowledge as well as family pride.

Floors Castle

Superbly set above Tweed, among grouped woods, Floors Castle commands one of the splendid views of Scotland. From the great, flat, green plateau of parkland below the house where black cattle, horses and sheep graze and wander, to Rennie's bridge over the river, the straggling waterside buildings of Kelso, and the Cheviot peaks on the horizon, the landscape seems to have arranged itself in perfect order for the painter, the poet and the passer-by with an eye for beauty. The site was certainly chosen with expert judgment, possibly by Vanbrugh, to whom the design of the castle is attributed. The builder of Blenheim Palace and Castle Howard in England, Vanbrugh, in his day, was accounted a better playwright than an architect. But his style, if sometimes massive, was grand and majestic and his talent for grouping brilliant. Floors Castle, built for the 1st Duke of Roxburghe, was started in 1721 and is Vanbrugh's only recorded house in Scotland. W. H. Playfair, the architect, ornamented, altered and added to the castle during the years 1838-49.

The Dukes of Roxburghe are descended from a long line of Border lairds whose family name of Ker is of Scandinavian origin. The first Kers (de Kari) are said to have landed with William the Conqueror, but the earliest record of the name in Scotland dates from about 1200. A century and a half later appears, as witness to a charter, John Ker of the Forest of Ettrick and Altonburn, ancestor of the two great Border houses of Ferniehirst, represented by the Marquis of Lothian, and Cessford, by the Duke of Roxburghe. The founder of the latter family was Sir Robert Ker—known as "Habbie" Ker—who, in 1616, became 1st Earl of Roxburghe. A born leader in war and politics, and respected by his English counterparts over the Border, he is described by the Archbishop of York as "... wise and valiant, but somewhat haughty and resolute." Born in 1570 while the Reformation was changing the ways and ownership of Scotland, Earl Robert was eventually given the lands which had belonged to Kelso Abbey—on which Floors Castle now stands. Before this time the family had occupied both Cessford Castle and Holydean, as well as Roxburghe Castle.

An older dwelling near the site of Floors, probably used by the Kelso monks, was pulled down in the late 18th century to build farm steadings, and the ruins of the religious house and gardens of the Greyfriars across the river were also demolished. Habbie Ker was the first to bring the news of Queen Elizabeth's death to James VI in 1603, and, on the King's accession to the English throne, accompanied him to London, where he held various high offices, becoming Lord Privy Seal in the time of Charles I. Predeceased by his only son, Earl Robert, by special grant, ensured that the estates and honours should be continued in the female line—a safeguard which led to many future legal entanglements. He was succeeded by his grandson, the child of his daughter Margaret and Drummond, Earl of Perth.

It was for John, 5th Earl and 1st Duke of Roxburghe, that Floors Castle was built. In his memoirs George Lockhart, who seldom praised without good reason, described him as "a man of good sense, improved by so much reading and learning that he was perhaps the best accomplished young man of quality in Europe, and had such a charming way of expressing his thoughts, that he pleased even those against whom he spoke." Cultured, travelled, progressive and a Whig, Roxburghe helped to bring about the Parliamentary Union with England in 1707, for which he was created in that year Earl of Kelso and Duke of Roxburghe. Like many of the new "Union" peers, Roxburghe began to think of building a new and grander house. Floors Castle, as shown in William Adam's *Vitruvius Scoticus* and in various old paintings and prints in the house today, was a solid, oblong building with towers at the four corners and a fore-court on the north side, flanked by east and west kitchen and stable pavilions. Laurence Whistler in his biography of Vanbrugh describes the original Floors as "a Gothic Castle Howard," and suggests it may have been an older building re-faced. This seems unlikely, however, from William Adam's plan, in which he himself may have had a hand.

If it was not the great Capability Brown himself who laid out the surroundings and foreground to the Duke's imposing new house, it was someone of talent and imagination for the job, which could hardly have been better done. The sketch for this great canvas of castle, setting and long view was now finished. It was left to W. H. Playfair, the architect of much of Edinburgh's Greek Revival, and to the growing plantations of hardwood, to complete the very grand present-day picture of Floors Castle. Playfair's transformation of the original rather plain Georgian building may not be admired by the New Puritans of architecture today, but no one could deny that in the setting it is an admirable conception, excellently carried out. Working from 1838-49, Playfair added a ballroom on the east side of the house, balanced on the west by an extension to the immense dining room, removing and rebuilding the main staircase. He also added the porte-cochère, several bay windows and the loggia between the main block and the east wing. But, above all, the character of the house is changed by the architect's exuberant vertical decoration of pepper-pot turrets, moulded corbelling, castellated parapets and ornamented water-spouts, crowding in near-Oriental splendour on the skyline. A less competent architect might have failed where Playfair succeeded in bringing the castle into its right perspective as the centre of this magnificent composition. He was obviously much influenced by the work he was doing at the same time at Heriot's Hospital and the new Donaldson Hospital in Edinburgh, even copying details of turrets, chimneystacks and tower parapets from the former and the carved decoration of Rose and Mullet which are the Heriot's Arms.

The builder's grandson, the 3rd Duke, whose portrait by Pompeo Batoni hangs in the dining room today, was also a man of culture who collected a fine library of books (the main part of which was sold in 1812 for £23,000) and gave his name to the famous Roxburghe

Literary Club, founded on his collections and papers. He died in 1804, unmarried, supposedly on account of a romantic attachment to an elder sister of Queen Charlotte, wife of George III, court etiquette disapproving an elder sister being the subject of a younger one. He was succeeded by his elderly kinsman, Lord Bellendean, who died the following year. A long lawsuit, known as "The Roxburghe Cause," brought by two rival claimants to the dukedom ensued, occupying English and Scottish Law Courts for several years. In 1812 the House of Lords judged that Sir James Innes of Innes had proved his case and he succeeded as 5th Duke. Over the library chimneypiece at Floors now hangs Raeburn's well-known portrait of this robust old man, to whom, in 1816, at the age of eighty-one, was born an only son and heir, and who, at the subsequent celebrations, "footed it with the youngest of them and snapped his fingers to the dancing of the Highland Fling." It was for his son, the 6th Duke, that Playfair remodelled the castle, where shortly afterwards Queen Victoria was entertained. His great-grandson, the present and 9th Duke, now lives at Floors with his wife and family.

The interior of the house is spacious and well proportioned, the main rooms on the ground floor running the length of the south face, overlooking the memorable view westwards towards Kelso and across the great park to the ruins of Roxburghe Castle over the river. The late Mary, Duchess of Roxburghe, an American by birth, who was much interested in decor, furniture and objets d'arts, became a connoisseur of various periods and mediums, from which she made several important collections, among them the 18th century French furniture, old tapestries and Chinese, Chelsea and Dresden porcelain. To some extent the house has been re-arranged since Playfair's alterations to show these to best advantage. Probably the finest and most valuable possession at Floors today is the beautiful 15th century Brussels tapestry depicting the Day of Pentecost, which hangs in the ante-room.

The vast ballroom was re-panelled and decorated in the 20th century to take the two Gobelins tapestries. French 18th century furniture can be seen in both rooms, but in the ballroom there are also many good English and Italian pieces of the 17th and 18th centuries, Chinese porcelain ornaments, Battersea enamel and family portraits by Lely, Reynolds, Raeburn, Kneller, Ramsay and Richardson. Round the chimneypieces the rich flower decoration, reminiscent of Grinling Gibbons's work, was carved by a local craftsman. Home-grown oak, ash and elm have been used for doors, panelling and wainscoting. Oak is particularly effective in the vast dining room which Playfair extended with a mullioned window. More intimate is the charming tiny needle room in the south-east tower, redecorated by the present Duke's mother in white and crimson in the French 18th century manner with its ormolu and Waterford glass chandelier and, in contrast, the cool colourings of the present Duchess's sitting room, dominated by the modern landscape of Kelso painted in 1958 by Raoul Millais, a grandson of the well-known Victorian artist.

Tapestry depicting the Day of Pentecost.

The tapestry room is hung with Brussels tapestries, collected and arranged by the late Mary, Duchess of Roxburghe.

Looking across the river Tweed to Abbotsford, set between the Tweed and the triple peak of the Eildons.

Abbotsford

ABBOTSFORD WAS OPENED TO THE PUBLIC in 1833, the year after Sir Walter Scott died. The forerunner by roughly a century of many country houses to follow suit, it is now one of the most visited and possibly the best known in Scotland.

Architecturally the building has fallen from grace since it was finished in 1824, although even in those days there were critics to spike the tumultuous applause which greeted its completion. Ruskin described it as " perhaps the most incongruous pile gentlemanly modernism ever designed," Hugh Miller called it " a supremely melancholy place " and Queen Victoria, who called on the family for tea in 1867, recorded in her Journal " it lies low and looks rather gloomy." But Abbotsford was then, as it is now, safe from all purist comment on its shape and style. Scott had built the house with his dreams and his love of the medieval past and lived in it with his family. That was enough recommendation for his friends and the vast public of his time, as it is for the thousands who visit the house today.

More than any house I know of, Abbotsford holds the living spirit of its builder. His fame as a writer, his greatness as a public figure and, above all, his lovable character are reflected in every room. Not only do the portraits by Raeburn, Landseer and others, and in particular, the excellent marble bust by Chantrey, present the warmth and charm of his physical presence, but the sort of devotion he inspired can be felt in the letters and presents he received from all over the world and the national relics left him by the families concerned. There are also the more personal reminders of his home life—paintings and drawings of his family, his trusted servants and his dogs, the desk he wrote at and the clothes he wore.

Looking back on this resplendent but humble figure which still stirs the heart of the public today, it seems that part of his charm lay in the modest estimate he had of his own literary powers. The first historical novelist proper in Europe, at the height of his fame he was by far the best known and most successful writer in the western world. His huge reading

Sir Walter Scott.

public in Great Britain, the Continent and America waited impatiently for the next instalment of his current novel and in London people read his last publication as they walked the pavements. The friend of George IV and chief organiser of his visit to Scotland in 1822, Scott did more to put Scotland on the map, politically, socially and culturally, than any man of his time. But the writer, the public figure and the " Shirra " of Selkirkshire were all subordinated to Scott's life-long desire to become a Border Laird. To own some acres of the countryside he loved, to build a house there and found a family, was his greatest ambition.

In 1777, Dr. Douglas, minister of Galashiels, received a letter from a friend telling him of the " extraordinary genius " of the little six-year-old Walter she had met at his father's house in George Square, Edinburgh. Dr. Douglas preserved the letter, never dreaming that 34 years later the same genius would buy his farm and make it famous. Scott bought the place in 1811, with 110 acres, for £4000. The farm, Cartley Hole (called Clarty—meaning dirty—Hole by the neighbours), " was poor and small, the steading inadequate and the drains defective . . . heather grew close to the doorway and a filthy evil-smelling duck pond lay in front." But Scott saw the possibilities of the site between the triple peak of the Eildons and a wide reach of the Tweed. Abbotsford, so named because in the old days the Abbots of Melrose, using the Roman road from the Eildons, crossed the river at a ford close by, was at first only to be the enlarged farm house. Scott wrote: " My dreams about my country cottage go on. My present intention is to have only two spare rooms with dressing rooms, each of which, at a pinch, will have a couch bed; but I cannot relinquish my Border principles of accommodating all the cousins and duniwastles who will sleep on the floor and in the hay-loft rather than be absent when folks are gathered together."

The drawing room. Over the mantelpiece is Raeburn's portrait of Scott.

A drawing of this charming Georgian cottage, with its pillared portico, standing to the east of the steading, which Scott presumably altered to his liking, is now in the drawing room of the private Victorian addition to Abbotsford. In the summer of 1812 the family moved from Ashiestiel, a country house up Tweed they had rented for some years, to their new home, in a picturesque and somewhat disorderly cavalcade " attended by a dozen rosy, peasant children carrying fishing-rods and spears and leading ponies, greyhounds and spaniels . . ."

Scott's first novel, *Waverley*, was not published till 1814. The foundations of Abbotsford were financed by the phenomenal success of his poems, *The Lay of the Last Minstrel*, *Marmion* and *The Lady of the Lake*. While the cottage was being extended, his duties as Sheriff of Selkirkshire and his legal work at the Edinburgh Court of Session filled five days of the week. When he returned to Abbotsford at the week-ends, he threw himself into the making of his new estate, superintending the building, laying out the garden and planting trees. He was also hard at work on his poem, *Rokeby*, writing at a desk in the window of the only living room, where the children had their lessons, the family dined and Mrs Scott entertained guests. Added to this, the place resounded with the din of workmen. " As for the house and the poem," Scott wrote, " there are twelve masons hammering at one and one poor noodle at the other."

But the cottage was too small to contain Scott's abundant hospitality. Two years later plans were made for the first addition between the cottage and the farm steading, while Scott's poem, *The Lord of the Isles*, and his second novel, *Guy Mannering*, were in progress. The immediate success of the latter confirmed Scott's future as a novelist. The growing estate absorbed alarmingly large sums of money and Scott's pen had to work faster than the mason's tools. By 1816 Abbotsford had increased to 1000 acres and two years later the imposing addition had engulfed the cottage in " a rural villa of some size and pretension." From this period till 1824, when the house was completed, Scott employed an architect and an interior decorator, and throughout the building and furnishing of Abbotsford he was continually advised by his friend Daniel Terry, the actor-playwright. Terry, who had studied architecture with a brother of James Wyatt, the builder of Fonthill and Lee Priory, was in part responsible for the English Tudor aspect of the final Abbotsford. The Edinburgh architect, Starke, had been consulted about the first addition but his plan was abandoned as " too greatly expensive."

Scott continued to buy land from his neighbours, sometimes at inflated prices, and in 1821, a year after he had received his baronetcy from George IV, he decided on the last and grandest addition to the house. The cottage was finally demolished to make room for " a manor house," which, in fact, is the main part of the house open to the public today, including the drawing room, dining room, library and study. This was designed by Edward Blore, a young English architect who later restored Glasgow Cathedral, worked at Buckingham Palace for Queen Victoria and rebuilt Lambeth Palace. Both Blore and Scott were antiquarians and Abbotsford, like many of Scott's novels, is set in the Middle Ages. The London decorator, William Atkinson, was responsible for the interior of the new wing, while Scott himself added the multitude of carved ornaments and fragments or copies from old buildings to the outside walls, including the door from Edinburgh Tolbooth, the porch modelled on one at Linlithgow Palace and the jougs from Threave Castle.

By Christmas, 1824, Scott's Abbotsford was complete—a romance in stone, part Tudor Gothic, part Scottish Baronial, part pure fantasy. " Abbotsford is all I can make it," he wrote, " so I resolve on no more building and no more purchases of land till times are safe again." Those times never came and of the seven years that remained to Scott, the last six were over shadowed by financial disaster, ill-health and family griefs.

But there was gaiety and merry-making at Abbotsford the following New Year when a Grand Ball was given to celebrate the engagement of Sir Walter's elder son. The family assembled and guests poured in from all quarters to see the new castle. Never had the Border Laird been a prouder or more entertaining host. When the house had been admired inside and out, visitors strolled round the garden surrounded by its medieval walls with a castellated gateway and portcullis designed by Blore, to see the curious sculptured stones and ancient ornaments. Farther afield, they were shown the wilder aspects of the property and the young plantations which were Scott's special care and pride. " I look back to the time when there was not a tree here," he said, " only bare heath; I look round and see thousands of trees growing up, all of which—I may say, almost each of which—have received my personal attention."

The amazingly varied collection of art treasures and antique relics Scott delighted in, and which has been added to since his death, is displayed throughout the house today—in the hall and armoury, in the drawing room with its hand-painted Chinese wallpaper, in the library where the pointed plaster roof is copied from the carved cedar-wood one at Roslin Chapel, and in the dining room where he died, looking for the last time on the Tweed and the green hills beyond. This splendid museum includes such diverse trophies as Napoleon's blotter and pen, taken from his carriage after Waterloo, Prince Charles Edward's quaich, Rob Roy's purse, a lock of Nelson's hair, a 15th century suit of armour worn at the battle of Bosworth Field, a tumbler which had belonged to Burns, with some of his verses scratched on it, and the last suit of clothes worn by Sir Walter.

After Scott's death nothing was done to Abbotsford till 1853 when the property came into the possession of Mr. Hope-Scott, who had married Sir Walter's grand daughter, Charlotte Lockhart. He restored the existing buildings to some extent, made some structural alterations to the grounds and in 1855 built the eastward addition, where the present representatives of the family, Mrs Patricia Maxwell-Scott and Miss Jean Maxwell-Scott, great - great - great - granddaughters of Sir Walter, now live. This wing is simpler and lighter in colour than the rest of the house and was built under the direction of the architect, William Burn.

Whether one goes to Abbotsford to see the house Scott built, or the countryside he loved, to look at the great museum he collected or the paintings and drawings of him and his family, it is certain to be a memorable experience. For in a rare and remarkable way, the character of the man himself, the gallant and beloved Border Laird who enjoyed Abbotsford so much more than his literary fame and his high offices of State, lives on in the house today.

TOP: *Abbotsford from the north-east showing, on the right, the final addition finished in 1824.*

CENTRE: *The dining room where Scott died.*

BOTTOM: *Mary Monica Hope-Scott, great granddaughter of Sir Walter, painted in 1855.*

LEFT: *The west entrance extension to Thirlestane Castle was built in 1673 for the Duke of Lauderdale.*

BELOW: *The original design for the west entrance front as shown in an old print dated 1673.*

Thirlestane Castle

THE ORIGINAL SPLENDOUR OF THE great west entrance front has been somewhat modified in appearance by Victorian alterations and additions, but Thirlestane is still very grand and imposing in rose-pink sandstone. A wide flight of steps leads to the little courtyard, almost dwarfed now by the massive enclosing walls of the central tower, the two flanking, square, turreted towers and the projecting north and south wings. This dramatic composition, reflecting the Restoration love of pomp and show, was built on to the old castle for the first and only Duke of Lauderdale by Sir William Bruce, the architect of many famous houses in Scotland, including Drumlanrig Castle, Kinross House and the modern part of Holyrood House. One of two old prints dated 1673 which hang in Prince Charles's room in the castle today, shows the original design for the entrance extension with two spacious courtyards and adjoining stables. By comparing this print with the present-day structure, the alterations completed in 1841 by the architect David Bryce are clearly shown.

The other print shows the south face of the old castle, built at the end of the 16th century and embellished at the same time as the west front was put up. The whole castle was then "heavilly stucco'd" and the formal garden consisted of three plots of grass adorned with statues. Today the garden, overlooking the banks of the River Leader, is laid out with a wide herbaceous border and a paved path dividing smooth green lawns. Perhaps the most picturesque view of the castle is seen from here—a long narrow building with three midway, and two tall, corner towers, and the steep roof, crow-stepped gables and carved dormer window-heads (ornamented with large thistles) typical of 16th century building.

Possibly Thirlestane stands on the foundations of old Lauder Fort, sometimes reported to have been built in the time of David I, sometimes by Edward I of England. But the ruins of the original Thirlestane Castle lie two miles east of the present house. The Maitland family, however, were settled in Lauderdale in the times of Edward I. They are still there today, and the castle is the home of the Dowager Countess of Lauderdale. One of the most famous and able families in Scotland, they have a long and honourable history of service to king, country, the law and the arts. Their first and chief seat in early times was Lethington Castle (now called Lennoxlove) near Haddington in East Lothian. There lived William Maitland, "Secretary Lethington" to Mary, Queen of Scots. It was in the time of his brother, the 1st Baron Maitland of Thirlestane, Lord Chancellor of Scotland, from whom the present family is descended, that the castle was begun, and the building was probably finished by the year 1600.

Baron Thirlestane's son was created 1st Earl of Lauderdale in 1642. The 2nd Earl and (later) only Duke of Lauderdale was one of the most important and controversial figures in the second half of the 17th century in Scotland, and after the Restoration of 1660, up to a short time before his death in 1682, was known as "The Uncrowned King of Scotland."

LEFT: *The south face of the old castle built for the 1st Baron Maitland of Thirlestane.*

BELOW: *A print of the south wing dated 1673.*

His lifetime covers one of the most agitated and entangled periods of Scottish history. And Lauderdale, as one of the three most powerful nobles in Scotland; as a leading Presbyterian and Commissioner for the Solemn League and Covenant (1643-46); later as chief Scottish adviser and confidant of Charles II, and a member of the Cabal Cabinet; and finally as Secretary of State and virtual dictator of Scotland (1660-80), was inextricably bound up with national history. Political documents and letters from and about this forceful, brilliant man are legion. But personal and domestic records are few or as yet unpublished. Of the building designed for him, or his day-to-day life at Thirlestane Castle and the guests he entertained there, nothing, it seems, was described by him or his family. This missing link between the Duke and his castle leaves posterity to guess or imagine the life he and his Restoration friends lived there.

"He was very big," according to a contemporary description, "his hair red, hanging oddly about him; his tongue was too big for his mouth, which made him bedew all that he talked to: his whole manner was boisterous, and very unfit for a Court." Before he was thirty Lauderdale was both the chief protagonist of Presbyterianism and the most promising diplomat in Scotland. The Scottish church (and the majority of the people), in their resistance to Episcopacy, the Bishops and the Prayer Book, pinned all their hopes on his success with King and Parliament. But Lauderdale was a staunch Royalist as well as a Presbyterian. He was with Charles during his exile in Holland and fought by his side at the Battle of Worcester in 1651 where he was taken prisoner, remaining in prison (when he "read a great deal of Divinity and almost all the Historians, ancient and modern") till the 1660 Restoration.

With his master the King back on the throne, Lauderdale came into the heyday of his power and glory. He was made Secretary of State for Scotland, and having complete influence over Charles (Pepys in his diary described him as "a cunning fellow: never from the King's ear or council"), enforced his will on the country without any fear of serious opposition. He aimed at making the crown absolute in church and state. But his devotion to Charles coincided with his desire to see the Scottish nobility secure and strong. Something had to be thrown overboard, and from then on his loyalties to the church and the people of Scotland weakened. A gradual degeration from uprightness to mere self-preservation set in, a process much hastened by his second wife, the beautiful and notorious Countess of Dysart, who, after her marriage to Lauderdale "carried all things with a haughtiness that could not have been easily borne from a Queen" in Scotland. She was a widow of forty-five when Lauderdale married her and the mother of eleven children (of whom only five survived), but "she had such an ascendant over his affections that neither her age, nor her affairs, nor yet the clamour of his friends and the people, more urgent than both these, could divert him from marrying her within six weeks of his Lady's decease."

Maitland was created Duke of Lauderdale in 1672. He continued to rule Scotland for another six years, even dissolving the Scottish

Parliament (in 1774) for nine months at the King's request. But this and other of his dictates not even Lauderdale's greatest supporters could accept, and his enemies were growing in strength and numbers. At length, under strong pressure from most of the Scottish nobles, the English Parliament and the Privy Council, the King deserted Lauderdale. He was forced to resign all his offices and retired to Tunbridge Wells to drink the waters for a paralytic affliction. Deprived even of his pension, he begged the king not to let his "old and faithful servant die in poverty." But it was of no avail. Some weeks before his death in 1682, he is reported to have said that "if he had been as faithful to his God as he had been to the King, He would not have shaken him off in his old age."

The castle was extended, ornamented outside and decorated inside at the height of Lauderdale's reign—the old prints bear the date 1673 and the interior was completed soon after. Probably no house in Scotland can

The long drawing room was decorated in the resplendent style of Restoration times for the Duke of Lauderdale.

boast of such resplendent decor in the almost baroque style of the time. In particular, the rich plasterwork ceilings in the first floor rooms are, of their kind, unequalled. Some of these were designed by the King's Master Mason, Robert Mylne, while Dutch craftsmen, brought from Holland by the Duke in 1675, were employed on the work. The ceilings are said to have taken five years to complete and to have cost £1500. There are very good collections of furniture and china at Thirlestane, many of the pieces being connected with family and national history, as well as old books, documents, fire-arms and other interesting relics. Most striking perhaps, and most lovely, are the variety of excellent paintings (both portraits and landscape) by Reynolds, Romney, Gainsborough, Lawrence, Hoppner, Bellotto, Guardi and others.

On the Duke's death in 1682, all the peerages conferred on him became extinct, the other honours and the Thirlestane property passing to his brother Charles, 3rd Earl of Lauderdale. Although the present family stem from the 3rd Earl, the succession has not been direct. The late Lord Lauderdale (the 15th Earl) was predeceased by his son, Viscount Maitland, who was killed in action in 1943. The present and 16th Earl is the Reverend Alfred Maitland, who lives in the south of England, his heir being his brother, Mr. Patrick Maitland.

George IV, by Sir Thomas Lawrence.

Eleanor, 8th Countess of Lauderdale by Romney.

Traquair House

THERE ARE MANY REASONS WHY Traquair should be perhaps the most interesting house in south Scotland, but these do not entirely account for its immeasurable charm and fascination. Those who have dreamt of waking up in another century and prying into the living past must find a visit to Traquair the nearest experience to such a fantasy. The first glimpse through the Bear Gates of this tall, solitary building, set among the green Peeblesshire hills is enchanting enough. But to stand in the courtyard and look up at the immense, white-harled walls pierced by tiny scattered windows and at the knife-edge roof rising steeply above turrets and dormers, is to realise the presence of another age. The two low little wings enclosing the north and south sides of the courtyard, so dramatically dwarfed by the great massif of the main house, complete this superb spectacle of rugged grandeur.

Traquair may well be the oldest inhabited house in Scotland. Originally a hunting lodge, it was used by the Kings of Scotland on sporting expeditions to the Forests of Ettrick and Tweeddale, the first royal visit being recorded in 1107. The earliest building was probably a rough stone tower standing above the river Tweed (since diverted to its present course), from the windows of which, we are told, salmon were caught—a peaceful occupation possibly for the royal hunters when they had tired of more strenuous pursuits. David I is said to have lived at Traquair between 1133 and 1142, and it was a favourite residence of William the Lion, who, while staying there in 1176, granted the charter which made Glasgow a burgh. Two English kings, Edward I and II, occupied Traquair with enemy garrisons, but it was restored to the Scottish crown with Robert the Bruce.

James III used the place as a sort of *bon bouche* for a series of favourites. The first presentation to Robert, Lord Boyd, was not a success. The second, to William Roger, his English " Master of Music," was disastrous. Roger was a fine musician, but the courtiers so violently resented his influence with the King that, under the leadership of " Bell the Cat," Earl of Angus, he was seized in 1482 with another royal favourite, Cochrane, and hanged over Lauder Bridge. Finally, the King gave Traquair to his half-brother, the Earl of Buchan, who in turn passed it on to his son, James Stuart, the ancestor of the present owners. Before he was killed at the Battle of Flodden in 1513, James Stuart had begun to enlarge the old keep which has now lost its identity, but must, in part, be buried within the present house.

The next stage of building was carried out by James Stuart's grandson, Sir William, who, in 1599, extended and heightened the house virtually as it stands today at the north end of the main block. Sir William, the second of four brothers who succeeded each other at Traquair, was M.P. for Peeblesshire and died in 1605. The eldest, Sir John Stuart, knighted by Mary, Queen of Scots, and Captain of her guard at Holyrood Palace, entertained the Queen and Darnley at Traquair in 1566. A human touch which has survived by hearsay is the story that Sir John had occasion to rebuke Darnley for his rudeness to the Queen. Various more solid relics of this visit are preserved in the house today, including a silk embroidered quilt worked by the Queen and her Four Maries, a late 16th century cradle in which she is said to have rocked her baby son, James VI, and her crucifix and rosary. James Stuart, the last of the four brothers, was succeeded by a grandson, John, whose melodramatic career emblazons the family history and whose bequest to Traquair is the finished picture—except for the wings—of the house today.

Born about 1600, John Stuart was educated under Thomas Sydserf, Bishop of Galloway, and at the age of 21 became Commissioner for Tweeddale. Greatly favoured by Charles I, he was made a baron in 1628 and, two years later, Treasurer-depute for Scotland. When the king paid a state visit north of the Border in 1633, he created Lord Stuart Earl of Traquair. His appointment as Lord High Treasurer in 1636 marked the peak of his achievement, for the cold war between King and Covenanters demanded of its leaders the steel of conviction or

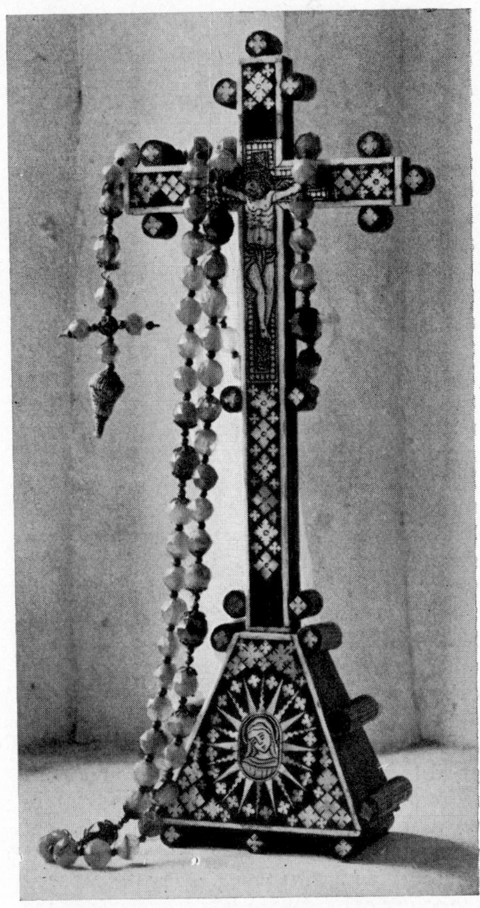

ABOVE LEFT: *A late 15th century cradle believed to have been used by the infant King James VI.*

ABOVE: *A rosary and crucifix which belonged to Mary, Queen of Scots.*

Part of the dining room with family portraits against wallpaper over 100 years old.

loyalty. Traquair, for all his brilliance, had neither. Striving to be all things to all men, he vacillated and was disowned by both sides. Divested of office, he was fined 40,000 merks and confined to his own lands.

After the Battle of Philiphaugh, when Montrose fled with a few followers to Traquair, asking for shelter, the Earl and his son " denied themselves " and would not unlock the door. In 1646, with a troop of horse, Traquair set out to rescue the King, whose favours had been restored, was taken prisoner at Preston and remained some time in captivity in England. Eventually released by Cromwell, the Earl returned to Scotland to find himself abandoned by friends and fortune. His last days were spent begging in the streets of Edinburgh, where he died in extreme poverty in 1659 in the house of a poor cobbler. His portrait, holding the rod of office as Lord High Treasurer, now hangs over the chimneypiece in the dining room.

But the ill wind which blew on the Earl after his fall from office in 1641 brought nothing but good to the old house. During his enforced retirement he extended the building southwards, adding the steep slate roof and dormer windows and completing the main block of the house as it remains today. He also changed the course of the Tweed, which endangered the foundations of the building, to its present bed, laid out the gardens to the south and east and, it seems probable, the formal terraces on the east side of the house with the entrancing little garden pavilion at each end.

The transformation from fortress to country house, carried out in the robust native style of the time, was made with the happiest results. Reminiscent of a French château cast in a Scottish mould, Traquair is unique as an almost complete example of this type of castle-into-house in Scotland. The low wings and wrought-iron gateway and screen enclosing the courtyard have been dated 1664, in the time of the 2nd Earl. A staunch Roman Catholic in a period of bitter religious strife, he first married the Marquis of Huntly's daughter and secondly Anne Seton, daughter of the Earl of Winton, both of the same faith. For this he was fined £5000 and imprisoned but, after his death in 1666, his widow continued to bring up her family as Papists and even to contrive a secret chapel with an escape stair. In 1688, a fanatical Presbyterian mob broke into the house, siezed what " Romish wares " they could lay hands on and burnt them at Peebles town cross. Among these, an " Inventar of what was gotten in my Lord Traquair's House, by the Laird of Kersland . . ." records " Two Marys and the Babe in a Caise," " The Queen of Peace curiously drawn," a " pot of Holy oyle," an altar, a chalice, relics, wafers, candles and some 130 books.

In the dining room today hangs a painting of Charles, the 4th Earl, and his wife, a sister of the Jacobite Earl of Nithsdale. Of their 17 children, only four married, two sons who in turn succeeded to the estate and two daughters. The rest, we are told, " vegetated between Traquair and Edinburgh," but, from all accounts, in a most elegant and sociable manner. Lady Mary became the (titular) Duchess of Perth and from Lady Catherine, who married her cousin, William Maxwell, is descended the present family of Maxwell Stuarts of Traquair. The 4th Earl was out in the 1715 Rising and his son, another Charles, who succeeded in 1741, actively supported Prince Charles Edward's bid for the throne in 1745 and was captured and imprisoned in the Tower of London for two years. Among the several stories of why and when the " Steekit yetts " were permanently closed is the vivid description of the Prince galloping down the long avenue from the house after soliciting Traquair for more help, and through the Bear Gates which were closed after him, never to be opened again till a Stuart sat on the throne.

The present appearance of the drawing room dates from the time of this Laird and his brother, the 5th Earl, although the room itself is much older and recent excavations have uncovered part of the original early 17th century beams and panels decorated with painted figures, garlands and Biblical texts in the manner of the period. The paintings over the doors are part of the 18th century re-arrangement of the room, one showing the Traquair arms and the other quoting a musical phrase from the traditional song " The Bush aboon Traquair." The following verse, written in 1724, describes an aspect of Traquair which has not been lost over the years:

The Bear Gates.

" And what saw ye there, At the bush aboon Traquair?
Or what did ye hear that was worth your heid?
I heard the cushies croon, Through the gowden afternoon,
And the Quair burn singing down to the vale of Tweed."

The Stuarts of Traquair paid dearly for their loyalty to the wrong side in politics and religion in the 17th century. Fines, losses and lack of remunerative appointments gradually impoverished the family. The 6th and 7th Earls lived much abroad and Charles, the 8th and last Earl, sold many of his lands and remained a recluse till his death in 1861. Traquair then passed to his sister, Lady Louisa Stuart, a friend and lively correspondent of Sir Walter Scott. A few days before her hundredth birthday, she made an expedition to Edinburgh to buy a new bonnet, caught a cold and died. The place was then inherited by Henry Constable Maxwell, great-uncle of the present Laird, who added the name of Stuart to his own.

The brew house, now in use after nearly 200 years.

In the King's Room, where Mary, Queen of Scots slept in 1566, is a gay baroque state bed with yellow hangings, brought from Terregles, the former home of the Nithsdale family. A most rare example of mural decoration in Scotland, dating from about 1550, remains on the walls of a room on the second floor, now used as a museum. Here is a fascinating collection of treasures and relics connected with the house and family over hundreds of years, including beautiful petit-point embroidery of about 1600, a Royal Missive dated 1565 to John Stuart, signed by Queen Mary and Darnley, letters from Charles I, a rare Amen glass of 1720-40, and an engraving of Prince Charles Edward done in Edinburgh during the '45. On the walls of the present chapel in the north wing hang a set of 12 carved wood panels dating from the 16th century, showing scenes from the life of Christ. Markedly Flemish in character, these may have been worked by a Scottish craftsman and were brought by the 5th Earl from the old chapel of Mary of Guise in Leith. The white marble altar is Italian.

Of particular interest in the stable block below the chapel is an unusually complete brew-house. The present owner has put it into use and it is now unique in being the only private domestic brew house in the country brewing and producing its own ale, " Traquair Ale," thus reviving a custom after nearly 200 years.

There is much else to see both inside and outside Traquair, which owes its miraculous preservation partly to the family's enforced retreat from state and public affairs some 300 years ago and partly to their continuing love and care of the place since then. In the time of the last Laird, the late Mr. F. Maxwell Stuart, the house was opened to the public for the first time. His son, the present and 20th Laird, Mr. P. Maxwell Stuart, with his wife, settled at Traquair a few years ago.

ABOVE: *The drawing room fireplace.*

BELOW: *An example of the early 17th century. beams and panels in the drawing room.*

The chapel in the north wing.

Broughton Place

BELOW: *Broughton Place from the south-east.*

PERHAPS THE ELLIOTT FAMILY WHO live at Broughton Place have forgotten what it feels like to see the house for the first time—to turn the last hair-pin bend on the steep road which twists up the hill from the old village of Broughton, near Biggar, in Lanarkshire, and come upon this fairy-tale castle gleaming white on the green hillside. But for the visitor the first impression is one of surprise—the sort of shocked delight that every theatrical producer hopes for when the curtain goes up on a new scene.

The element of surprise is even more dramatic if the visitor arrives with a few facts about this remarkable house—knowing, for instance, that although the site is ancient and historic, the building itself was only finished in 1938. Here are the old trees planted round the house that stood on the site more than two centuries ago—there is the magnificent setting among rounded grassy hills, and the long views beyond Broughton towards Tweedsmuir and the heights of Broad Law and Dollar Law. And in the centre of the stage stands this spectacular modern stronghold, wholly traditional in outline but little more than thirty years old.

The house was built for Professor and Mrs. Elliott by Sir Basil Spence, the architect, whose design was chosen in 1951 for the reconstruction of Coventry Cathedral, but whose work had been widely recognised in Scotland for some time before. His plan for Broughton Place is daring in conception, not because it is a new idea to go back to 17th century Scottish Baronial for inspiration, but because it is precisely what the Victorian builders did with such deplorable results. Basil Spence has chosen his own way back and with the help of a splendid site has achieved striking success.

The massive front, harled white, with its towers and steep corbie-stepped roof, its dormer windows ornamented with carved pediments and its simple stone doorway, embodies the spirit of Scottish Baronial building. Yet the design evades mere imitation both in construction and detail (such features, for instance, as the larger windows divided by astragals, the decorative work by Hew Lorimer on the wall plaques, and the interior planning, are all strongly individual), and the whole is vigorous and imaginative.

John Murray of Broughton, or "Mr. Evidence Murray," as he was known after his downfall, once lived at Broughton Place, and it was he who planted the trees which stand round the new house today. More than a hundred years before, his ancestor, who had been knighted by Charles I, acquired the lands of Stanhope and the Barony of Broughton. John Murray, whose father, "a person of great worth and honour," had also supported the Stuarts, was born in 1715. A student of law, he was educated at Edinburgh University and at Leyden in Holland, after which he visited Rome, where he met many exiled Jacobites.

On his return to Scotland in 1738 he took up the Stuart cause with energy and purpose, and soon became one of the chief liaisons between the Jacobites in Scotland and on the Continent. The same year he bought back the family estates at Broughton, which had been sold in Cromwell's time, and married a Miss Fergusson of Nithsdale, who was much admired for her beauty and spirited support for "the King over the sea." Mounted on horseback, with drawn sword and white-cockaded hat, her public declaration of loyalty to Prince Charles Edward, in the streets of Edinburgh, was remembered and recorded by many different people.

Murray visited the Prince, who regarded him as "ane of the honestest, firmest men in the whole world," in France in 1743, discussing with him the chances of an imminent rising. Although the Scottish Jacobites were practically all against an immediate attempt, Charles Edward had made up his mind. Murray was appointed Secretary, and seems fully to have justified the trust put in him as a devoted servant and able administrator. In August, 1745, he joined the Prince soon after he landed at Moidart, never leaving him till shortly before Culloden.

After the debacle, Murray decided to charter a ship and escape to Holland with Lochiel. Disguising himself as a drover, he travelled south on foot, but, passing through Broughton, caution deserted him and he could not resist calling on his aunt at Kilbucho Place. The servants, becoming curious about a tattered drover being so lavishly entertained in the dining room, rumours soon spread through the village. Pushing on to his brother-in-law's house, Polmood on Tweed, he arrived in an exhausted condition and slept soundly for a few hours. By five o'clock next morning the dragoons were at the gate. Murray of Broughton was hustled down to the Tower of London.

If his story had ended there, Secretary Murray would have come down to history as a hero of the '45. Death on the battlefield he might have faced bravely, but within prison walls he had time to reflect. He turned King's Evidence, and brought Lord Lovat and others to the gallows instead. In 1748 he was pardoned and given a pension of £200 a year, but life was dearly bought. Shunned and disowned by his friends, branded as a traitor and forsaken by his wife, there could be no home for him in Scotland. After remaining at Broughton for a decade or more, he sold the estate and sought a new life in England, where he died in 1777. Yet he kept in touch with Charles Edward to the end, and at a secret meeting with him in London in 1763, remarked to his nine-year-old son, "You have seen your King!"

It was Sir Walter Scott's father, an Edinburgh lawyer, who negotiated the purchase of Broughton Place in 1764. Hence the well-known story of how Mrs. Scott, becoming curious about her husband's mysterious client, burst in on them one day with an offer of tea. When Murray had gone, Mr. Scott threw the cup he had drunk from out of the window with the words, "Neither lip of me or mine comes after Murray of Broughton's!"

In 1775 the old house was burnt to the ground, and 1780 the whole estate was bought by Lord Braxfield, the "Hanging Judge," immortalised in Robert Louis Stevenson's *Weir of Hermiston.* His descendants remained in possession, though there was no house for residence, until after the First World War, when the estate was broken up for sale in 1921 to the several tenant farmers. Eventually, in 1937, Professor and Mrs. Elliott acquired the farm of Broughton Place and built anew on the actual site of the old house of the Barony of Broughton. Professor Elliott, up to his death in 1961, and his family have done much to recreate Broughton Place and to bring new and active life to an old and historic setting.

The large and charming drawing room of the house.

The hall on the ground floor, showing the traditional spiral staircase.

Glamis Castle, near Kirriemuir in Angus, from the south-west.

Glamis Castle

GLAMIS HOLDS A UNIQUE PLACE AMONG the royal castles of Scotland. Not only were its beginnings royal some nine hundred years ago, but in this century a daughter of the house has brought back to the castle a live and regal enchantment. As the family home of the Queen Mother today, Glamis is better known than ever before in its long history. Buildings are not always worthy of having this sort of greatness thrust upon them but Glamis has an important heritage in its own right, both architecturally and historically. It has something more, as clearly defined as the soaring turrets and immense walls—in the true sense of the words, it has a romantic character.

The approach to the castle by a long straight drive through level green fields where cattle graze and wide lawns surrounded by woods, gives a distant perspective of the building, unusually set on flat ground. Most castles of a certain age are built on high defensive sites. The traditional explanation for the low-lying setting of Glamis in Strathmore is that the castle was started on the top of Hunter's Hill near by. But the place was already inhabited by fairies who every night scattered the stones which had been built up during the day until the humans admitted defeat and brought their foundations down to the present site. The first castle, however, said to have existed in very early times, must have been constructed of earthworks and timber. From the 11th to the 14th centuries Glamis was a hunting lodge for the Scottish kings and some time during that period the first stone dwelling, probably a peel tower, must have been built.

In 1372, Sir John Lyon, ancestor of the present owners, married Dame Joanna, daughter of King Robert II. The White Lyon, as he was called because of the fairness of his hair, and his bride were given the Barony of Glamis and the family has remained there for nearly 600 years. Sir John Lyon's grandson was created the 1st Lord Glamis. Attributed to these early Lyon lairds is the oldest masonry in the present castle, in the crypt and the old kitchen, dating back to the 14th century. But the structural bones of the existing building, begun by Patrick, Lord Glamis, in the first half of the 15th century, were completed by his widow between 1459-84. It must have been a stalwart and desirable castle, for 50 years later it was seized by James V who, with his Queen, Marie of Lorraine, and the court, moved in and lived there in great splendour for four years.

The great hall, now the drawing room.

Looking down from the crypt to the spiral staircase and iron yett.

The whole episode casts a dark shadow on the King, who was considered democratic and on the whole respected by his subjects. On a trumped-up charge of witchcraft, the widowed Lady Glamis, who was born a Douglas, and her young son, Lord Glamis, and second husband, Campbell of Skipnish, were imprisoned in Edinburgh Castle. Campbell tried to escape and was killed on the ramparts. Lady Glamis, found guilty of the outrageous charge, was burnt alive on the Castle Hill on December 3, 1540, " with great commiseration of the people, being in the prime of her years, of a singular beauty and suffering all though a woman, with man-like courage, all men conceiving that it was not this fact (witchcraft) but the hatred which the king carried to her brothers."

Meanwhile, during her imprisonment, the King not only lived in great state at Glamis but ransacked it of most of the costly furniture and silver. " Twelve great silver flagons " were melted down also and the Lyon rents annexed to pay the expense of the court. The young Lord Glamis was kept under close arrest until the King's death when the impoverished estate was restored to him, the castle practically empty of furniture and everything of value gone. There is a charming portrait of this young Lord Glamis at the age of eight, by the French court painter Clouet, in the castle drawing room today.

Later in the century, in 1562, Mary Queen of Scots stayed at Glamis on her way north to quell the Huntly rebellion. The weather was " extreame fowle and colde " and all the roads almost impassable, but the English Ambassador recorded that " I never saw her merrier, never dismayed." The Queen was accompanied by her four Maries, her half brother, James Stewart, and " the whole nobility " and presented her host's sister, Lady Margaret Lyon, with " a watch in a gold case, ornamented with filigree." One wonders whether the Queen's gesture made any amends to the family for her father's misdeeds. At the time of this visit, the castle consisted of a central stone keep with out-buildings, surrounded by a wall of enceinte defended by towers.

It was Patrick, 9th Lord Glamis, afterwards 1st Earl of Kinghorne, who began the remodelling of the castle as we see it today. He started the work about 1600 when the great hall or drawing room was begun on the second floor. Before this time the vaulted hall on the first floor, now called the crypt, was used as the living-dining room. The massive 16-foot walls, tiny slits of windows and narrow stair up from the entrance, must have made this earlier great hall almost impregnable from outside attack. Lord Glamis attended the court of James VI in London and there probably met Inigo Jones who designed Whitehall Palace. There is a tradition that this great English architect was employed to make plans for the reconstruction of Glamis, but evidence is lacking. James VI, who often visited Glamis, arranged the marriage between Lord Patrick and Dame Anna Murray, daughter of the Earl of Tulliebardine, which took place at Linlithgow Palace " with greite triomphe " in the presence of the King and Queen. Above the window of the great hall and in other places on the walls at Glamis are the initials of Patrick and Anna, by that time Earl and Countess of Kinghorne.

Earl Patrick's son John, 2nd Earl of Kinghorne, continued his father's work at Glamis by decorating the high vaulted hall ceiling with plasterwork designs, carried out by travelling craftsmen. These same Italian artists also worked at Craigievar and Muchalls Castle and have left some of the finest examples of such decoration in Scotland. But, once again, Glamis fell on evil days and the re-building was halted. The 2nd Earl, a friend of the great Montrose, backed the Covenanters with both his loyalty and his fortune. It was said "he came into his inheritance the wealthiest peer in Scotland and left it the poorest." This generosity was meanly repaid by Cromwell's troops who, when they were quartered at Glamis, used it as roughly as a stable and once more destroyed most of the furniture. The Earl died in 1646 and his widow re-married the Earl of Linlithgow who squeezed every last penny from the estate for his own use. When the young Laird, Patrick, later 1st Earl of Strathmore, came of age, he was confronted by a debt of £400,000 and the advice that "his estates were irrecoverable."

Far from crushing the young man's spirits, this desolate prospect spurred him on to remarkable achievements. It is astonishing that over many years of hard work and good management, the Earl not only repaid his debts but finished the great reconstruction of Glamis begun by his grandfather. Between the years 1671-89, he built the west wing of the castle, re-roofed the east wing, raised the central tower, laid out the garden with statues and a sundial, erected the surrounding walls and planted many trees. He also decorated and furnished the rooms and built the chapel, employing the Dutch artist, Jacob de Wet, to paint the panels. De Wet and another Dutchman, Jan Van Santvoort, who probably made the carved chimneypiece among other things at Glamis, had come to Scotland to work at Holyroodhouse. Apart from these two foreigners, only local craftsmen were employed at Glamis and the Earl's diary seems to indicate that he was his own architect. "Tho it be an old house," he wrote, "and consequentlie the more difficult to reduce the place to any uniformity, yet I did covet extremely to order my building so as the frontispiece might have a resemblance on both syds, and my great hall haveing no following was also a great inducement to me for reering up that quarter upon the west syde which now is, so having founded it, I built my wall according to my draught . . ."

In Defoe's *Tour of Great Britain* the writer who saw the castle early in the 18th century recorded that "Glamis is indeed, one of the finest old built Palaces in Scotland, and by far the largest; . . . when you see it at some Distance it is so full of Turrets and lofty Buildings, Spires and Towers, some plain, others shining with gilded Tops, that it looks not like a Town but a City; and the noble Appearance seen through the long Vistas of the Park are so differing that it does not appear like the same Place any two Ways to-gether.

"The great Avenue is a full half Mile, planted on either side with several rows of Trees; when you come to the outer Gate you are surpriz'd with the Beauty and Variety of the Statues, Busts, some of Stone, some of Brass, some gilded, some plain . . ." In the drawing room of the castle today is a painting

Patrick, 3rd Earl of Kinghorne, with his sons.

In Malcolm's Hall the plasterwork ceiling dates from 1620.

The 17th century sundial on the lawn.

The crypt. In the archway are the state chairs used by James V and his Queen.

of the Earl, wearing flesh-coloured armour, with his sons, pointing to the castle and the gardens he had recreated.

In 1716 the " Old Chevalier," son of James VII, spent a night at Glamis where no fewer than 88 beds were prepared for his retinue. He was entertained by the 6th Earl of Strathmore, a boy of 16, whose brother had been killed fighting for the Stewart cause. In the chapel, the Chevalier " touched for the King's Evil," and it is said " all his patients recovered." Although a Jacobite, the 8th Earl was not actively engaged in the '45 Rising and so escaped fines and the loss of his title.

In 1767, the 9th Earl married Mary Eleanor Bowes, heiress to large estates in the north of England, and the family name was changed to Bowes-Lyon. Some years later, towards the end of the 18th century, the grounds at Glamis were modernised on the lines of the fashion-

RIGHT: *The main doorway and stair tower built into the angles of the old castle.*

The Queen Mother's bedroom.

ABOVE: *Portrait of the 16th Earl's elder brother the late John Patrick, Master of Glamis.*

ABOVE: *The Glamis Chien Lung china.*

BELOW: *The bed hangings in the Queen Mother's bedroom.*

able " Capability " Brown and his followers. The walls round the castle were taken down except for two towers which still remain on the lawn, the gateways removed and the avenues " greatly mutilated." The *New Statistical Account* reported that " altho a fine park of upwards of 200 acres has been formed, yet not in keeping with the venerable castle and the period to which it belongs." Sir Walter Scott, who had visited the castle as a young man, protested more loudly at the change " which under the pretence of improvement deprived that lordly place of its appropriate accompaniments, leaving an ancient dome and towers like these, beggared and outraged."

Alterations were made to the castle in 1811 and 1849 after the west wing had been burnt down. It was during the rebuilding of this wing that the stone gables were replaced by the present " Gothick " cornice on the east wing also. The dining room was remodelled at the same time, it is thought under the direction of the architect James Wyatt. In 1891 an extension at the east end of the castle was built in the Victorian baronial style, now facing on to a formal Dutch garden designed by the 14th Earl and Countess of Strathmore, parents of the Queen Mother. It is in this stately castle that the present 16th Earl and Countess live today.

Although so much furniture at Glamis has been ravaged, plundered and scattered in the past, a certain number of original pieces have been found and returned. There is a large collection of family portraits from early times and among other paintings, a memorable one by Kneller of John Graham of Claverhouse who was a friend and neighbour of the Strathmore family. Interesting sets and pieces of china in the house include a fine Glamis Chien Lung collection from which H.M. the Queen's wedding present was taken. There are also many intriguing relics, such as (in the crypt) the two state chairs used by James V and his Queen when they were in residence, a bullet-proof coat of pressed antelope hide, laced with silver, used by Claverhouse and the cap and bells belonging to the family Jester—said to be the last one maintained in Scotland.

In the Queen Mother's bedroom, part of the present royal suite, is a four-poster bed, the hangings of which were worked by her mother, the 14th Countess. Along one side of the canopy the names of her ten children are embroidered. Of these only the two youngest daughters, Rose, Dowager Countess of Granville, and Elizabeth, the Queen Mother, survive. For the Queen Mother when she visits Glamis, this room must have many memories. Like a fairy-tale youngest daughter, she became a Princess and a Queen, but fairy stories seldom follow the heroine till she becomes a Queen Mother and a grandmother. Glamis, where kings and queens have stayed for a thousand years and which has been enlivened and desolated by history in every century, will not forget this well loved daughter of the house whose life has been as eventful and perhaps more romantic than any of her ancestors.

The east wall and tower from inside the old courtyard, showing the present house.

Airlie Castle

THE APPROACH TO AIRLIE BY THE HUGE towering eastern facade is dramatic enough to halt most visitors for a few moments before the arched entrance in the gate-house. An immense wall of rose-red sandstone, 30 feet high and 10 feet thick, pierced only by gun-loops, stretches southwards from the narrow, fortified gate-house with its three tiny windows and slim, corbelled turret. Coming out on the west side of the wall, into what was once the castle courtyard, the scene changes to green, terraced lawns set before a Georgian house on the north side of the square. In terms of architecture, Airlie Castle is a remnant of a 15th century stronghold with older foundations and with a late 18th century house built along the old north elevation. In terms of history, it is part of the long and eventful story of the Airlie family.

The earliest known owner of Airlie was the Mormaer of Angus who forfeited his lands to the crown in the time of William the Lion. A century later they were held by Simon de Preston in lieu of military service, and about 1378, Robert II conferred the "lands of Eroly" on John de Cappella, "Keeper of the King's Chappel," and later on William de Camera, the "Camerarius" or chamberlain. In 1411 Sir John Stratoun of Lauriston was given the property "for the service of one knight" and either rebuilt or added to the original castle. Twenty years later Airlie was bought by Sir Walter Ogilvy, 2nd son of Sir Walter Ogilvy of Auchterhouse, and founder of the present Airlie family.

The young Sir Walter was as shrewd and capable as he was ambitious and industrious. He had married Isobel Durward, the rich heiress of the Barony of Lintrathen, and with money, good judgment and a flair for what today would be called the property market, Sir Walter acquired large tracts of land in Angus, Perthshire and beyond. Confidence in his ability and power is reflected in the offices to which he was appointed by church, state and king. He was made Baillie of Arbroath Abbey, Lord High Treasurer and Master of the Household of James I.

In 1431, only a few months after Sir Walter's acquisition of Airlie, the King granted him a licence to erect "his tower of Eroly" in the form of a castle. Built on a promontory of land above deep ravines falling to the river Isla and the Melgum Water, the castle stood on a strong defensive site with free access only on the eastern side. The east wall, which remains standing today, was stoutly defended by buttresses at the south end and by the gate-house tower with a drawbridge and portcullis at the entrance. Sir Walter died in 1440. His grandson, Sir James, who had travelled widely in Europe in his youth, was later sent as Ambassador to Denmark, where he "with sich dexterity and wisdom performed his business to the King's contentment, so that for his guid service at his return he was created Lord Ogilvy." He also held the appointments of Baillie and Justiciary of Arbroath Abbey and was given by the Abbot the Barony and Castle of Bolshan, which, for the next 200 years, became the principal home of the family. Airlie Castle was used as a summer residence or lived in by the eldest son when he married.

The 1st Lord Ogilvy's great-great-great-great-grandson, another James, was destined to see the virtual destruction of Airlie Castle. This James was born in 1586 and educated, first under a tutor and then at St. Andrews University, where he was "teachit to handle the bow for archerie, the glub for goff, the batons for fencing, also to rin, to leape, to swoom, to warsell." He returned to live at Airlie Castle in 1611 on his marriage to Isabella Hamilton, daughter of the first Lord Haddington, the distinguished judge.

Like many of his forebears and descendants, James Ogilvy became a right-hand man to his sovereign, Charles I, who entrusted him with the administration of Central Scotland. When the Civil War broke out in 1638 Ogilvy was

TOP: *The entrance in the old east tower showing the only remaining wall of the castle built in 1432.*

CENTRE: *The vaulted dining room.*

BOTTOM: *A short staircase leads to a bathroom in the old tower, converted from the room where Lady Ogilvy defied Argyll.*

summoned to York and given command of a cavalry regiment, and "for his own great merit and eminent services and for the great loyalty and fidelity of his ancestors," he was created Earl of Airlie. But his active assistance to the King in trying to force Episcopacy on Scotland made him a target for the opposing Presbyterian party. In June, 1641, a commission of "Fire and Sword" was granted to the Earl of Argyll, the leader of the Parliamentary forces, who made swift and deadly use of it. With 5000 men he set off for Airlie Castle and, after plundering it, reduced the building to a smouldering ruin. It is said Argyll himself "took the hammer into his own hands and knocked down the hewed stone work of the doors and windows till he did sweat with heat."

At the time of the attack Lord Airlie was at court, but his young daughter-in-law, Lady Ogilvy, who was there, escaped with her children across the river Isla to Dundee, where a few days later a daughter was born to her. The 1st Earl, who, during his lifetime, had sold Bolshan Castle and Farnell and lost Airlie and Forfar Castles by the hands of the Covenenanters, died at Cortachy Castle, which he had bought in 1625 from a kinsman, and which, since then, has been the chief family home.

For a century and a half Airlie Castle remained a ruin until in 1792-3 the present house was built by David, 12th Lord Ogilvy and titular Earl of Airlie. He is perhaps the most romantic figure in the family story and one of the best loved. While studying in Edinburgh, he eloped at the age of 16 with Margaret, daughter of Sir James Johnston of Westerhall in Dumfriesshire, who was three months his senior. The bride's uncle, Lord Elibank, interceded for the couple with Lord Airlie, who seems to have been a most reasonable parent.

David, however, did not want to give up his education. "Dear Papa," he wrote from Edinburgh on the 27th of December, 1742, "I am very sensible of your goodness in writing at all and shall always retain the highest gratitude of the favour. You mention in your letter that we shou'd live together and board in some place, but as that wou'd be quite giving up my education, I hope, my dear Papa, that you won't press it for some time at least; but let me go on as formerly for the session, and I give you my word that, instead of laying aside my books, I shall double my diligence. . . ."

Lord Airlie agreed to this, but a year later packed his son off to a military academy in France until he came of age. David was popular at the French court where he was known as "Le Bel Ecossais" although he was only one of the many young Jacobite countrymen there. His own enthusiasm for the Stuart cause was stirred by meeting Prince Charles Edward and in the summer of 1745 he returned to Angus and there raised the Ogilvy Regiment in support of the Prince. With the Jacobite army David Ogilvy shared the early triumphs of the Rising and the final defeat at Culloden. He survived the battle (although Lady Ogilvy was captured and imprisoned in Edinburgh Castle for five months) and escaped to Sweden and thence to France.

The old Earl died in 1764 but David, Lord Ogilvy, was not pardoned or allowed to return to Scotland till 1778 and never legally inherited the Airlie titles. He was nevertheless overjoyed to be home again at Cortachy Castle and immediately set about finding the survivors of his regiment and helping the dependants of those killed. He and his family had lived so long in France that they had adopted many of the country's ways. They kept a French cook and butler at Cortachy and David wore the dress of a French colonel, spoke the language perfectly and his native tongue with a French accent which he tried hard to overcome. Although he entertained his friends from abroad when they were in Scotland, Lord Ogilvy preferred now to live quietly and unostentatiously. His youngest daughter, Joanna, finding this altogether too tame after the gaieties of Paris, returned there where she lived till her death in 1826.

The ruins of Airlie Castle with all its family memories and historic interest appealed forcefully to David Ogilvy's imagination. Lack of funds forbade the full scale rebuilding of such a castle, but in 1792-3 the east wall and tower were restored and the present house built over the old north wall and surviving ground floor. This long, narrow range, welded at the north-east corner to the ancient tower, is built of the rose-red stones of the old castle and rises to two storeys with attics and half basement. The decorative focus of the unpretentious south front, with its symmetrical sash windows and four little dormers jutting out from the roof, is the sedately charming front door at the top of a double flight of balustraded steps. Above the oval-topped doorway with its "Gothick" window is a heraldic plaque on which is carved the Airlie arms and on either side of the door hang two wrought-iron lanterns. Lord and Lady Airlie have recently moved the entrance westwards to the centre of the house. They have also added a low one-storey wing running west from the Georgian house, which can be used as a self-contained flat.

The front door now opens into what was originally the dining room which, like all three reception rooms on this floor, extends to the width of the house with windows north and south. The panelled walls, woodwork and ceiling are, today, painted white, the windows framed in crimson damask curtain. Over the Regency chimneypiece, outlined in decorative plasterwork designs and garlands, are set the Airlie arms and a coronet in high relief, painted in rich colours of crimson, gold, blue and black. The paint has never been re-touched since 1793 and the heraldic bulls are without collars, signifying that the family was then attainted. In this room, hang portraits of James, 2nd Earl of Airlie (1610-1646), in whose time the castle was destroyed by Argyll, and of David, Lord Ogilvy of the '45, builder of the present house.

The drawing room at the west end of the house is typically and enchantingly Regency in character, with its ornamental plasterwork chimneypiece in the Adam manner, the restrained detail round the china alcove and wainscot and the good proportions of windows

The entrance hall opens into the panelled front hall, originally the dining room.

ABOVE: *The Regency drawing room with family portraits on the walls.*

BELOW: *The bedroom in the east end of the house. The four-poster is a copy of Darnley's bed at Holyroodhouse.*

and doors. The Aubusson carpet in shades of pink, brown and sand gives the room an agreeable grandeur with golden brown silk curtains and pelmets. The pretty white and silver crystal mirror over the fireplace is modern but the pictures, china and most of the ornaments are family possessions.

The library, east of the entrance is a comfortable, lived-in room of which three sides are lined with bookshelves. A moss green carpet, pale green silk curtains and oatmeal coloured furnishings make a good background for the vivid colours of the petit point embroidery on chairs and a stool worked by Lady Airlie. Downstairs in the semi-basement, the vaulted, white-washed dining room has lately been converted from the old castle kitchen. A George III dining table and sideboard and a set of Chinese Chippendale "Cockpen" chairs link the Georgian period of the main part of the house with this much older room. Out of the main spare bedroom on the first floor, a short staircase leads to a bathroom in the old tower, converted from the room where Lady Ogilvy defied Argyll when he attacked the castle in 1641.

The attainder was reversed by Act of Parliament in 1826 when the titles and honours were restored to Lord Ogilvy, nephew of "Le Bel Ecossais" who became the 8th Earl of Airlie. The present and 12th Earl's grandmother, Blanch, Countess of Airlie, in her later life dwelt for many years at Airlie and is much associated with the house and garden. "My match-box," she sometimes called it, and Augustus Hare, one of her numerous literary friends described it as "the finest castle in the world." There are many smaller castles in Scotland but few more charming and more convenient in this age than Airlie.

The present Earl and Countess who now live in the castle—reversing the family tradition, for Lord Ogilvy, their eldest son, is established at Cortachy—have, in the last few years made various improvements to this most historic, most delightful home. Lord Airlie, who served in both world wars and has been Lord Lieutenant of Angus since 1936, is Lord Chamberlain to the Queen Mother and Chancellor of the Order of the Thistle. Among many other appointments he has been Chairman of the British Legion for Scotland and both he and Lady Airlie are actively interested and well known in different spheres of public work.

The library, east of the entrance, Three sides of this room are lined with bookshelves and it makes a comfortable and lived-in Room. The chairs and a stool are covered with petit point embroidery worked by Lady Airlie.

THERE ARE FEW MORE EXCITING discoveries than an unimagined perfection. Yet, "the lovely is the familiar," wrote the poet, Walter de la Mare, and even when one is astonished into admiration and pleasure, there is usually something at least subconsciously familiar to evoke the response. Such is Stobhall—a unique architectural experience, both strange and enchanting and, as a whole, quite without parallel in Scotland. But as soon as the eye has become accustomed to this small group of buildings clustered round the green plot of grass in the middle of the courtyard, familiarity is established with most of the individual shapes and outlines. As if some brilliant director had assembled a cast of traditional actors to dance a ballet or sing an opera. Stobhall

The Dowery House from the courtyard.

Stobhall

The 16th century toy cottage, now the kitchen.

presents a spectacular collective pattern. Possibly there were other similar groups of buildings within a courtyard in medieval Scotland which have not survived.

Standing high up on the left bank of the river Tay, some eight miles north of Perth, Stobhall is surrounded by walls, overhanging a precipitous ravine on the north-east, and enclosing three stone buildings irregularly placed between the upper and lower courtyards. The approach from the north-west is bordered by the long, formal garden stretching from the windows of the Dowery House and set out with clipped, shaped yew trees between rose-beds and lawns, much as it was fashioned in the mid-17th century. The entrance to the courtyard is by a stout gateway, and from thence a wide, flagged path runs alongside the walls. Green grass is laid like a carpet between the Dowery House on the west side, the chapel and adjoining turreted house almost opposite and on the south a tiny toy cottage, once the laundry and now the kitchen, its slated roof and crow-stepped gables only a few feet from the ground. A miniature yew tree planted on the grass outside the Dowery House looks as if it had been put there by a child and become rooted. An immense peace surrounds this courtyard of grey stone and green grass between great woods of beech, elm, lime, sycamore and oak and—far below —the dark waters of the Tay.

The chapel and adjoining turreted house.

Most historians agree that Malcolm Beg, Steward to the Earl of Lennox between 1225 and 1251, is the authentic founder of the Drummond family. His son first took the surname of Drummond, which, it is thought, derives from their lands of Drymen or Drummane in Strathearn. Malcolm's great-granddaughter, Margaret Drummond, "a very beautiful dame," became successively mistress, wife and, in 1363, divorcee of King David II. Lands were granted to the family from the king, and hereafter the Drummonds

The east end of the chapel, showing the medieval lancet window on the left, the ancient altar slab and the painted ceiling.

rose in importance. John Drummond, brother to Queen Margaret, is designated " of Stobhall," which is evidence of some sort of dwelling there, although there are no indications of a fortified castle. In 1365 John's daughter Annabella, who, like her aunt, Queen Margaret, is described as " of great beauty," married the King's cousin, John Stuart of Kyle, and 25 years later, when he ascended the Throne of Scotland as Robert III, a second Drummond wife became Queen.

By the middle of the 14th century, the Drummond family had evidently moved from Dunbartonshire to Perthshire, but it is difficult to be sure exactly when they began to live at Stobhall. Certainly Dame Margaret, widow of Sir William Drummond, lived there, for a document dated 1445 states that " the said Dame Margaret shall have the lands of Stobhall during her life with the wood and grass." While it is here established as a dower house, there is strangely no reference to a main family residence in contemporary records. In 1491, in the time of the 1st Lord Drummond, the family built and settled at Drummond Castle, some 25 miles away in the vale of Strathearn, near Crieff. It was here in 1502 that a tragic fate overtook Lord Drummond's three daughters, Margaret, Euphemia and Sybilla, when they all died of what was almost certainly food poisoning. The poisoned breakfast dish had been meant only for Margaret, who was the mistress of James IV and had, in 1497, borne him a daughter. It is said that the King wanted to marry her but that a number of jealous nobles did not approve of a third Drummond Queen.

It was in the time of David, 2nd Lord Drummond, and his wife, Lilias Ruthven, that the chapel and adjoining house in their present form took shape. A small lancet window with a trefoil head in the north wall of the chapel suggests that the main walls of the building date from the 14th century or earlier. But a reconstruction was carried out when the tower, porch and rooms were added to the chapel in 1578—the date on the lintel of a room on the top floor beside the initials of David Lord Drummond and his wife, Dame Lilias Ruthven. The chapel and dwelling house, standing at right-angles with a corbelled turret squeezed into the corner, are in fact built on the familiar L-plan with modifications. This semi-domestic, semi-ecclesiastical hybrid is as rare as it is charming and merits Bacon's observation that " there is no excellent Beauty that hath not some strangeness in the proportion." Inside, the chapel is white-washed, the stone floor covered with rush mats. Against this simple background the boldly painted ceiling (executed *circa* 1642 and restored in 1858) stands out vividly, depicting kings of many countries on horseback, among them Charles I, Philip IV of Spain and Gustavus Adolphus of Sweden, animals, other designs and, over the doorway, the Drummond arms. On the ancient and massive altar slab stands an Italian crucifix, and on the left in the north wall is an aumbry or cupboard, the fine timber door left unpainted. An old water-stoup engraved with a cross stands by the door, and the font, found in a nearby garden, is medieval work. The chapel is today once

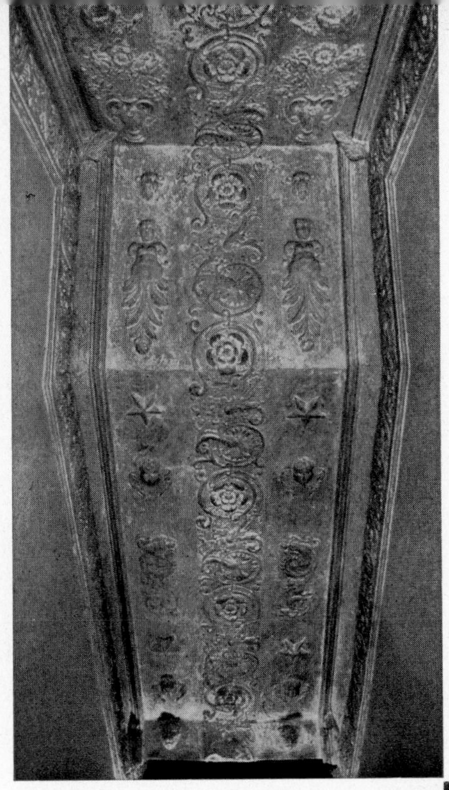

more used—as it was from 1685 until 1827—for Roman Catholic services.

On the ground floor of the building, a narrow stone passage divides the chapel from two small bedrooms, now used for guests. In one of these, formerly the priest's room, the ceiling beams also bear painted decoration, this time of fruit, flowers, sea-serpents and mythical monsters. Gold chintz curtains and bed-hangings splash colour against the simple austerity of white-washed walls and a grey stone moulded fireplace, and through the tiny sunlit window there is an expansive view of the river and beyond. A winding stone staircase leads up to the main bedroom (used by the painter Millais when he stayed at Stobhall in mid-Victorian times), which has a quite small chimney-piece quaintly carved, probably in the 17th century. Above this, in a room at the top of the house, is the fireplace inscribed with the date 1578 and the initials of the builders. From this period, too, must date the entrancing miniature cottage standing close to the chapel-house which may have started life as a kitchen, has been a laundry and brew-house, and was lately re-converted to a present-day kitchen by Lord and Lady Perth, who have added the low covered-in passage-way to the Dowery House. The south side of this cottage is on a lower level, opening on to the courtyard overlooking the Tay.

In the 17th century the Drummond family continued to support the Stuart Kings, and their fortunes fluctuated with those of that royal house for the next 150 years. Over the doorway of the Dowery House are carved the initials of John, 2nd Earl of Perth, and his wife, Lady Jane Ker, daughter of the Earl of Roxburghe, and it was in his time that the present house was built, although it may have been finished after his death in 1662.

It has been suggested that the Dowery House was built during the occupation of Drummond Castle by Cromwell's troops soon after 1650, but nothing is certain. Rubble-built in a warm brownish-grey stone flecked with pink and black, the house is two-storeyed (attic windows have recently been added on one side by Lord Perth), long and low, with chimneys at the top of each crow-stepped gable. Four plain dormer windows rise above the roof-line, which is considerably longer than the wall space. A moulded stone surround emphasises the entrance doorway with the suggestion of a porch, and today two wrought iron lamps flank the heraldic carvings over the door. Otherwise the exterior of the house is quite simple and unpretentious. Set back from but adjoining the west wall of the house, the entrance gateway gives the whole composition depth and distance.

The interior is equally simple on plan. There is a room on either side of the front door (once the kitchen and parlour), opposite which a straight staircase rises to the upper floor, originally occupied by bedrooms. The low, narrow strip of ceiling over the staircase is gorgeously adorned by plasterwork decoration—the only such work remaining in the house. On either side of the rich scroll-work pattern of roses and thistles, there are fleur-de-lys, stars, cherubs' heads with the faces of old men, lions' masques, urns of flowers, naked half-human figures and other designs.

At the top of the staircase the present drawing room in the south-west corner of the house is panelled and painted white and has

ABOVE: *A strip of the decorated plaster-work ceiling above the staircase in the Dowery House.*

RIGHT: *Formerly the priest's room, now used as a guest room.*

BELOW: *Part of the ceiling in the chapel. Charles I is depicted in the top-right-hand corner.*

three deep-set windows, the woodwork dating from about 1700. As in the rest of the house, most of the fittings, the furnishings and decor have been arranged by Lord and Lady Perth during the last few years after a careful and complete restoration of the structure was carried out. A pretty Louis XV marble chimneypiece of the 18th century has been inserted, yellow silk curtains reflect the gleam of a large gilt mirror and Italian candle-brackets and there is French and English furniture, old and new. The tranquillity which is so much a part of Stobhall pervades this charming and memorable room with its historic associations, long views over woods and fields to high blue hills, and its present individuality completed by books and a widely different choice of paintings—there are landscapes by Landseer and Anne Redpath.

In the ground floor dining room, which has been converted from the sitting room, a set of Georgian mahogany chairs is covered in magnificent Scottish needlework of about 1600, worked in soft blues, pinks and browns on a darker brown background.

Although the Drummond family suffered with other Royalists during the Civil War, their fortunes rose again with the Restoration of Charles II, and the peak of their power and fame was reached in the time of James VII and II, who made the 4th Earl Lord Chancellor of Scotland. This Earl lived the last years of his life in exile with his King at St. Germain in France. It was there that the deposed James VII created Drummond Duke of Perth in 1690, a title held by five of his successors and honoured in Scotland and France, at least in Jacobite circles. His son, the 2nd Duke, was out it the 1715 Rising, later attended the exiled King and died in France.

The 3rd Duke fought in the '45 and was " one of the Prince's bravest and most capable officers." He died on the return voyage to France in 1746. The titular dukedom passed to a brother and two uncles and in 1760 became extinct. The Drummond estates were confiscated after the '45 although some of the family were allowed to live on at Stobhall, including the old Dowager Duchess, widow of the 2nd Duke, who remained there till her death in 1773 at the age of 90.

In 1784 the Drummond estates were restored to James Drummond of Lundin, a cousin of the last Duke. Ten years earlier his father had made his home at Stobhall, and his sister, Lady Rachel, and an aunt, Lady Sarah Bruce, lived on there till the last years of the 18th century.

In the 19th century Stobhall passed to Lord Perth's daughter Clementina, who married Lord Willoughby D'Eresby, and was inherited by her descendants, the Earls of Ancaster. Although the family never lived in the house, the place was carefully kept and cherished and was let to various people and lived in for a time by the factor. The turret on the garden side of the Dowery House was added by Lady Willoughby D'Eresby, who also restored the chapel. In 1853 the attainder on the earldom of Perth was reversed and, in 1902, inherited by Viscount Strathallan, a descendant of the 2nd Lord Drummond.

The present drawing room in the south-west corner of the Dowery House.

In 1953 Stobhall was made over by the Earl of Ancaster to the present Lord Perth, thus re-joining the title and property. The place was then in a state of some disrepair, and Lord and Lady Perth spent several years restoring it to its present perfection, and now use the Dowery House as a home.

They have also recently built a library in matching stone, on the site of the earliest building, long vanished, which is behind and to the south-east of the Chapel block.

Lord Perth, who is the 17th Earl was Minister of State for Colonial Affairs for five years from 1957, and is now 1st Crown Estate Commissioner.

The ground floor dining room.

The east entrance front of Blair Castle, showing Cumming's Tower on the extreme right.

Blair Castle

Blair castle, vast and white-harled, is set among high, green-wooded hills, patched in autumn by heather and tawny bracken. A long straight lime avenue leads through parklands studded with old trees, to the great terraces and lawns surrounding the entrance. The line of the castle, horizontal as well as vertical, massive yet well-grouped, shows many of the vicissitudes of its seven centuries. Here Edward III of England stayed in 1336. Two centuries later, Mary Queen of Scots was entertained there with a hunt when 360 red deer and five wolves were killed. Prince Charles Edward spent a few days at the castle soon after his arrival in Scotland in 1745. But not even Queen Victoria, who paid a visit to the 6th Duke in 1844, saw the building as we see it today.

The castle has presented three very different faces even in the last three hundred years—before that it is more difficult to reconstruct the shape. It was first mentioned in 1269, when David Strathbogie, Earl of Atholl, complained to the king that John Comyn of Badenoch (grandfather of Bruce's enemy) had begun to build a fortress at Blair in his absence. No doubt the foundations of what is now called Cumming's Tower, at the north end of the castle group, dates from that time. The hall range (clearly visible only from the west front) is said to have been built by the 3rd Earl in 1530. Two drawings made in 1736 when the 2nd Duke was laying out the grounds as they remain today show us this pre-Georgian stronghold. After the scars inflicted by a Jacobite force commanded by Atholl's younger brother, Lord George Murray, in 1745, the Duke completely re-modelled the castle in the classical manner, chopping off steep gables, turrets and whole attic floors, making a new entrance hall and replacing all the old windows in the building with 18th century sash windows. The castle was now re-christened Atholl House to show that even in the Highlands of Scotland the predominance of classical architecture was recognised.

But fashion is a fickle mistress, and not much more than a century after this, in 1869, the 7th Duke employed the well-known Victorian architect, David Bryce, to obliterate or subdue the out-moded Georgian features of the exterior and to regain its original baronial character. Accordingly, Bryce, always industrious and competent, but seldom so successful as here at Blair, restored height to Cumming's Tower, replaced bartizans and crow-stepped gables and altered the 18th century entrance to the present neo-Gothic composition, reconstructing the hall inside, and, later, in 1871, building the ballroom.

Up to the 17th century the earldom of Atholl never remained for very long in one family. The first earls of the royal Celtic blood had died out by 1211, when the earldom passed through the female line to David Strathbogie. But, for opposing Robert the Bruce, his descendants forfeited the title and lands, which were next held by Robert II and his son Walter. In 1457 the earldom was granted to a half-brother of King James II, Sir John Stewart of Balvenie, who is the ancestor of the present Atholl family. Only the name changed in 1629, when John Murray, Master of Tulliebardine, whose mother, Lady Dorothea Stewart, had been heiress of the 5th Earl of Atholl, succeeded.

It was ten years after this Royalist Earl's death, in 1652, that Blair Castle was captured by Cromwell's troops and held till the Restoration, eight years later. But the Athollmen who supported Montrose in 1644 were not at the Battle of Killiecrankie, fighting for King James, because the 1st Marquess of Atholl was a William of Orange man, probably on account of his wife's cousinship to the Protestant Prince. The 2nd Marquess, created 1st Duke of Atholl in 1703 by Queen Anne, continued to uphold the House of Hanover throughout the 1715 Rising, although three of his sons, including his heir, the Marquess of Tulliebardine, joined the Stuart cause. Thus, on the Duke's death in 1724, he was succeeded by his second son Lord James Murray, the Marquess of Tulliebardine having been charged with high treason and attainted by Parliament.

On the 30th of August, 1745, Prince Charles Edward arrived at Blair Castle and stayed there two days on his way to Perth. Although the 2nd Duke, apparently absent, was still a Hanoverian supporter, his three brothers, many relations and most of the families and clans of the Stewarts of Atholl were Jacobites.

Early in 1746, the Duke's brother, Lord George Murray, probably the most able commanding officer in the Prince's army, with a small force, laid siege to his old home, Blair Castle, which, by this time, was occupied by Government troops under the command of Sir Andrew Agnew, an English officer. Lord George, "a man of original and powerful character," according to Sir Walter Scott, ". . . was tall and hardy and robust, and had that intuitive acquaintance with the art of war, which no tactics can teach." Knowing the strength of the castle, Lord George counted his "light field piece" and his handful of men useless in attack. So he decided to besiege the place, he and his "Atholl Brigade" firing on anyone who showed themselves on the battlements. But just as famine had nearly broken the defences, the blockade was raised. Lord George, appealing unsuccessfully for more men and hearing of Hanoverian reinforcements on their way from Perth, decided to withdraw his forces.

ABOVE: *A 17th-century Dutch cabinet with engraved mother-of-pearl and ivory inlay.*

ABOVE LEFT: *Some of the flower-decorated Crown Derby exhibited in the china and lace room.*

LEFT: *The chimneypiece in the large drawing room. The painting of the 2nd Duke's two daughters, Lady Jean and Lady Charlotte, has now been moved.*

RIGHT: *The dining room, formerly the banqueting hall, was redecorated in the 18th century.*

CENTRE RIGHT: *The red bedroom.*

Although the new south-east stable wing with its toy-like white-washed tower, had been built in 1743, the main Georgian transformation was carried out between 1747 and 1758. The magnificent classical interior, fortunately left unaltered in Victorian times, was designed and decorated by various different craftsmen, as was then the custom. Most of the plasterwork, for instance, was executed by Clayton, an able English artist. The woodwork is by Abraham Swan and the chimneypieces by Thomas Carter, the London stonemason. A good deal of the 18th century and Regency furniture is also English. Of all these distinguished and elegant rooms, each filled with so much to interest and delight, I liked best the exquisite white and gold small drawing room with its pillared marble chimneypiece and overmantel, the beautifully carved door pediments and its informal atmosphere. It would be invidious to choose, however, between the different enchantments of the thirty-two rooms.

Besides the historic and architectural interest, outstanding at Blair Castle is the number of excellent collections housed there, ranging from the very fine furniture, paintings and china to the numerous valuable books and documents, the splendid display of embroidery and lace of all periods and several countries, and the astounding exhibition of trophies and treasures gathered by the Atholl family over the centuries. There is also a natural history room, full of stuffed birds and beasts, some quaint and rare, others—such as the wild cats—really terrifying. Although the pictures do not, as a whole, reach the high standard of the furniture collectively, there are some delightful family portraits and conversation pieces by Hoppner, Zoffany, David Allan and Davison. Here, in fact, is a sort of Highland Victoria and Albert Museum where one could easily spend a week without exhausting even the most important subjects. I have never before seen so many different collections of quality under one roof in Scotland.

In the ballroom is a portrait by Guthrie of the 8th Duke of Atholl, who raised and commanded the Scottish Horse in South Africa during the Boer War and also in Gallipoli during the First World War. He died in 1942, and was succeeded by his brother, the late Lord James Murray. The present and 10th Duke, who is a descendant of the 3rd Duke and whose father, Lt.-Col. G. A. Murray, was killed in action in 1945, succeeded in 1957, and now lives for some months every year at Blair Castle.

RIGHT: *The gold and white small drawing room.*

The entrance to Arbuthnott House showing the central Georgian portion flanked by the 16th- and 17th-century wings.

Arbuthnott House

THE PRESERVATION OF ANCIENT records is seldom characteristic of a country with a stormy history—and Scotland is no exception. It is rare to find a Scottish family holding such full documentary biography over eight hundred years as the Arbuthnotts of Arbuthnott. Early in the 12th century the lands of Aberbothenoth in Kincardineshire belonged partly to the crown and partly to the church. Towards the end of that century the founder of the present family was given the crown lands by Walter Oliphard, the church lands remaining the property of the Bishopric of St. Andrews until 1544. On becoming Laird of Arbuthnott, Hugo de Swinton changed his name to Arbuthnott. The oldest document possessed by the family today is a record, dated 1206, of a dispute between Hugo's son, Duncan, with the church concerning his property, in which the dispute was decided in favour of the church.

The approach to Arbuthnott House, once between a long beech avenue facing the house, was reconstructed in Regency times so that the drive might sweep over the handsome new bridge before the final elegant curve to the entrance. The central portion of the house, built in 1754-56, at the same time as the north wing, was subsequently altered in the 19th century by the addition of a porch, an outer hall to replace the entrance and an inner hall including a staircase and cupola. The coat of arms was, in all probability, added to the front at this time. This central section is flanked by a north and south wing set at right angles. The south wing, an addition to the 15th century castle, is in three distinct parts, the more recent of the three being built in 1650, the centre part around 1580 and the remaining part possibly 15th century. The rest of the castle consists of old buildings, today used as out-houses, and at the back of the house there is an old bake-house which bears the date 1588 and the initials A.A. standing for Andrew Arbuthnott who was Laird at that time. It is likely that it was he who built the central section of the south wing.

This castle was begun by Hugh Arbuthnott in 1420 for his personal protection after he had been accused with several others, of the murder of Melville of Glenbervie, Sheriff of the Mearns, by having him boiled in a cauldron. The document bearing the remission for this murder is now in the Advocates' Library in Edinburgh. The castle was finished by Hugh's great-grandson about 1480. Of the first 13th century castle practically nothing is known.

Hugh le Blond, the Laird who was hero of a ballad (unfortunately fictitious in date, at least) included in "The Minstrelsy of the Border" by Sir Walter Scott, was buried in Arbuthnott church about the end of the 13th century. The stone figure of a recumbent knight in the Arbuthnott aisle is thought by some to represent the gallant Hugh le Blond. The stone figure is almost certainly 13th century, whereas the base of the tomb is later in date, probably 14th century. On the tomb are carved the arms of the Arbuthnott, Douglas and Johnstone families, and there are indications that other shields have been cut away.

The church, dedicated to St. Ternan, is one of the oldest in use in Scotland today, the chancel and possibly part of the knave dating from 1242. The next building, which includes the Arbuthnott aisle, was carried out

A plasterwork figure in one corner of the drawing room ceiling.

in the late 15th century, and finally, after a fire in 1889, in which fortunately none of the original structural features suffered, part of the church was restored by the well-known architect, the late Mr A. M. Mackenzie.

Robert, who finished building the castle in 1480, was outstanding among the Arbuthnott lairds. Not only did he make many improvements to the estate but he endowed his family with the Arbuthnott aisle—"verie gorgious bothe in craft and materiallis", and two bells. "And that this wark micht be the better exceptid of God . . . he carrit the stonis, lyme and all the rest of the materiallis with his avin horses and would tak no help off his tennantis as the custom was". Most valuable to posterity was his commissioning of the Arbuthnott Missale, finished in 1491 by the Vicar of Arbuthnott, James Sybbald, and now the only complete Scottish Missal of this type in existence. The priest, who worked in a little room above the Arbuthnott aisle of the church, also wrote out and beautifully illustrated the Arbuthnott Prayer Book and Psalter. These three precious and exquisite documents, saved from the general destruction at the Reformation, were sold by the family in 1894 and are now in Paisley Museum.

Many good deeds are recorded of Robert Arbuthnott and his wife Marion. In 1482 they were granted a Plenary Indulgence for their contributions to the Turkish Crusade, and five years later were received into the Order of the Friar's Minors of Observance, with participation in all its benefits. And in 1490 they were granted a licence to carry about with them a portable altar and to say Mass at any time and place convenient to them. Both James III and IV liked and trusted Robert Arbuthnott, and a natural son, Patrick (he also had twelve lawful children) who had studied Medicine in France, became physician to James V. From the accounts of the Lord High Chancellor comes this entry—" Item, to Doctor Arbuthnot, the Kingis mediciner,

An old print of the Arbuthnott Missale, showing the figure of St. Ternan, patron saint of the church.

awatand daily on the Kingis service, to his expens be the Kingis precept—£240." He also received £26 13s. 4d. for fodder for his horses per annum, and eventually a yearly pension of £66 13s. 4d.

Principal Alexander Arbuthnott, one of the moving spirits of the Reformation, was a grandson of the good Robert. First Protestant Principal of King's College, Aberdeen, and twice Moderator of the General Assembly in the difficult years of the 1570s, Alexander found time during his short life to write a history in Latin of the Arbuthnott family as well as some of the best poetry of the day. His brief poem, *On Luve*, is worth repeating:

" He that luifis lichtliest,
Sall not happin on the best.
He that luifis langest,
Sall have rest surest.
He that luvis all his best,
Sall chance upon the gudliest.
Qua sa in luif is trew and plaine,
He sall be lufit weill agane."

Dr. John Arbuthnott, Scottish mathematician and physician is remembered chiefly as a friend of Swift, Pope and John Gay. He was physician to Queen Anne from 1705 till her death in 1714. His literary works are mainly satirical and include *The History of John Bull*, published in 1712.

In the 17th century south wing of the house, on the first floor, is situated the long, rather narrow drawing room overlooking the ancient garden. Here is one of the most curious and splendid ceilings in Scotland. The bold magnificence of the designs is emphasised by the unusually low ceiling for such a room, and the baroque grandeur thrown into relief by the simplicity of the rest of the house. Although Italianate in feeling and execution, some of the plasterwork masques and grotesques are quaintly individual in character and suggest an enterprising craftsman with a strong sense of humour. The pine panelling in this room which, unlike the usual varnished pinewood, has a soft creamy-yellow natural polish, also dates from the 17th century. There are much plainer plasterwork ceilings in two of the bedrooms on the floor above. The dining room, where hang many interesting family portraits, is in the 18th century part of the house, as is the central staircase with its charming Regency balustrade.

The 1st Viscount, created in 1641, was a Covenanter, and when the Royalist troops under Montrose marched through Kincardineshire, the lands of Arbuthnott were not spared. Lord Arbuthnott complained to Parliament in 1645 that he " hes bene maist maliciouslie opprest and almost ruinated, for in the moneth of Merch, 1645, his landis . . . wes brunt and waisted be James Grahame and his adherentis, enemies to this Kirk and Kingdom. And his losses at that time did exceede all those of his qualitie where he lived . . ." Eventually Parliament exempted Arbuthnott from the " Levie bothe of horse and foote . . . and that in respect of his constant affectioune and of his former extraordinary sufferings."

The garden at Arbuthnott House, laid out in the 17th century and in perfect order and beauty today, is, in my experience, unique—partly because of the unusual layout and partly in the meticulous preservation of its former glories. Grass lawns sloping down to the burn at the bottom are intersected by long, criss-cross grass paths, each with its special vista. Shaped box yews, cedars, Wellingtonias, holly and fruit trees grow among borders of flowers, banks of roses and flowering shrubs. And the great lime trees ringing the wood and the rising fields to the south remind us still of the Jacobite sympathies held by the Arbuthnott family in the 18th century.

The present and 15th Viscount, Major-General Robert Keith Arbuthnott, who has been Lord Lieutenant of Kincardineshire since 1961, now lives in this historic house with its rare and enchanting garden.

The drawing room in the 17th-century wing.

This photograph of Crathes Castle was taken before the Georgian wing was destroyed by fire in 1966.

Crathes Castle

MOST PEOPLE WHO COME TO SCOTLAND for the first time have in mind a vague and sometimes sadly brief list of what they want to see—Holyrood Palace perhaps, the Forth Bridges, Loch Lomond, Abbotsford and so on. There is no doubt that Crathes Castle should come near the top of all such lists, not only for the stranger but for every Scot who is interested in his own history and architecture. The castle is in the care of The National Trust for Scotland, to whom it was handed over by Sir James and Lady Burnett of Leys in 1951. Sir James the 13th Baronet, had a distinguished military career; he commanded the 2nd Gordon Highlanders and was G.O.C. Highland Division from 1931 to 1935.

Standing high on the north side of the River Dee under the green Hill of Fare, the castle is surrounded by fine trees and overlooks a glimpse of rolling, wooded uplands stretching beyond the village of Banchory. A first glimpse of it is unforgetable — this great Jacobean tower, harled and sand-coloured, rising from its base of solid strength to a magnificence of corbelled turrets, gables, chimneys and a rich fantasy of ornament. Begun in the reign of Mary, Queen of Scots, Crathes is the perfect example of the transitional castle-into-house built at a time when the need for defence (and that only against troublesome neighbours) was beginning to give way to a new demand for comfort and beauty. The simple and satisfying Georgian wing which the 3rd Baronet added to the south wall of the tower, together with a later Victorian addition, was destroyed by a fire in January 1966. What manner of building is to arise from the ruins is a problem which The Trust now faces.

The family Burnett of Leys is one of the oldest in Scotland. They and their next door neighbours, the Irvines of Drum, were supporters of King Robert the Bruce, who in 1323 rewarded the Burnetts with a gift of land in exchange for service as coroners of the Royal Forest of Drum. A jewelled ivory horn which was the badge of office for this appointment is preserved at Crathes today.

In early times the Burnetts lived in a crannog or lake-dwelling in Banchory Loch (since drained) and the title "of Leys" which belongs to the head of the Burnett clan, refers to the land on the Loch shore. In the year 1553 (some 50 years before the Privy Council decreed that all such lake-dwellings or "crannakis in the Ylis" should be surrendered to the King), Alexander Burnett started to build Crathes. Finished in 1596, it is the earliest and one of the most lovely and ingenious of all that large group of Scottish Jacobean castles which represents the last and best phase of the old native style of building.

It is largely due to the skilful and imaginative restorations made by the former owners that one can glimpse today many aspects of the castle as it must have looked when the 1st Laird and his Lady, Alexander Burnett (great-grandson of the founder) and Katherine Gordon set up house more than three and a half centuries ago. A lavishly carved oak bedstead and two armchairs bear their initials—all exceptionally interesting specimens of the scanty Scottish furniture of the time. The long gallery at the top of the tower (a fashion borrowed from England) with its unique oak panelled ceiling, was once used as the Court of Barony. Most rare and exciting of all the original features are the painted ceilings, discovered in 1877 in the upper floors of the tower under Georgian plaster.

These depict a series of quaint figures of undoubtedly North German ancestry, sumptuously dressed in clothes of the period (the colours—bright blues and greens, glowing reds, terra-cottas and flesh-pinks—are all as fresh as if they had been painted yesterday), accompanied by Gothic-lettered inscriptions, pious, proverbial and whimsical, such as (in the Muses Room) "HOP IS A VERTUE OF CINGULAR GRACE," and (in the Green Lady's Room):—

> " Thryce happy is the man indeed
> That weds ane vertues wyf
> She is the blessing of his seid
> And comfort of his lyff."

ABOVE: *Section of the painted ceiling in the Green Lady's Room.*

LEFT: *The Horn of Leys, a jewelled ivory horn, was given to the Burnetts, as the badge of office, for their services as coroners of the Royal Eorest of Drum by King Robert the Bruce.*

BELOW: *The carved oak bedstead belonging to the 1st Laird and his wife.*

Although these may be attributed to foreign workmen who were not uncommon in Scotland in the early years of the 17th century, it is perhaps significant that one of the Laird's brothers was at this time Professor of Philosophy at the University of Basle in Germany.

Whoever the artist, they are among the finest things of their kind in Scotland. A few years ago, however, the boards of Memel pine which bear the paintings, had seriously deteriorated. Pests were damaging the timbers, and the lucent tempera colours were flaking and fading. With the aid of special funds, notably from the Gulbenkian Foundation, The Trust was able to arrange for an artist to be trained in the special techniques of restoration. What began as an operation to save the Crathes ceilings has since grown, at Stenhouse Mansion in Edinburgh, into a project which may become a conservation centre for works of art in Scotland.

But the hall with its vaulted roof of granite boulders, great Elizabethan chimneypiece and old oak doorways, is still the heart of the castle. It is an enthralling room—grand, massive and yet comfortable with a kindly Scottish splendour. Oak and walnut furniture, old rugs, family portraits and flowers vivid in contrast, are perfectly set off against the rough stone walls. Alterations and re-arrangements have been made since the 1st Laird's time; finally—and I think superbly—Sir James and Lady Burnett revived much that is vigorously Jacobean in character.

One of the remarkable things about Crathes is its uninterrupted history, for it seems to have escaped all but the lightest scars through the religious broils and Civil War of the 17th century and during the Stuart Rebellions of later times. This was due to family characteristics rather than to chance or design. The Burnetts were in the main peace-loving, reasonable men with a zest for culture and education (the younger sons figure largely in the church and the professions) and with nothing less than a genius for friendship which often triumphed over political and religious differences. Sir Thomas Burnett who was knighted in 1620 and became a Baronet of Nova Scotia in 1626 did not altogether avoid trouble with the Covenanting Party although he was by no means opposed to them. It was Montrose who stayed at Crathes in 1644, when he had turned King's man, who put his life-long friend and host to some inconvenience. However, apart from a skirmish with a band of Highlanders from Aboyne who attacked the castle and cost Sir Thomas £67,000 (Scots) in damage, Crathes escaped the destructive vengeance of the Covenanters. So both life and property were saved time and again from the fate that befell many Scottish estates and families.

Sir Thomas was succeeded by his grandson in 1653 who apparently found less favour in the countryside. The Laird of Brodie recorded in his diary:—" When I heard that the Lord of Leyis Burnett, being a sober, grave man, had a

ABOVE: *The great hall.*

successor so profane, dissolute and naughty, my heart said "what do I travel for under the sun?" How is it true of Soloman, men know not what shall come after them, whether a wyse man or a fool?". This Laird had little time to vindicate such admonition for he died at the age of 26, leaving an infant son, another Sir Thomas (1663-1714) in whose time the estate prospered. A strong supporter of William of Orange, he was marked down for a peerage but the King died before this materialised.

It was his son who added the Georgian wing to the tower—where perhaps he lived more securely a little removed from the ghostly haunts of the old castle where the Green Lady's Room is said to be haunted by a mother and child found buried under the floor, for it is recorded that he suffered from " broodie fears."

The gardens at Crathes which are the loveliest and the richest I have ever seen, were also originally laid out in the 18th century—the great yew hedges were planted in 1702. From the topmost point of the tower one can visualise the original plan and extent of the lay-out—eight separate geometrical enclosures divided by yew hedges and bounded on the north-east by high stone walls. Within this formal pattern many different pictures must have been framed. Among the now world famous collection of rare plants are many which need special care and encouragement in so northerly a climate and some which have never been successfully grown there before. But strange and foreign plants mingle with the older inhabitants in the most natural

ABOVE: *Jamesone's portrait of Sir Thomas Burnett of Leys, 1st Baronet and 15th Laird.*

LEFT: *The hall of the old keep.*

way—a way known only to the true craftsman whose masterpieces, however intricate in the making, suggest the almost effortless perfection of nature.

A memorial panel on a granite wall in the Pool Garden records the great contribution made to the garden by Sir James and Lady Burnett: " His renowned collection of shrubs and her unique gift for colour, design and planting added much to the interest and beauty of their old established garden." Sir James collected rare plants and shrubs from all over the world, and the garden was already famous when he died in 1953. Lady Burnett continued to devote her skill to the work until her death in 1960.

To describe in detail or to sum up the whole in so short a space would be an impossible task. Each garden has its own beauty of form, colour and design. At random, my October impressions include the Pool Garden—a stone-edged pool, flashing with goldfish, set in a surround of grass and gay flower-beds, the White Border which in summer must be dazzling, a festival of dahlias blazing against the dense blue-green of a yew hedge, and in the Trough Garden, a corner where indigo blue gentians and waxen, white colchicums dimmed memories of summer in autumn glory.

Sir James and Lady Burnett lost both their sons before and during the Second World War. The heir to the remainder of the estate is the son of their only daughter. When he succeeded in July, 1966, he assumed the name of Burnett of Leys, thus continuing a tradition which stretches back to Bannockburn.

ABOVE: *The main entrance guarded by an iron yett.*

LEFT: *The gardens at Crathes. Among the now world famous collection of plants are many which are rarely found in so northerly a climate. These foreign plants mingle quite successfully with older inhabitants.*

BELOW: *The long gallery at the top of the tower has a unique oak panelled ceiling and was once used as the Court of Barony.*

Drum Castle

DRUM IS ONE OF THE MOST REMARKABLE castles in Scotland, and in importance must rank with the first half-dozen in the country. That is if the word "importance" represents here (as I mean it to) the triple distinction of age, beauty and a long and continuous family connection. Taking these qualities in that order, first look at the upstanding keep, dwarfing the other courtyard buildings like a giant in a midget show. With its twelve-foot-thick walls and dizzy parapet more than seventy feet high, it has all the characteristics of a 14th century tower and may be even older. Next, walk round the corner to where, facing south, stands one of the loveliest 17th century additions I have ever seen, with knife-edge roof, carved dormer windows and unevenly placed towers and turrets, many of the enchanting features of that time. And lastly, inside the castle the present Laird can show you the original charter of the place, presented in 1323 to his ancestor, William de Irvine, by King Robert the Bruce.

Originally crown property, the Forest of Drum was granted by Robert the Bruce to his supporters, the Irvines and the Burnetts of Leys. It is an astonishing fact that both these neighbouring families should still remain here after more than six hundred years—for although Crathes Castle has recently been handed over to The National Trust, the Burnett family live in one wing. William de Irvine, the 2nd son of the Norman Laird of Bonshaw Tower in Dumfriesshire, was secretary to the King and a devoted follower through all his vicissitudes. Thus, with the chieftainship of that family, the 1st Irvine of Drum settled in Aberdeenshire.

This period, so far away in time, is continually kept alive at Drum by the overpowering presence of the keep. The original movable wooden staircase leading to the entrance on the first floor is now replaced by a stone stair. Once inside the tower, although internally it has been much altered, one is quickly submerged in the formidable past in the chill darkness of the vaulted basement dungeon and in the narrow, spiral stairs twisting up to the great hall, also cool and dim, yet still retaining some of its austere grandeur in such features as the huge chimneypiece and the deeply recessed stone window-seats. This room was originally divided horizontally by wooden floors, thus adding, above, a private hall for the Laird, and bedrooms beyond. Walking round the parapet on top (the uneven steps are said to have been made expressly to keep the night watchman awake), one looks perilously down on a clutter of tall chimneys, almost perpendicular gables and lichened turrets, rising as it were from the far-away green grass carpet of the lawn.

ABOVE: *The Jacobean part of the castle facing south, with the old keep projecting to the east.*

Although small outbuildings grew up by degrees round the keep in the courtyard, it was three hundred years before the great Jacobean house was built on the south side. The 10th Laird—one of the nineteen Alexander Irvines of Drum—was now in possession and the family fortunes prospered. At the beginning of the 17th century the Irvines were the largest landowners in Aberdeenshire, Kincardineshire and Angus. But the Laird, a man of many parts, was not entirely taken up with worldly goods. In 1612 he received a letter from King James VI with "very hearty thanks for service done in the north part of that our kingdom," and some years later he was appointed sheriff-principal of Aberdeen. Irvine also founded several bursaries at Marischal College and at Aberdeen Grammar School, "Because it hath pleased God the Lord, of His mercy, to prolong my days for the education and provision of all my bairns, and both then and since that time hath blessed and increased my means, whereof, lest I should prove forgetful in not rendering back a part for sacred and pious uses, I leave ten thousand Scots money."

Still guarded by an iron yett, but now covered in by a 19th century hall, the main entrance to Irvine's new house, built in 1619, is in the south-west corner of the courtyard. But the long lovely front flanked by square towers faces south across the wide expanse of lawn. Typical of the period is the more symmetrical arrangement and shape of the windows, varied only by individual ornament. The interior, altered in mid-Victorian times by the architect David Bryce (who also made some exterior additions on the courtyard side), follows in the main the 17th century plan, with an added corridor, staircase and larger hall. Characteristically, all the spacious principal rooms are on the first floor, under the bedrooms, which were originally reached by several small staircases. The Laird's private rooms adjoining the drawing room have a secret staircase leading to an outside door in one of the towers—so that he might entertain visitors without the notice of the rest of the household. In fact, these two parts of Drum—the old keep and the Jacobean house, separated by three centuries—perfectly contrast the social as well as the building customs of their times.

The Laird who succeeded in 1630 lived through stern times, and by his loyalty to the King and his refusal to sign the Covenant, saw the prosperity of Drum decline and the place battered and plundered in the Civil War by five hundred of Argyll's rampant Irish troops who were quartered there for some time. Nor did Irvine escape a term of imprisonment in Edinburgh Tolbooth for his convictions. Unluckily, the Restoration brought little compensation, although an earldom was offered and refused. The Irvines actively supported the Stuarts and fought in both the '15 and the '45 Rebellions, thereby forfeiting more of the property, which was further diminished by a series of lawsuits in the early 19th century. Possibly, however, the ill wind has blown something good into the present, for landowning on a large scale now carries heavy burdens. And Mr. Quentin Forbes Irvine, the 24th Laird of Drum, who lives there with his wife today, inherit perhaps the longest partnership of name and place in Scotland.

BELOW: *The old iron yett.*

ABOVE: *The drawing room in the 17th-century part of the house.*

BELOW: *Family portraits hang in the long dining room.*

BELOW: *One of the decorated dormer window-heads.*

The great hall on the first floor. This room has a groined vaulted ceiling covered in elaborate plasterwork ornamentation and the walls are half-panelled in carved oak.

Craigievar Castle

Craigievar has the completeness and natural beauty of something grown to perfection rather than achieved by man-made effort. Halfway between Alford and Lumphanan in Aberdeenshire, the castle stands high on Craigievar Hill, surrounded by old trees in a glen carved out by the Leochal Water. Against the green background, the tower of pinkish harled granite rises to a height of seven storeys from its massive base to an extravaganza of turrets, chimneys, cupolas and gables jostling for space at the top. Triumphantly balancing fantasy with realism, Craigievar is undoubtedly the supreme example of a tower-house in Scotland.

The lands of Craigievar belonged to the Mortymer family in the last half of the 16th century and to them is attributed the beginnings of the castle. Financial troubles led to the sale of the property in 1610 to William Forbes of the neighbouring Forbes family of Corse, a younger brother of the famous Bishop Patrick Forbes. " Willy the Merchant," as he was called, had " made a goodly pile merchandizing at Dantzig " in the Baltic and gradually acquired other properties in Aberdeenshire and farther south. He was a rich man when he started work at the unfinished castle on Craigievar Hill and his money commanded the best builders and craftsmen of a peak period in Scottish architecture. At this time the stout stone keep had developed from a military stronghold to a domestic tower-house in which the importance of comfort, convenience and beauty of design had all but replaced the need for defence. At Craigievar the traditional form remains—a substantial L-shaped keep—while the ancient war-like features have been diverted to points of ornament. Thus the balustrade at the top of the square tower replaces the early roof parapet from which boiling oil and other missiles were hurled down on the grounded enemy; the corbelled turrets, once used to support the parapet, have descended gracefully below a diminishing gable and the cannon-like projections represent the old water-draining spouts from the roof.

So much for the formula of a fashionable laird's house of the time, the success of the finished building depending on individual craftsmen. It is certain that the Laird of Craigievar, a cultured man with an Edinburgh University degree and a wide knowledge of foreign parts, had a hand in the designing of his new castle. But most of the credit for this dramatic tour de force must go to the master-mason. Although he left no written record at Craigievar, I. Bel, who had remodelled Castle Fraser in 1681, is generally acknowledged to be the man. One of a family of succeeding generations of master-masons, the Bels were mainly responsible for the brilliant group of Aberdeenshire castles, including Midmar and Fyvie, built in the early 17th century.

Among these Craigievar is unique in remaining today almost exactly as it was finished in 1626, virtually without alterations and additions to smudge the original picture. It is a picture which clearly shows that although the framework of the castle is traditional, Scots builders were already familiar with Renaissance ideas of decoration such as the bell-shaped cupolas topping two turrets and the classical balustrade above the tower. At Craigievar these two contrasting styles have been supremely welded. The rounded corners of the lower walls give continuity to the bulging turrets above and the knife-edge roof of lichened Foudland slates (which replaced the original stone slabs in the early 19th century) stabs out a horizontal pause among the aspiring pinnacles and chimneys.

William Forbes died the year after his castle was completed, being succeeded by his son, another William who was created a Baronet of Nova Scotia by Charles I in 1630. But when the Civil War broke out, his sympathies were with the Covenanters and he fought at both battles of Aberdeen, in 1644 and 1646, and was taken prisoner on each occasion by the Royalists, having escaped from his first captivity by breaking parole and hereby smirching his reputation. In the year between he was appointed a member of the Committee of Estates and in 1647 became Sheriff of Aberdeenshire. Sir William, who died in 1648, was painted by Jameson, " the Father of Scottish Painting," and the portrait hangs at Craigievar today with that of his son, known as Red Sir John. Although this description probably applied to his colouring or temperament, Red Sir John had a reputation for rough justice in the barony courts of Craigievar, which were sometimes held in the great hall.

Not all the Forbes lairds were men of war. There were also writers and poets as, for instance, Alexander, born in 1700, who was described as " a child of ardent spirit and of so strong and beautiful a genius that in the 12th year of his age, he has wrote poems which are read of all with admiration." The 5th Baronet married a daughter of the 13th Lord Sempill and two generations later the 8th Baronet, who served in the Crimean War, succeeded to the title in 1884 in the right of his grandmother.

The interior of the castle perfectly equals the glory of the outside and here the richness of the decoration more markedly reflects Renaissance influence. The only entrance, on the ground floor, opens into a little hall with access to three vaulted rooms, one of which is still used as the kitchen. From here a straight stair leads up to the great hall on the first floor. This splendid room with its groined vaulted ceiling covered in elaborate plasterwork ornamentation, the walls half-panelled in carved oak and a piper's gallery at the east end, is the only one in Scotland to retain its original form practically intact. Over the chimneypiece is a magnificent presentation of the Royal Arms in stucco, flanked by two demi-figures. We are told that William Forbes " plaistered it (Craigievar) very curiously " and this applies in particular to the medallion portraits of Biblical, Greek and Roman heroes, including David with his harp and crown, Hector of Troy and Alexander the Great. The same English travelling craftsmen who had worked at Muchalls Castle and Glamis a few years earlier were employed at Craigievar and some of the plasterwork is identical. The heraldic

arms of Willy the Merchant with the initials of his wife, Marjorie Woodward (a daughter of the Provost of Edinburgh), are displayed and also those of his grandson, Red Sir John.

Opposite the great hall, the small cosy withdrawing room, panelled in 18th century Memel Pine (one of the few innovations to the interior) has a beautiful plasterwork ceiling, low enough to be admired in detail. The centre moulding depicts St. Margaret. A reminder that life in the most sophisticated dwelling of the time was not entirely without incident, is the heap of earth under the floorboards of this room which, it is said, served to deaden the cries of prisoners in the dungeon below. From the first floor two spiral stairways ascend to the top of the tower leading to bedrooms at different levels and the long gallery, once used for social occasions or barony courts and now re-arranged to display family charters, books and weapons.

One of the grandest bedrooms is the Queen's room on the fourth floor with its bold plasterwork ceiling. Carved on the bed-head of another bedroom is the Craigievar motto: "DOE NOT VAKEN SLEEPING DOGS." Over the chimneypiece hang portraits by Raeburn of Sir William Forbes, 5th Baronet (1755-1816), and his wife, Sarah, daughter of the 13th Lord Sempill (1762-1799). There is also a photograph of Raeburn's receipt: "Received from Mr. Leith sixteen guineas for the portraits of Sir Wlm. and Lady Forbes. Henry Raeburn." Along with this there is a receipt for the frames which cost six guineas.

Another of the rare alterations is a compact bathroom on the second floor, converted

Craigievar Castle, a superb example of the tower house in Scotland.

from a box bed. Most of the furniture dates from a later period than the house and some of it was made by the estate carpenter of one time and another. Many of the carpets are in Forbes tartan as is much of the upholstery work. As lately as 1842 the main rooms were every day covered in fresh rushes, these also providing wicks for the multitude of lamps.

Any doubt about a tower-house being necessarily cramped is dispelled by the spacious planning at Craigievar. Partly this is achieved by the greater width of the top half of the building, partly by small rooms eked out of the thick walls, but mainly by the soaring vertical amplitude of the plan akin to the sky-scrapers of modern times. In 1963 The National Trust for Scotland acquired Craigievar with 30 acres of ground round the castle and restrictive agreements over a further 560 acres of agricultural land. The 19th Baron Sempill, who was also Sir William Forbes, 10th Baronet of Craigievar, died in December, 1965. By invitation of The National Trust, his widow, Cecilia Lady Sempill, continues to live at Craigievar.

The withdrawing room.

The Queen's bedroom on the fourth floor with its bold plasterwork ceiling.

Castle Fraser from the south-west.

Castle Fraser

CASTLE FRASER IS THE LARGEST AND most spectacular of that superb group of Aberdeenshire castles which grew up towards the end of the sixteenth and the beginning of the seventeenth centuries, roughly within thirty years and fifteen miles of each other. Crathes, Craigievar, Drum, Midmar and Castle Fraser—these were the masterpieces of a school of granite masons whose genius for design has never been excelled in the old Scottish style of building. To see Castle Fraser, set among level green grasslands and surrounding trees, rising in solemn grandeur to the ordered fantasy of its topmost peaks and pinnacles, is to forget for a moment the practical purposes of a house. Architecture has been described as frozen music, and here, at any rate, the contrasting vigour and delicacy and the modulated rise and fall of massed shapes has something akin to a great symphony.

The castle as it stands was mainly devised and built by Andrew Lord Fraser and his master-mason between about 1595 and 1636. But the royal coat of arms on the south wall dated 1576 once adorned an earlier and plainer castle. This consisted of the present west block and perhaps part of the central block—a simple fortified tower with an addition built out at right-angles. The Frasers, who originally came from France, possibly with Henry II, and soon after settled in the south of Scotland and Stirlingshire, migrated to Aberdeenshire in the mid-14th century. Thomas Fraser received a charter of the castle—then called Muchall-in-Mar, from James II in 1454.

Andrew Fraser, the 7th Laird, born in 1570, was a comparatively rich man and, like so many of the Scottish nobles and gentry whose pockets had been filled by the wealth drained from the church since the Reformation, he planned to enlarge and alter his rather austere and war-like home. Building at the turn of the century was mainly influenced by two factors. Firstly, gunpowder and the use of small arms had pierced the former inviolability of the great stone wall as a defence; and, secondly, people were beginning to demand convenience, comfort and beauty of design in their homes as well as some measure of security.

One of the plans evolved to meet these needs consisted of a group of two or three buildings welded together and slightly overlapping each other so that one block might be defended by fire directed from the next. Between fifty and sixty of these so-called Z-plan castles were built at this time in Scotland, a third of the number being in Aberdeenshire. Of these, Castle Fraser is undoubtedly the supreme example.

Thus the castle, in all its astonishing beauty and dramatic force, was based on practical needs—a formula however apparently incompatible which has produced most great architecture.

But, from the general to the particular, Andrew Fraser was extremely fortunate in his choice of a master-mason. A small panel at the base of an heraldic tablet on the north side of the castle bears his signature and the date:

1617
I.Bel
MM (an engraved heart) F.

the last line of which has been translated as "master-mason in leal service to Fraser." Less than five miles away, in Midmar kirkyard, a granite tombstone is inscribed with the words: "Heir Lyis Georg Bel Meason Deceisit in Balogy Ano 1575." Midmar Castle (formerly called Ballogie) is ascribed to Georg Bel, who must surely have been related to I. Bel (possibly they were father and son), for the two buildings present an unmistakeable family likeness.

The central block, most dramatically seen from the south side, was probably finished by 1618, and is built in the elaborate and highly developed style of the time, the old defensive features being translated into rich and fantastic yet wholly vigorous ornament. Only the base of the castle remains typically stolid and plain. Thus a mock-embattled parapet runs round the building as a decorative belt,

ABOVE: *The vaulted great hall on the first floor.*

BELOW: *High up in the round tower, one of the rooms has an early Victorian décor.*

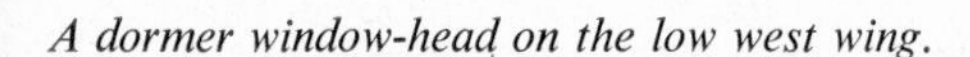

A dormer window-head on the low west wing.

beyond which rise carved dormer window-heads, two-storey corner turrets, angled chimney-stacks and the massive bulge of the round south-east tower swelling above the knife-edged roof. On the north side, where two long low wings (not finished till after 1630) run out to form a courtyard enclosed by a gateway, the aspect is different. For the soaring central block falls gradually and serenely to the lower level of the courtyard, which shows signs of Renaissance influence.

Opening from the courtyard into the old north-west tower is the original entrance, and high above it, under the window of a one-time oratory, a sculptured panel with an angel carrying a shield which bears the "five wounds

ABOVE: *The Laird's bedroom above the great hall. A copy of the portrait by Raeburn, of Miss Elyza Fraser, hangs on the left.*

LEFT: *Set into the walls of the old tower is a sculptured panel.*

of Christ." The important position of the panel and the Flemish cast of the touchingly meek angel suggests a pre-Reformation date for this feature. The dormer window-heads are all embellished with the "fraise" motif, three strawberries (the name Fraser is derived from the old French "freze": strawberry), and those on the west wing are inscribed with the initials of Andrew Fraser and his first wife, Lady Elizabeth Douglas. On the corresponding side of the east wing, which was completed after he was made a peer in 1633, Lord Andrew Fraser has proudly added an L above the letters A.F. and a D (Dame) for those of his wife.

The Lord Fraser, a great Covenanter, succeeded in 1636. His son married, as his first wife, a kinswoman, Katherine Fraser, daughter of Lord Lovat, from which time dates the connection between these two families. Charles, 4th Lord Fraser, came of age in 1683, and in the same year married Lady Marjory Erskine, widow of Simon Fraser of Invercallochy. He left his affairs in great confusion when he was accidentally killed by falling down a rocky hillside where he was wandering in hiding after the failure of the 1715 Rising. He had no children, and the estate was inherited by William Fraser, a descendant of his wife, Lady Marjory, by her first husband.

William's brother Charles, the next Laird of the castle, outlived his three sons (the eldest fell at Culloden), so that his spinster daughter, Elyza, succeeded about 1795. Miss Elyza had very definite ideas about modernising the castle in the elegant mode of the time. The present main entrance was then opened up on the south side below three large windows let into the great hall on the first floor. To this south wall she also removed (from the north side) two old coats of arms, adding her own. Her considerable additions on the courtyard side have judiciously been removed. A more worthy memorial is her very fine embroidery, which, in perfect condition, still adorns some of the castle furnishings. Miss Elyza was followed by her grand-nephew, Colonel Charles Mackenzie-Fraser, who died in 1871. His son was the last male representative of the Castle Fraser family.

The inside of the castle is so excellently preserved that it gives the impression of an immense clarification of the interior plan and detail of the time. The vaulted ground floor of the central three-stepped building contains the original kitchen and cellars. On the first floor, the great hall, also vaulted, is a long high room with white-painted plaster covering the granite walls and a huge chimneypiece set across the east end. Most impressive is its simple, uncluttered grandeur, regained through the admirable restorations carried out by the Hon. Clive Pearson and the late Dr. Kelly of Aberdeen. Sir Walter Scott's description of "the Laird's Lug" (i.e., a small opening in the wall of the great hall which connects with a wall closet on the upper floor, used for eavesdropping) in *The Fortunes of Nigel* was taken from the unusually large example at Castle Fraser. (James VI is said to have had one made in the Tower of London and afterwards built up, "the rather that my back is sair with sitting in it a whole hour!")

The castle has not been lived in since 1921. The following year it was acquired by the first Viscount Cowdraw, and since 1947 has belonged to his grand-daughter, Mrs. Michael Smiley, and her husband, who live today in the charmingly converted stables nearby. Major and Mrs. Smiley are interested and active custodians, and are doing much, with knowledge and care, to preserve this splendid castle.

Leith Hall

The south front. The corner pavilions and the ground floor were built 40 years earlier in 1756.

ALTHOUGH LEITH HALL HAS GREAT charm and interest architecturally, perhaps the place most of all owes its guarantee of preservation to a complete and lively family history, figuring largely in national events and illustrated by an entrancing collection of treasures, relics and portraits to be seen in the house today. For these in their right setting can enlighten and touch future generations (as well as present-day visitors) far more effectively than the dispersed and dusty instruction of library or museum.

The Leith-Hay family of Leith Hall are directly descended from William Leith of Barnes, who was provost of Aberdeen in 1352. He was also steward of the royal household of Queen Joan, wife of David II, and when the King was taken prisoner at the Battle of Neville's Cross in 1346, Leith, with several others, went to England as a hostage. He was a man of outstanding character, and part of William Leith's memorial in St. Nicholas' Church, Aberdeen, is still intact today.

Three hundred years later, in 1650, the Provost's descendant, James Leith of New Leslie, built the north wing of Leith Hall on the site of an older house, known as Peill Castle, near the village of Kennethmont. Typical of the time (although there are some 19th century alterations) is this north front with its steep roof, carved dormer window-heads and the little peak-hatted turrets bulging out at the corners. The next stage in the construction of the house, dating from about 1756, was the addition of a low, one-storey building ranging round a central courtyard with little pavilions at each corner. This plan, although altered and added to since, still gives the house its very individual character today. A south wing built up in 1796 by General Alexander Leith-Hay follows, in the main, the lines of the original block but with such deliberate Regency features as the large elliptical windows on the first floor. Some years later, the same Laird extended the east front. The

The staircase and lobby in the south wing.

interior of these two wings, with their rounded walls, high-ceilinged rooms and Adamesque decoration, is in complete contrast to the 17th century house.

Meantime, in the century and a half between these two dates, the family, now rooted at Leith Hall in Strath Bogie, were making their mark on the country. Active Jacobites, the four brothers of the Laird of the time were all out in the '45 Rising. Andrew Hay of Rannes, a giant of over seven feet, whose sister married John Leith of Leith Hall in 1730, was also a supporter of the Stuart cause and evidently a great personal friend of Prince Charles Edward. The night before the Battle of Culloden the Prince gave him a Shagreen Etui, made in Paris, containing writing material including an ivory tablet bearing a message in his own handwriting. This is preserved in the house today. Also in the house is one of the very rare written pardons signed by George III which Hay obtained in 1780 after spending many years abroad in exile. On his death, nine years later, the name Hay was added to Leith, for when the family were in financial straits, Andrew Hay of Rannes had bought Leith Hall, making his great-nephew, Alexander Leith, his heir.

In 1763 the Laird of Leith Hall was killed in a duel in Aberdeen. He left a young widow, Harriot, whose letters tell the story of her early struggles to bring up three young sons. The eldest boy, John, was consumptive and the doctors advised her to take him abroad. "No matter what the inconvenience or expense, I will have to take him," she wrote to her uncle, Andrew Hay. The inconvenience was certainly considerable. She embarked at Aberdeen in a sailing ship with John and his younger brother, Alexander for France, but the trip was so rough that she and the little boy were continuously sick and "of little use to John." The invalid's luggage included his chaise, a shee-ass and several goats to keep him supplied with milk. They arrived safely, but in spite of her care John died at the age of twenty. He was succeeded by his brother Alexander, who rose to be a Lieutenant-General (the same who built the south and east wings of the house) and is remembered in the north for his raising of the 109th Aberdeenshire Regiment in 1794, the colours of which remain in the house today. His younger brother, General Sir James Leith, who is buried in Westminster Abbey, distinguished himself in the Peninsular Wars and in 1814 was made Governor-General of the West Indies.

General Alexander Leith-Hay's son, Andrew, who was later knighted, diverged from the established military traditions of the family (although he fought in the Napoloenic Wars) towards other achievements. A Member of Parliament, he was also a gifted writer and artist, and among other things wrote a detailed history of the Peninsular Wars and the charming *Castellated Architecture of Aberdeenshire*, both illustrated by his own drawings. Sir Andrew's son, who commanded the Argyll and Sutherland Highlanders in the Crimean campaigns and at the Indian Mutiny, brought back many fascinating trophies from far places. One of these—not on view today, alas!—was a white cockatoo from India which lived at Leith Hall for over fifty years. It was this Laird who added the west front in 1868 in the Scottish Baronial style of the time.

Finally, the east porch and entrance hall were built on in 1900 by the late Mr. Charles Leith-Hay, who was Laird of Rannes and Leith Hall for thirty-nine years and died in 1939. He also improved the estates, added to the gardens and laid out the enchanting rock garden. His son, the last and 27th Laird, lost his life on active service in 1939 at the age of twenty-one. The house was given to The National Trust for Scotland, by the late Mrs. Leith-Hay in 1945, who over the past years has successfully managed to preserve the many treasures of Leith Hall.

Already the visitors' book records hundreds of names from all over the world. The gradual building up of Leith Hall from one generation to another and the unfolding of its history in stone, paint and family treasures gives the place a peculiarly human appeal beyond mere beauty of outline or documentary interest. Few visitors can fail to sense this particular charm.

The drawing room in the south wing has rounded walls typical of the Regency period. This south wing was built up, in 1796, by General Alexander Leith-Hay and has such deliberate Regency features as the large elliptical windows on the first floor.

Haddo House

ABOVE: *William Adam's design for Haddo House, dated 1732.*

SINCE IT WAS BUILT MORE THAN TWO hundred years ago, the architectural importance of Haddo House has always been somewhat overshadowed by the history and lives of its owners, the Aberdeen family. National figures and men of stature in almost every generation, they fill a large canvas upon which Haddo, one of their Scottish homes, has made less mark than it merits. The design by William Adam, included in *Vitruvius Scoticus*, shows a sedate, elegant, three-storied building linked to lower wings by short curving colonnades of arches. A double flight of steps sweeps up to the first floor entrance under the central, solemn pediment adorned by three Grecian vases, and four solid chimney-stacks complete this charming Early Georgian composition. The house was begun in 1732 for the 2nd Earl of Aberdeen.

The origin of the Gordon family, represented by the Duke of Richmond and Gordon, the Marquis of Huntly and the Marquis of Aberdeen, goes back to very early times where fact mingles with legend. The Gordons of Haddo are directly descended, not from the senior branch, but from Sir John Gordon, who was a Royalist hero of the Civil War in Scotland and the first man to be legally condemned and executed in Edinburgh for his loyalty to the crown.

"And albeit," wrote a contemporary, "Haddoche wes ane loyall subject to the King; hardie, stout, bold in all haserdis; freind to his freind, and terribill to his enemy, of a goodlyf and conversation, moderat, temperat, and religious . . . ane good nichtbour, loving, kynd to his tennantis . . . yet thus he ended."

His Place of Kellie, the precursor of Haddo House, was destroyed by the Covenanters, but at the Restoration Charles II made amends to the family and returned the estates to Sir John's son and heir, Sir George, who became a member of the Scottish Bar in 1668. Scholarly, industrious and possessed of that integrity and sense of justice which distinguished so many of his descendants, Sir George was raised to the Bench ten years later with the title of Lord Haddo, and now "sat in the very city and judgment seat where his father suffered so sad and unjust a sentence." In 1682 Lord Haddo became Lord High Chancellor of Scotland and was created 1st Earl of Aberdeen.

It was for the 2nd Earl, who had strong Jacobite leanings, that Haddo House was built from the design by William Adam, father of the more famous Robert and three other sons, and the finest and most fashionable architect in Scotland. It is now almost certain that the new house was built up from the remains of the old Place of Kellie, and it seems probable that the ancient keep walls are incorporated in the present walls of the square drawing room. Very little is known, unfortunately, of the interior finishing and furnishing of the Adam house. In 1745 the 3rd Earl, sometimes called the Wicked Earl, succeeded. As staunch a Hanoverian as his father had been Jacobite, he was a good manager, ran his estates well and increased the family wealth and property. He bought three large houses, Cairnbulg and Ellon Castle in Aberdeenshire and Wiscombe Park in Devonshire, settled a brown-eyed mistress in each and raised three flourishing families. His wife and Haddo House he eventually deserted, and during the rest of the century the original Adam furniture and fittings disappeared either to Lord Aberdeen's other homes or to the sale rooms.

The Wicked Earl survived his eldest son and was succeeded in 1801 by his twelve-year-old grandson, George, who was to become the most eminent member of the family. Lady Haddo with her fatherless children had moved south after the death of her husband, and, somewhat naturally, was not on friendly terms with her father-in-law. When she died, while George was still in his early teens, the boy lived between the homes of his two guardians, Henry Dundas, afterwards Lord Melville, and Mr Pitt, who was then Prime Minister. The influence of these two powerful men and their political and social circles shaped the boy's life even more than his schooldays at Harrow and his scholastic success at Cambridge University. On his return from the Grand Tour in France, Italy, Greece and the Near East, George, now the 4th Earl, attained his majority in 1805 and travelled up to Haddo House, which he had not seen since he was a child of eight. He was given a warm welcome by his tenants and neighbours, but his first impression was not a happy one.

"The scene before him was certainly cold and cheerless," his son later wrote of this arrival, "the short, lime avenue before the house terminated in a dreary and extensive peat moss . . . stacks of fuel and sheds of lumber were piled against the walls of the house itself . . . The neighbouring lairds . . . were uneducated and had little in common with 'Athenian Aberdeen' (Lord Aberdeen had founded the Athenian Club, of which Byron was a member) . . . a particular small kind of raw turnip appeared on the table as the winter dessert. Stores of salt meat were laid in for winter use . . . Women habitually assisted to draw the plough; and the houses of the peasantry and even the smaller farmers were of the poorest description . . ."

If the young Earl thought he had come into a barren inheritance, the old family huntsman had his own reservations about the new Laird, who, he said, would have been a fine man "gin they hadna ta'en him to England and *spoiled his education.*"

Six months later Lord Aberdeen married Lady Catherine Hamilton, a daughter of the Marquis of Abercorn. It was a love match and the years of their tragically brief married life were the happiest he ever knew. On her first visit to Haddo in 1806, Catherine Aberdeen wrote to her father: "My dear Papa, you need not believe one word of what Lord Aberdeen says about this place, for I can assure you that there is nothing to complain of. I never was so surprised in my life as when I first saw it, for I had been told so much about it by everybody, that I expected a thing not fit for a human to live in, placed in the middle of a barren, black moor, without a tree or anything near it but a bog; instead of that I saw a great many very good trees about the house, which is not regularly beautiful on the outside, but very comfortable in the inside . . . it is really very strange that everyone should have thought it so depressing; they said it was useless to do anything but build, for that we could never make it tolerable, but with a good chair and sopha or two, and new curtains to the drawing room, I do not wish for anything better; and what do you think,

TOP: *The garden front with (left) a Victorian wing and (right) the chapel.*
ABOVE: *George, 4th Earl of Aberdeen, by Lawrence.*

The grand drawing room, now used for large parties and practices of the Haddo Choral Society.

I have got two little tame fawns . . ."

Lady Aberdeen died in 1812, and her husband now threw himself into the diplomatic and political work in which, by his knowledge of foreign policy, sound judgment and absolute integrity, he eventually rose to the greatest height. After the defeat of Lord Derby's Ministry in 1853 he was sent for by the Queen and accepted office as Prime Minister of the Coalition Government which was in power during the Crimean War. Reserved and somewhat aloof in personal relationships, Aberdeen was loved and respected by all, irrespective of party, and on his memorial in Westminster Abbey is written the Greek word meaning "Most Just." As he grew older, Aberdeen became not only reconciled but devoted to his Scottish home, which, unfortunately, his second wife never found congenial. He made immense improvements to the land and the farms, laid out the grounds and gardens at Haddo, and by the end of his life had planted some 14,000,000 trees. Queen Victoria, whose long friendship he cherished, visited Haddo in 1857, of which Aberdeen wrote: "The visit passed off very prosperously. The Queen was in great good humour, was very gracious, and expressed herself to be much pleased."

In the year 1878 the Premier Earl's grandson, the late Marquess of Aberdeen, brought his bride, Countess Ishbel, to Haddo for the first time.

In their two volumes of Memoirs, *We Twa*, Lady Aberdeen tells how "A.'s grandfather had been wont to say that he must leave the overhauling of the *inside* of the house to his successor—*he* had devoted himself to the transformation of the 1700 acres of policies from the bare neglected state in which he found them into a demesne of varied beauty and charm."

Soon after this Lord and Lady Aberdeen carried out an extensive restoration of the house, making several alterations and additions under the direction of the architect, C. E. Wardrop. Bathrooms and modern plumbing were installed, and servants' quarters and new nurseries added by building out a south wing on the garden side of the house. A front hall was also built at this time and a new internal staircase so that guests might arrive more conveniently on the ground floor. But the original horse-shoe shaped stone stairs were taken down and replaced by a long balustraded veranda supported by pillars and a new front porch. The adjoining chapel, designed by G. E. Street, with a stained glass window by Burne-Jones, was built in 1882 and is still the only undenominational church in Scotland. The redecoration of the house was then undertaken by the London firm of Wright and Mansfield. This tremendous operation has not been recorded in any detail, so that it is difficult to know how much of the interior decoration may have been originally designed by Adam.

The 7th Earl and his Countess Ishbel, who are well remembered not only in Aberdeenshire, have already become a legend. No two people can surely have accomplished more in so many spheres of public and private life in their 57 years of marriage. Twice Lord-Lieutenant of Ireland, Governor-General of Canada between the years 1893-98, and an outstanding Liberal Peer, Lord Aberdeen was an active supporter, one might say, of almost every good cause, as was his wife, and instigator of many new ones from late Victorian days right up to the 1930s.

One sentence from Lady Aberdeen's Memoirs illustrates the cross-section of her interests. "Thus it came about," she wrote, "that discussions over the speeches of Mr Gladstone, Mr Bright, and Mr Disraeli, and over the sermons of Mr Moody and the singing of Mr Sankey, seemed to become quite natural features of my talks with ball-room friends, to be continued during rides in Rotten Row and at garden parties. I can recall many lifelong friendships which began in this fashion . . ." Yet perhaps fullest of all was their family and social life and their personal relationships with an immense and international circle of friends which included many of the great figures of the time. Liberal in politics, with a strong Christian faith and a deep interest in education and the arts, wealth and position to these two were only the means of enriching others and establishing a real democracy not only among their tenants and neighbours but at every point of the world they touched.

Today Haddo has come into its own architecturally. The Georgians are admired as they never were in their own or in Victorian times, and 18th century building and decoration are, of all traditional tastes, the most cultivated. One of the main glories at Haddo is the long vista made possible right through the house by the two large central reception rooms divided by double doors with french windows to north and south. The grand drawing room overlooking the garden has a coved ceiling with plasterwork decoration in Adam colours of gilt, green, pale blue and cinnamon. On the walls, covered with blue watered-silk paper, hang family portraits, landscapes, including one by Claude Lorraine, and paintings by Murillo and Van Dyck.

In the smaller but formal ante-room above the entrance stands a marble bust of Queen Victoria presented by her to the Premier Earl, whose portrait by Lawrence also hangs on the wall here. In the long dining room, now used only for special occasions, is a decorated ceiling and frieze in the Adam manner in shades of smoke grey, pale green, cinnamon and apricot, the walls being covered in apple green silk. Among the family portraits predominates a painting by Edward Marsh of the present Marquess of Aberdeen, 8th Earl. The morning room, with its chintz covers and curtains, book-cases and mixed Regency and modern furniture, is the most informal room and has a large bow window added in Victorian times. There is no museum-like preservation at Haddo. The whole house today is used and lived in, perhaps to a greater extent than ever before.

Haddo House is now the home of Major David Gordon, Earl of Haddo, who is a son of the present Marquess of Aberdeen, and his wife and family. It is due to them that Haddo is now famous for what one might call the Northern Festival of Music. In 1946 the Haddo House Choral Society was formed by a group of tenants and villagers to sing carols in the chapel where services are held every Sunday. Trained and conducted by Lady Haddo, who is a professional musician, the choir (now with over 100 members) and orchestra, sponsored by the Arts Council, every year perform a series of concerts. These take place in the Canadian-looking timber hall, built by the late Marquis and Countess Ishbel as a working men's club, which can accommodate 600 people. International artists come to sing, play and conduct at Haddo. The society has launched out into a serious study of Shakespeare plays, which are given on a replica of the original Globe stage, and also light opera. Probably the most ambitious venture was a performance of the *War Requiem*, by Benjamin Britten, in conjunction with the Scottish National Orchestra. Lady Haddo trained the choir and Alexander Gibson conducted the performance. This society celebrated its 21st birthday at Christmas, 1966. Large audiences are drawn from all over Scotland, and the Queen Mother is a regular attender of the summer performances.

TOP: *The corridor in the north wing. The hand painted china service was given to the 7th Earl and Countess by the people of Canada.*

ABOVE: *The long dining room has a decorated ceiling and frieze in the Adam manner. This room is now only used on special occassions.*

The more informal morning room has modern and Regency furniture and has a large bow window added in Victorian times.

Barra Castle with (right) an 18th century addition.

Barra Castle

Aberdeenshire is rich in grand castles built in the Golden Age of Scottish domestic architecture. Barra Castle, two miles south of Old Meldrum, bears out Ben Jonson's conviction that "In small proportions we just beauties see; and in short measures life may perfect be," and that the talent and skill of the 16th and 17th century masons and craftsmen were not withheld from the smaller, less important buildings of the time. Rebuilt from 1593-1614 with a later north wing, Barra stands round three sides of a central courtyard entered from a doorway in a low wall, adorned with stone urns, enclosing the fourth side. This is the sedate and charming face turned to the main road beyond a short, straight approach. But it is the southern garden facade with its conical-topped turrets, crow-stepped gables and steep, lichened roof which embodies the spirit of Scottish Baronial building. Round towers carried up from the ground with very little corbelling, jutting gable-ends and high, uneven walls jostle each other for space with informal unconcern. Even the jumbled stones (pinkish-brown and black) of the rubble-built walls heighten the characteristic effect of crowded disorder miraculously moulded to a unified pattern.

Although a dwelling does not seem to have been mentioned until the present castle was built in 1614, Barra is certainly older than its Jacobean reconstruction suggests from the outside. The entrance to the castle in the south-west corner of the courtyard opens into the oldest part of the house, and the kitchens and cellars here may date from a considerably earlier period.

It is only a legend that Robert the Bruce slept in the castle, but legend mingles with fact in accounts of the battle of Barra (which took place on Christmas Eve, 1307 on what is called to this day the King's Field, slightly to the north-east of the castle) when Bruce routed Comyn, Earl of Buchan.

By 1445 the lands of Barra belonged to the family of the King, who were apparently co-portioners with the Blackhalls of that ilk. Blackhall House, of which no trace remains today, was the main seat of this family, who were hereditary Coroners and Foresters of the Garioch, and probably Barra was a minor tower on the property.

The first Blackhall of whom there is documentary evidence is mentioned in 1460 as "the good man of Barra-Blackhall." Alexander, last of Blackhall and Barra, owned the property between 1574-92. After this the family seem to have melted into obscurity except for a descendant, William Blackhall, a minor Latin poet and a Papist who was removed from his post at Aberdeen University in the mid-17th century for his religious views. He was "accusit of what religion he wes and of what Kirk he wes," we are told, and "Efter sum ansueris at last plainlie and avovitlie declarit he was ane Roman Catholik and wold byd be the samen, to the astonishment of the haile heirarus, being ane uther profession as appearit, and so pertile to manifest himself so." Evidently he outraged the Presbyterian University authorities, for it is recorded that he was "ane of the Regentis of Colledge Marschal, a prompt scoller, bred, borne and brought up in Aberdene, and never yit out of the countrie," and yet he "refussit to subscrive to the countrie covenant, as the rest did, whereupon he was deposit of his regency; thereafter he livit simply in sober maner within the toune."

The Kings of Barra, co-portioners with the Blackhalls, do not figure largely in national or local records until the 16th century, when they came into conflict with the law, for not paying their taxes, for not appearing in court, and finally for the murder of Alexander Seton, the young Laird of Meldrum. For this last offence their lands of Barra were forfeited to the crown in 1590 and James King was arrested with threats of worse punishment, but eventually pardoned by James VI after a plea by the Earls of Mar and Melrose that "divers of his

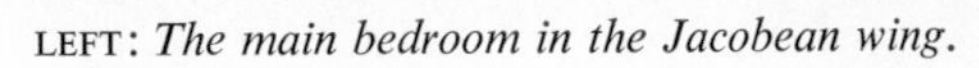

LEFT: *The main bedroom in the Jacobean wing.*

ABOVE: *The small dining room.*

CENTRE LEFT: *The sitting room in the Georgian addition.*

BOTTOM LEFT: *Part of the wide stone staircase (right) within the south wing.*

BELOW: *The old "great hall" or living room, now the drawing room.*

kindred and friendis has bene killed" and "his haill goodis intromettit with, and himself compellit at last to sell his landis and leving far shorte of the half value. . . ." Divested of property and home, James King's son left Scotland and, like so many Scots of his time, joined the Swedish Army, where he became a colonel. His cousin, another James King, achieved an even more distinguished career in the Swedish army, returning to Scotland to fight in the Royalist cause against the Covenanters, and in 1642 was created Lord Eythin.

Meanwhile, the King-Seton feud smouldered at home, and in 1595 one of the King family in Edinburgh was disposed of by George Seton, Tutor of Meldrum, who must have given some good reason for his action as three years later, in 1598, he was granted by James VI "all the properties . . . named in the sunny half of Barra . . ." as well as "the shadow half of the same lands owned by William King and his son James, King of Barra." Finally, in 1615, the crown renewed the charter to George Seton, now Chancellor of Aberdeen, "all the lands of Barra . . . for incorporation as a free barony of Barra when Barra Castle was ordained to be its chief seat."

By this time the south-west portion of the present house must have been begun, presumably under the direction of George Seton, although nothing is recorded of his personal supervision. From this time dates the wide stone circular staircase within the south wing, the hall and withdrawing room on the first floor, and the bedrooms and garrets above. Although the hall—now the drawing room—has been altered from time to time, it is possible to imagine its original aspect, the windows with deep embrasures cut through the thick walls and large open fireplace which retains the 17th century stone surround.

ABOVE: *Looking west up the terraced garden.*

LEFT: *The southern facade overlooking the garden.*

Today, after the final restoration of the castle, carried out by the late Mrs. Forbes Irvine in 1910-11, it has both the charm of age and the comfort of the present. A timber floor is covered with old mats, French, Italian and Georgian furniture are informally mixed, paintings and china well set against dark panelled walls, and the south-east turret makes an entrancing little corner writing-room. The actual dimensions are probably not those of the first hall, but the authorities are still undecided whether the withdrawing room adjoining (now the dining room) was at one time part of the "great hall." A door now leads into this small cosy room with its white painted walls and two windows overlooking the courtyard. From the south end of the room a narrow pantry has been converted. In the main bedroom on the first floor, where the original panelling remains, a coverlet on the four-poster bed dates from the time of William and Mary.

The Setons did not live long in their new castle. Barra was sold in 1630 to James Reid, whose descendants remained there for more than a hundred years, during which time a baronetcy (extant till 1885) was conferred on the family. In 1753 John Ramsay of Melross and Leithers acquired Barra and the estate of Straloch near by, and it was he who heightened the west block of the castle and built the wing on the north side of the courtyard. Although the exterior of this 18th century addition is plainer and simpler than its Baronial counterpart to the south and the stonework somewhat different, there is no abrupt change of plan or outline and the whole composition is one of unity. During much of the 19th century Barra was lived in as a farm house and the north addition used to provide bothies, corn loft and storage room. From a state of disrepair following occupation, the north wing has recently been rescued by the present owner, greatly helped by a grant from the Historic Buildings Council, and it is hoped that further interior restoration will be possible. The sitting room on the first floor, with its good proportions and Georgian panelling, has already regained a comfortable elegance.

Mrs. Quentin Irvine's son, Major Francis Charles Quentin Irvine, now Laird of Barra and Straloch, is a direct descendant of the first John Ramsay of Barra. Twice the property was inherited by an only daughter, first in 1787, when Mary Ramsay married John Innes of Maisley, who changed his name to Ramsay, and secondly when Major Irvine's grandmother, Mary Agnes Ramsay, was left the estates. She married Francis Hugh Forbes Irvine of Drum, parting the name of Ramsay from Barra and Straloch, and on her death in 1938 was succeeded by her son, Quentin Hugh. Mrs. Quentin Irvine, who now lives in the castle, has continued to revive the old as well as the new building and to cherish the delightful terraced garden in the south stretching beyond Barra's fairytale facade which makes the castle one of the most enchanting and memorable of its period in Scotland.

Darnaway Castle

LEFT: *The original 15th century open timber roof of the banqueting hall.*

BELOW: *The passage and staircase in one of the ground floor wings.*

TRADITIONALLY THE EARL OF MORAY was a royal title bestowed on kings' sons or near relatives in Scotland. Between 1314 and 1562 it was held by six different families, and there are few earldoms that can boast as many names famous in national history. Robert Bruce created the title for his nephew, Thomas Randolph, who fought at Bannockburn with him and became one of his most trusted generals. It was later held by Dunbars, Douglases, Stewarts and Gordons, and finally, Mary Queen of Scots granted it to her half-brother, James Stuart, in 1562. From this Earl, afterwards known as the Regent Moray, the present family are descended.

Darnaway Castle stands on the site of Thomas Randolph's ancient stronghold, not far from Forres, in the county of Moray. The oldest part of the present house is the open timber roof of the banqueting hall, which dates from about 1450, when Archibald Douglas built his grand castle there.

In 1810 a new house was built in front of, and connected with, the old hall. Solid and symmetrical, with a castellated roof line, the new castle faces east, overlooking open fields ringed by great woods of oak, beech, sycamore and birch. The interior is spacious and pleasantly laid out and contains good collections of books and paintings, including a fascinating series of royal Stuart portraits, and some interesting furniture. But the banqueting hall (rather misleadingly called Randolph's Hall) is still the heart of the castle. Today, against the dark oak beams of the roof, family banners present the ancestral arms in a blaze of gay colours. Here a thousand guests were entertained one night when the floor was carpeted with rushes and six-foot logs crackled in the two vast fireplaces. Here Mary Queen of Scots held a council in 1562 after spending a night at the castle.

It is this chapter of Darnaway's long and varied history which immediately kindles the imagination. For the reign of Mary Queen of Scots is perhaps the most dramatic span in all Scottish history. The documentary evidence is too slight to leave us a whole picture, and (because we Scots live passionately in the past) controversy still rages over the characters. One of these was James Stuart, ancestor of the present Moray family through the female line.

An illegitimate son of James V by Margaret Erskine, daughter of the Earl of Mar, he was born in 1533 and destined for the Church.

Darnaway Castle, near Forres, Morayshire, from the north-east.

The pillared entrance hall. On the left is a painting of Charles I by Van Dyck.

When he was only three years old he was presented to the Priory of St. Andrews. But his inclination and abilities lay elsewhere. He became the leader of the Protestant party, and at first worked hard and unselfishly for the unity of the country. When his half-sister the young Queen landed at Leith in 1561 with such high hopes, he was whole-heartedly her right-hand man. He was loyal, strong and gentle with her. It was he who stood with his back against the door of the Queen's private chapel that first Sunday, facing an angry mob, so that she might worship according to her own faith.

As time went on, however, ambition seems to have corroded his morals. But for the accident of his birth he would have been king—and he knew himself capable of ruling Scotland. Yet he had to stand aside and see a headstrong girl with more charm than wisdom plunge from mistake to disaster, until Scotland was torn in two by civil war. Embittered by his role, he opposed the marriage with Darnley, approved Rizzio's murder, and diplomatically visited France while Darnley was disposed of. When he returned he was appointed Regent for the infant Prince—it is said at the Queen's request. But Moray now played openly for her betrayal, and at Langside triumphantly defeated the royalist forces.

It was a short-lived triumph. Scotland without a queen became a quagmire of treachery, revenge and ruthless butchery. As he passed through Linlithgow one day in 1570, Moray was shot at from a window by a Hamilton, and died a few hours later in Linlithgow Palace. The Protestant party made a last gesture, proclaiming him innocent of complicity in Darnley's murder, and John Knox preached " ane lamentable sermond " about him. What a play Shakespeare would have made of this complex character—noble in its beginnings, tragic at the last.

In Randolph's Hall hangs the gruesome painting of the dead body of " The Bonnie Earl of Moray," showing the gashes and wounds inflicted by his murderers, the Huntlys. The Bonnie Earl, " a comely person, strong of body as a kemp of champion," and well liked by everyone, was a son-in-law of the Regent Moray. Some say the king was jealous of his good looks and popularity (the ballad hints at an intrigue with the Queen), and incited his hereditary enemies, the Huntlys, to the murder. With a large force, they surrounded the Morays' house at Donibristle on the shores of the Forth one night, set fire to it, and waited with drawn swords. Moray himself was attacked by Gordon of Buckie, who left the Earl of Huntly to make the final thrust. But Moray had the last word. " You have spoiled a bonnier face than your own," he said with his dying breath. The portrait, dated 1591, is said to have been painted by order of Moray's mother, and sent to the king at Holyrood.

"*He was a braw gallant,*
And he played at the ba';
And the Bonnie Earl of Moray
Was the flower amang them a'."

Darnaway is famous for its magnificent forests stretching for many miles beyond the castle. In the latter half of the 18th century thirteen million trees were planted, including a million and a half oaks. The present Earl, who, after retiring from the Royal Navy, farmed in South Africa, succeeded in 1943, and now lives at Darnaway with his wife and family.

An old oak chair, possibly 17th century Scottish workmanship.

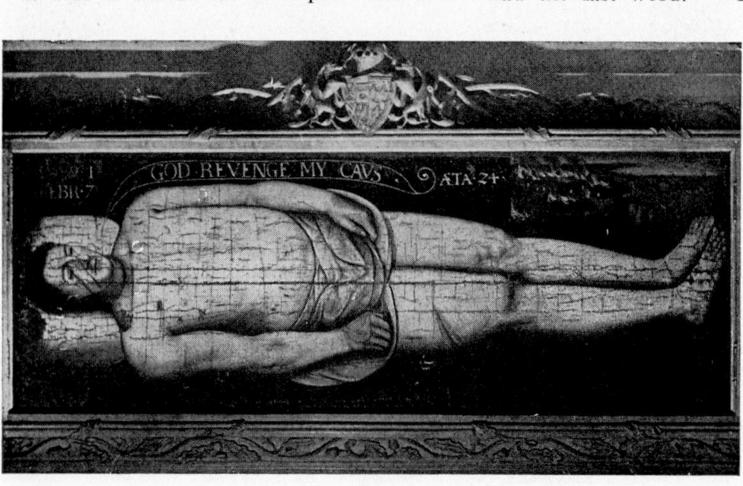

LEFT: *Painting of the dead body of the "Bonnie Earl of Moray".*

The banqueting hall. From the far end of the hall, the banners represent: (left) Randolph, Earl of Moray, the Huntlys, the Luttrells of Dunster, the Pleydells of Milborne: (right) the Stewarts of Doune, the Argylls, the Elphinstones, and the Douglases of Cavers.

Cawdor Castle, Nairnshire, from the south-east.

Cawdor Castle

It would be unfair both to the stones and the story of Cawdor Castle to say that Shakespeare alone put it on the map for all time. Yet millions of people outside Scotland connect the name with the play *Macbeth* more than with the castle near the shores of the Moray Firth. To them the Thane of Cawdor "is a prosperous gentleman" whose rank was promised by the witches to Macbeth and who, on the eve of execution for treason, died nobly—for "nothing in his life became him like the leaving it."

Shakespeare was not unduly concerned with historical accuracy. Macbeth was dead before the Norman Conquest, and it is most improbable that the title (first given in Scotland to Saxon and Norman Crown vassals), the property or a castle of Cawdor even existed in his time. The earliest documentary evidence of Cawdor occurs in a charter of King Robert I dated 1310, renewing a grant of tenancy of the crown lands of Cawdor to Thane William, on the same conditions and to the same family that held them in the reign of Alexander III. The first recorded Thane of Cawdor may thus be placed in the second half of the 13th century.

Recent investigations suggest that the present keep at Cawdor was built at the end of the 14th century. But the brooding splendour of the castle today has puzzled and misled, as well as delighted, many admirers at first sight. In 1454 James II issued a licence to the Thane of Cawdor to fortify the castle (on condition the king and his heirs have entry when desired), and it has usually been assumed that the fortress was entirely built at that date. The additions and fortifications then made by William, 6th Thane, such as the rounded corner turrets set out from the parapet, are undoubtedly 15th century features of castle-building as is the capehouse and at a first glance give the tower a spuriously late look. The original ground floor entrance to the tower would have been approached by a stone-built fore stair; here is the iron yett, older than the keep, being of 13th century date and coming from Lochindorb. The arch of the usual first floor entrance can be seen with a later window built into it. This, like the other windows of the keep, is of 17th century date.

William, 6th Thane, was King's Chamberlain beyond Spey, and a "loved, familiar squire" to James II. Enriched by his public work, he added substantially to the family estates, and from this time the Calders of Calder (the name was later changed to Cawdor) held a high position in the north. But it was left to William's great-great-granddaughter Muriel, who inherited Cawdor before she was a year old, to effect an even greater change in the fortunes of the family. Under the direct protection of the King, who appointed the Earl of Argyll her guardian, Muriel somehow escaped the plots and intrigues hatched by her own relatives, who very much disliked the idea of a female Thane of Cawdor. The child was kidnapped by the Campbells to spend her early years in the west until she was of age to marry into the Chief's family. When asked what would happen if she died before reaching marriageable age, a Campbell spokesman is said to have answered, "She can never die as long

In the dining room, once the great chamber, is the carved chimneypiece, executed circa 1670 to commemorate the marriage of Muriel Calder to Sir John Cambell in 1510.

as a red-haired lassie can be found on either side of Loch Awe." When she was twelve years old Muriel was duly married to Argyll's second son, Sir John Campbell, and the eagerly awaited lands of Cawdor added to his considerable estates in Argyllshire.

By this time the Argyll family was one of the most powerful in Scotland. Thrusting and ambitious, they were also good and able administrators and had acquired great possessions in the west. While Sir John built up the estate of Cawdor to ever more prosperous dimensions, his grandson, another John, added Isla as well as large territories of church land in the west as a result of the Reformation. But this John Campbell came to a tragic end by trying to grasp more than he could reach. Once again a struggle arose over the upbringing of a child—this time the young Earl of Argyll, who had been left in charge of Cawdor, and Campbell of Ardkinglass. After the latter's death, Cawdor seized the boy and kept him by force to make sure of the control of the House of Argyll. But in 1591 the Laird of Cawdor was "shot at night by three bullets from a hagbut fired through a window . . . in Lorn," by order of Ardkinglass's jealous son.

During the 17th century the north and west wings of the castle were altered and enlarged to accommodate the growing and grander company, and the reconstruction, in the main, fashioned the shape and aspect of the present castle. In 1639 a contract for building " The Auld Hall and Kitchen of Cawdor " was signed by Colin Campbell, brother and tutor of the laird, who suffered and never fully recovered from a mental illness. Local masons were entrusted with what was a fairly comprehensive restoration of the old castle as long as the " armes, names and siferis upon the windockis were wrocht to the said Colin Campbell his contentment." While not competing with such contemporary masterpieces as Heriot's Hospital, Castle Fraser or Craigievar, the Jacobean architecture at Cawdor does credit to the Nairn craftsmen. In the latter half of the 17th century the next Laird, tutor Colin's eldest son, Sir Hugh Campbell, continued the remodelling of the north and west wings, adding such decorations as dormer windows with carved pediments, coats of arms and chimneypieces.

With Sir Hugh's lairdship—he came of age in 1660, the year of the Restoration—the pattern of living at Cawdor seems suddenly to come out of the shadows of medievalism and to link up, however distantly, with our own times. Sir Hugh, a graduate of Glasgow University, married Lady Henrietta Stuart, daughter of the 3rd Earl of Moray. Their

The Tapestry Room has the sombre, solid grandeur characteristic of the Restoration period. This room is low-ceilinged with Flemish tapestry hangings on all four walls.

sons were sent to college and afterwards abroad on the Grand Tour; their daughters learned to dance and to play the virginal and the viol da gamba, to embroider and make pastry at a select Edinburgh school. The Laird, much engaged with his estate work, including the breeding of cattle and horses on Isla, the preservation of deer, rabbits and blackcock and the laying out of the present garden, sometimes regrets that " rambling abroad in the country hunting and hawking have taken him from reading and study, except for divertisement." But he also found time to represent Nairnshire in Parliament for some years. Among the very full collection of papers, bills and accounts covering this period at Cawdor, an interesting point is the omission of any reference to Highland dress, arms, ornament or tartans. The Thane of Cawdor's dress was then apparently indistinguishable from that of an English or French gentleman of the day.

Sir Hugh died in 1716. The new Laird had married a Welsh heiress of Stackpole Court in Pembrokeshire and there, for more than a hundred years, the family made their chief home. Although farming and tree-planting were carried on under supervision, the castle itself became a picturesque outpost; absence, neglect, wind and weather left their mark on the whole place.

But the solitary years at least left the old outline intact. By the first quarter of the 19th century the sport, scenery and wild life of the Highlands were fast becoming fashionable. When John Campbell, 19th Thane, who, in 1827, had been created Earl of Cawdor, returned to live in the Scottish home of his ancestors, he wisely made few alterations to the exterior of the castle. The four dormer windows and turret on the north of the drawbridge, however, which date from 1855, are exceptionally well carried out. Inside, where restoration was obviously necessary, a certain amount was done in Victorian times, including the replacement of a ceiling in the dining room (formerly the great hall). The Blue Room on the first floor, however, with its original panelling and curious, baroque chimneypiece dated 1667, cannot have changed very much in two and a half centuries. The Tapestry Bedroom, too, low-ceilinged with Flemish tapestry hangings on all four walls, four-poster and old oak furniture, has the sombre, solid grandeur characteristic of the Restoration period.

Today Cawdor is cared for, lived in and cherished. The present and 5th Earl, who now lives there, has done much to preserve and bring new life to this enchanting and historic castle. Immense and grey, its gables and rooftops touched with golden lichen, the castle stands amidst great woods, the Queen Anne garden stretching south-wards in a long formal vista towards the park. The square, solid keep, now nearly six hundred years old, rises like a sturdy veteran among the later wings and courts, the gateway, drawbridge and surrounding dry moat. The whole composition, although largely remodelled since, is still a splendid picture of a 15th century castle, and as such, rare in Scotland.

Castle Leod from the south-west

Castle Leod

ON A FINE DAY, WITH THE SUN DIScovering creamy-yellow and grey and crimson patches in the weathered rose-pink stone, Castle Leod has a breath-taking quality of near-perfection. It is a quality which has nothing to do with the technical perfection of a blueprint. For the plan of the castle, rebuilt on older foundations in 1616, was disturbed very soon after by the addition of a south wing (in which the entrance doorway is now set), and there is a more modern extension, added to in 1914, on the north side. Partly, its beauty lies in the magnificent setting between the towering grandeur of Ben Wyvis and the distant Cromarty Firth, partly in the power and imagination of Baronial building in Scotland at that time. Looking at this tall, robust stone tower, built for (Sir) Rorie Mackenzie of Kintail—from whom the family of the Earls of Cromartie is descended—one senses the timely serenity of a work of art. For the skilled craftsmen and masons of the 17th century in Scotland were no less than artists.

Of Celtic stock, the Mackenzies, after recent investigation, can trace their ancestry back to long before the 13th century. They were for long the vassals of the Earls of Ross, but at the beginning of the 15th century the earldom came into the hands of the powerful

The south-west angle turret decorating the south wing.

The old banqueting hall, with part of the south wing, forms the present drawing room.

Macdonalds, who held vast property on the west. But in their pride and strength the Macdonalds set themselves up against the crown, and in 1493, after several rebellions, were crushed by royal forces and the Lordship of the Isles forfeit. After this the old earldom of Ross was divided between Rosses, Munros and Mackenzies. Alexander Mackenzie of Kintail, who had consistently refused to support the Macdonalds against the King, was rewarded by royal charters for his lands and laid the foundations of the clan's future power and importance. During the 16th century the Mackenzies gradually moved from west to east, where the land was very much more fertile. John Mackenzie of Kintail was created Lord Mackenzie by James VI.

Lord Mackenzie's brother (Sir) Rorie Mackenzie, who built Castle Leod, had been given the lands of Culteleod by his father in 1585. In 1605 he married Margaret Macleod, daughter and heiress of Torquil Macleod of the Lewis. Their initials are carved on the dormer windows on the north side of the castle with the date 1616. An older castle once stood on the site where Rorie Mackenzie built his house—for, in fact, it was more of a house than a fortress by that time, even in the Highlands. The points of fortification, for instance, had become part of the traditional pattern of domestic building rather than of actual defence. But it was still built on the old L-shaped keep plan with an open parapet and bartizans at the angles. The line of this corbelled parapet was soon after interrupted by the addition of a south wing, fitted between the original south and east walls and raised a storey higher than these. The main purpose of the addition was to provide a wide, straight staircase to the first floor and some extra bedrooms. Ornamental dormer window-heads and conical-roofed turrets decorated the new wing and were very probably added to other parts of the castle then too. The position of the main entrance was altered to its present place in the new south wing at this time, and the old coat of arms set up above it.

Sir Rorie is usually known as the "Tutor of Kintail," for, on his brother's death, he undertook the care of his nephew, the 2nd Lord Mackenzie, then only a child. He also looked after the Kintail estate and, unlike the proverbially unscrupulous and designing relatives of wealthy minors, did so well and skilfully, eventually handing it over to his nephew in excellent condition. In 1625 Lord Mackenzie was created Earl of Seaforth. The Tutor was also given the task of subduing Mull, Morven and Tiree, which he successfully accomplished in two years. Sir Rorie was knighted in 1619.

Two years after his death in 1619, his son John was created a Knight Baronet of Nova Scotia and granted 16,000 acres of land in the Colonies, called the Barony of Tarbat. It was probably in his time that the south wing was added. Parts of the interior, such as the main staircase and little entrance hall, remain unchanged today. Elsewhere there has been some alteration. The ground floor contains the kitchen in the wing and the cellars in the main block. Above the cellars was built the great hall which now forms the larger half of

Top of the original east tower.

Portrait of "The Tutor of Kintail" at Tarbat House.

ABOVE: *The larger of the Spanish Chestnut trees.*

RIGHT: *The entrance doorway with the Mackenzie coat-of-arms above.*

BOTTOM RIGHT: *The stone staircase in the south wing leading from the entrance to the first floor.*

the present drawing room. Decorated in Regency times, this delightful room, white-painted, with its polished timber floor, old and new furniture and family portraits, combines an atmosphere of the past with present comfort and grace. There are a number of smallish bedrooms on the three upper floors. At present the castle is undergoing repairs and the present Earl lives mainly in the Victorian addition.

Sir John died in 1654 and was succeeded by his son, George, who was educated at St. Andrews University and King's College, Aberdeen. An active Royalist, he lived abroad for some time before the Restoration of 1660, when he became chief adviser to Lord Middleton, King's Commissioner in Scotland. In 1661 he was made a Lord of Session with the title of Lord Tarbat, and in the same year was elected Member of Parliament for Ross-shire. Under Queen Anne he became Secretary of State for Scotland, and in 1703 was created Earl of Cromartie. He lived to be an old man, and Swift wrote of him that, "after four score, he went to his country house in Scotland with a resolution to stay six years, and live thriftily in order to save up money that he might spend it in London." He died in 1714.

In the time of the 2nd Earl, the estate became financially entangled, and in 1724 was sequestered. This may have been partly due to Cromartie's first wife, Lady Elizabeth Gordon (divorced in 1698), who run up large debts for "meat, drink, cloathes, abulziments, rings, bracelets and jewels of great value." The 3rd Earl, a cousin and intimate friend of Simon, Lord Lovat of the '45, supported Prince Charles Edward in 1745, was captured at Dunrobin Castle and taken to the Tower of London. He was tried and sentenced to death and his estates forfeited. But, luckier than his notorious cousin Lovat, his life was spared, mainly through the efforts of his wife. He was allowed to live with friends under supervision, and spent some years in Devonshire. But it was not a happy exile. Poverty crushed his spirit. In 1759 he wrote, "we feel daily the miserable situation we are in. I am afraid we shall have to be put to the utmost extremity soon, perhaps not to have a house to go into or a bed to lie on, and no hope of any amendment to this, our very distressed situation for some time." He died in 1766, leaving ten children, the youngest of whom, Augusta, was said to have been born (in 1746) with the mark of an axe and three drops of blood on her neck.

The family estates were restored in 1789 to the 3rd Earl's eldest son, John, Lord Macleod, who fought with the Swedish and Prussian armies in the Seven Years' War and in 1777 raised a Highland regiment, then called the 73rd Foot, later the 1st Battalion of the Highland Light Infantry, for service in India. On his return home he was made a Major-General. In the 19th century the succession passed three times through the female line—thirdly to Anne Hay-Mackenzie, who married in 1849 the Marquis of Stafford, later 3rd Duke of Sutherland. In 1861, Anne, now Duchess of Sutherland, was created Baroness Macleod of Castle Leod, Baroness of Castlehaven, Viscountess Tarbat and Countess of Cromartie. Her granddaughter is the present Countess, also in her own right. Lady Cromartie, who now lives mainly at Tarbat House on the Cromarty Firth, has among the achievements of a long and eventful life, written a number of books, including *The End of the Song*, published in 1904. Her son, the 4th Earl of Cromartie, who lives at Castle Loed, served in the Seaforth Highlanders during the last war, when he was awarded a Military Cross. He was taken prisoner at St. Valery in 1940 and, while in captivity, compiled further material for a family history. His *Picture Catalogue and Historical Notes of the Mackenzies, Earls of Cromartie*, was published in 1937.

Among the many fine old trees round Castle Leod are two Spanish chestnuts planted in 1550 by John Mackenzie, 9th Chief of Kintail, who was Privy Councillor to James V and a great-grandfather of the builder of the castle, Sir Rorie Mackenzie. When last recorded in 1850, the larger of these trees measured 36 feet in girth at the base and 107 feet in height. There are also some of the largest and rarest ornamental trees in Britain today.

Dunrobin Castle

DUNROBIN CASTLE IS ONE OF THOSE houses not easily translated either by paint brush or camera. This is partly because the building presents several very different architectural aspects impossible to capture in one glimpse, and partly because there is magic not only in the superb site and setting but also in the vaster, wilder surroundings.

But, as one climbs the steep ramparts to the castle and comes face to face with first one line of solid building and then another, the fairy-tale castle vanishes. A triangular facade of Victorian Gothic work rises high round the south and east of the building, while on the west the Jacobean house emerges with the simplicity of an original theme among variations. Oldest of all is the keep at the north-east angle, the foundations of which are thought to date from about 1275, the time of the 1st Earl.

The Sutherland family is the most ancient in Scotland and the earldom second only in seniority to the premier earldom of Mar. One of King David I's Norman supporters, Freskyn de Moravia, who lived in the early 12th century, was the common ancestor of both the Sutherland and Atholl families. He was sent north to conquer Moray, the home of the Macbeths. Possibly Freskyn's children settled in Sutherland as governors in a land which had long been held in dispute between Norse Vikings and Celtic chiefs. At any rate it is certain that his grandson Hugh held lands there before 1214 and was known as "Lord of Sutherland." Hugh's son, William, was created 1st Earl of Sutherland some twenty years later.

The first time Dunrobin Castle is mentioned by name is in a charter dated 1401 to which Robert, the 6th Earl put his seal. Possibly the castle was called after this Earl who probably built up and enlarged the keep. During the 15th and 16th centuries Dunrobin was first and foremost a stronghold, dominating as it does the ancient roads and bridle paths between the hills and the coast leading up the north-east of Scotland. The Freskyn line ended with the death of the 9th Earl who "was weak of judgement, deprived of naturall wit and understanding, being able to govern neither himselfe nor others; bot his sister Lady Elizabeth Sutherland (the wyff of Adam Gordon of Aboyne) was full of spirite and witt." In fact, it took all Lady Elizabeth's "witt" to prevail over other contestants to the earldom and to establish her own right. Having done so however, she kept her husband's name and henceforth the second line of earls were Gordons.

The Gordon Earls of Sutherland were well written up by the family historian, Sir Robert Gordon, an influential councillor at the court of James VI, a man of learning and literary talent and at one time tutor to the 13th Earl. He tells us the dramatic tale of a dinner party at Helmsdale Castle given by Lady " Issobell Sinckler " to which she invited John, 10th Earl of Sutherland with his wife and heir Alexander. The Earl and Countess duly drank their prepared potions of poison, but the slip between cup and lip was one of rough justice this time, for young Alexander Gordon arrived late from the hunting field and so was warned of treachery by his dying father. Meantime Lady Isobel's son for whom she had planned the Sutherland earldom, took the poisoned cup from an ill-formed servant and died with his guests.

From Sir Robert's account books which he kept during his tutorship at Dunrobin, much information of the social life of the day can be gleaned, including the daily activities of the young Earl John Glas, from his studies at Dornoch to his archery practice, his golf and his hunting expeditions in Glen Sletadale. The Earl was admitted to St. Salvator's College, St. Andrews, on January 16th, 1627—the same day as his contemporary, the great Marquis of Montrose. Earl John Glas built a new staircase tower at Dunrobin and was mainly responsible for the Scottish Baronial house which he extended west and north from the old keep round an inner courtyard.

The Sutherlands supported the Government in both Jacobite Risings. Dunrobin was captured by Prince Charles Edward's troops in 1746 and although the Earl escaped to sea at the last moment, the Countess remained a prisoner while the castle was looted. Both Lord and Lady Sutherland died, however, the same year (and are buried in Holyrood Abbey) leaving an only surviving child of little more than a year old, Lady Elizabeth Sutherland. Once again the earldom passed to a women—but not without dispute even in late Georgian times. Sir David Dalrymple, later Lord Hailes, the famous historian, defended " The Sutherland Case " which came before the House of Lords in 1771 and was decided in favour of Lady Elizabeth. There was great jubilation in Sutherland when the result was known and the factor presented a large bill for " whisky and other drink, bread and cheese, powder and shot, consumed by above 500 of the Countess' tenants who had met at Golspy to rejoice in her carrying the peerage."

Countess Elizabeth lived a long and eventful life. In 1785 she married George Granville Leveson Gower, eldest son of the Earl of Gower, who five years later was appointed British Ambassador to France. The Countess was presented to Marie Antoinette and found her charming. Not long after, when the Queen and Louis XVI were imprisoned by an angry mob, the Countess befriended her, smuggling in her own clothes and linen at great personal risk. In 1803, her husband succeeded as 2nd Marquess of Stafford and twenty years later, for his support of the Reform Bill, was created 1st Duke of Sutherland. It is said the Duke chose the designation in honour of his wife who, on the contrary was extremely displeased and afterwards insisted on being called the Duchess-Countess. From this time the two titles (Duke of Sutherland in the peerage of the United Kingdom and Earl in that of Scotland) have been held concurrently by their descendants.

Before the end of the 18th century the Duchess-Countess built up the south and west sides of the courtyard, so completing the tall house begun by Earl John Glas. Between 1835 and 1850 Duchess Harriet,

Formerly the Duchess of Sutherland's bedroom, this room is now used as the school sickroom.

The long dining room in the Barry addition.

wife of the 2nd Duke, commissioned Sir Charles Barry, the architect of the Houses of Parliament at Westminster, to enlarge the castle. These additions, built to provide a royal suite for Queen Victoria and the Prince Consort, rise round the east and south of the old house, and were copied from the French Château de Chenonceaux.

Her Majesty also stayed at Dunrobin in 1872 with the 3rd Duke and Duchess Annie who later became not only Mistress of the Robes, following in the footsteps of the 2nd Duchess, but also for a time the sole companion and personal confidant of the widowed Queen. It is said, in fact, that Gladstone strongly objected to affairs of state being " decided in the drawing room between the Queen and the Duchess." While Dunrobin was an Auxiliary Naval Hospital during the First World War, the Barry addition was gutted by fire. Sir Robert Lorimer was called in to reconstruct the building, the work being completed in 1919.

Both the 2nd and 3rd Dukes were great reformers and decisive men of action. The family was then one of the richest in Great Britain and fortunes were spent on agricultural improvement, on land reclamation schemes in the peat bogs of Lairg and Kinbrace, on road-making and the pioneering of the railway system in the north. Until quite recently the Dukes of Sutherland possessed several historic houses in England including Cliveden in Buckinghamshire, Lilleshall and Trentham in Shropshire and Hampten House and Stafford House in London, now all either owned or lived in by various public bodies. In Stafford House the Sutherlands gave probably the most brilliant receptions of the 19th century. " I come from my house to your palace," remarked Queen Victoria to the Duchess one evening. The late Millicent, Duchess of Sutherland was also a great social and political hostess of the late Victorian and Edwardian era.

The 5th Duke, the 21st Earl of Sutherland, had a distinguished political career and was, like his ancestors, actively interested in many good causes. On his death, in 1963, the castle was converted to a boy's public school by his niece Elizabeth, Countess of Sutherland, the family keeping only the one wing in the 17th century part for their own use. The school now has 80 boys and eventually it is hoped to accommodate 300.

TOP: *From the west terrace a glimpse of the 17th century Jacobean house.*

RIGHT: *The 21st Earl of Sutherland and his brother, by Ellis Roberts.*

CENTRE: *Harriet, wife of the 2nd Duke and her daughter Elizabeth, by Sir Thomas Lawrence.*

FAR RIGHT: *William, 17th Earl, by Allan Ramsay.*

Duntrune, on its rocky peninsula, to the north of Loch Crinan.

Duntrune Castle

THE FIRST STONE CASTLES IN SCOTLAND were introduced by the Normans during the 12th century, built in the current European style and lived in by a number of powerful barons whose job it was to enforce law and order for the crown. Few of such early fortresses remain anywhere in Scotland today, except in the Highlands and Islands, where they were less likely to be replaced by more modern buildings. The solitary silhouette of Duntrune Castle, standing stark and grey on a tongue of rock to the north of Loch Crinan, is one of the rare remnants of this period. Since then the castle has been rebuilt at various times, but the great curtain wall sweeping round it, and part of the foundations, date from the late 12th or early 13th century.

Facing the Sound of Jura on its rocky peninsula, Duntrune Castle commands a wild and splendid panorama of sea and landscape which can change in a matter of moments from dark ferocity to dazzling brilliance. Both from within and without, the castle has a dramatic force which seems to dominate every other aspect of the place.

It is rare in Argyll to find a castle which was not originally a Campbell home, and Duntrune is no exception. Duncan Campbell had a charter of Duntroon from King Robert the Bruce. Duncan's father was the famous "Cailean Mor"—Great Colin—who supported Bruce in his claim for the Scottish throne against John de Baliol, and was knighted in 1281.

The L-shaped dwelling house which now stands at the south end of the courtyard was probably built in the 16th century over an older house, parts of which are incorporated in the present structure. The remains of an early 19th century addition may also be seen. The tall, steep, uncompromising walls and crow-stepped gables are characteristic of the tower-house of the period, but the roof has been modernised. Inside, the form of the Jacobean house, with its great hall on the first floor and bedrooms in the wing, can easily be reconstructed, for, although the present Laird and his wife have converted the interior to an elegant, comfortable and up-to-date house, many features of the old building remain.

The castle escaped devastation in the 17th century by a curious means, related in perhaps the best-known story about Duntrune, which was then called the Castle of the Turrets. Coll Macdonell of Ireland, an ambitious desperado who had a debt to pay off in Argyll, decided to invade Scotland from the west. His mother, a daughter of the Earl of Argyll, had eloped with his father, considered to be a person of lower rank and thus not eligible for his wife's dowry. But Coll Macdonell thought he would enforce the family claim for this sum of money by stronger means than argument. His Chief, the Earl of Antrim, was displeased with Argyll for joining the Covenanters, and readily agreed to help the expedition by raising 3,000 men from Ulster. With this army, Macdonell landed in Kintyre and moved northwards, destroying the castles and properties of every Campbell in Argyll. From Castle Swin, he approached the Bay of Crinan, intending to attack Duntrune Castle. But he had sent ahead his piper to gather information. The piper was received into the castle, but, finding it strongly defended and that the narrow winding stair could only be climbed by one person at a time, concluded that his Chief would have little success there. Being himself suspect by this time, he was confined to one of the upper turrets of the castle, from where, in due course, he saw Macdonell's forces approaching. Hoping to warn them of the danger, he played on his bagpipes the pibroch, now known as "The Piper's Warning to his Master."

"*Dearest Coll, shun the tower, shun the tower:*

My beloved Coll, shun the tower, shun the tower:

I am in hand. I am in hand" (i.e., I am a prisoner).

The warning was well understood by Macconell and his men, who turned northwards along the Strath of Kilmartin near the ford of Lochaw, destroying and plundering everything in their way. Some say the faithful piper had all the fingers of his right hand slashed off by the sword, others that he was immediately put to death.

Captain Neil Campbell of Duntroon and Oib was the last to hold the land of his forebears. He had hoped to save Duntrune from the debts incurred by the failure of the Ayr Bank in 1785, of which he was a shareholder. But soon after his death in 1791 the castle was sold by the trustees. Two of Captain Campbell's sons, General Sir Neil Campbell, K.C.B., and General Patrick Campbell, became important soldiers, the former being appointed to attend Napoleon at Elba as British Commissioner. Memorials to all three remain today in Kilmartin Church. In 1792 the estate of Duntrune with other lands was bought from the Campbell trustees by Neill Malcolm, 12th Laird of Poltalloch, ancestor of the present owner, Lieutenant-Colonel G. I. Malcolm. The Malcolms, for many centuries near neighbours of the Campbells of Duntroon, were settled in Argyll from early times, and Donald 1st Laird of Poltalloch, had a charter of the property in 1562. The family first lived in Kilmartin House, which was followed by Old Poltalloch House, built in the late 18th century but never lived in. The 2nd Poltalloch House, built about 1850 by Neil Malcolm, 13th Laird, near the mouth of Kilmartin Glen, was demolished in 1959 when Colonel and Mrs. Malcolm made their home in Duntrune Castle. John Wingfield Malcolm, who died in 1902 and whose portrait hangs in the castle today, was in 1896 created a life peer with the title of Baron Malcolm of Poltalloch for his parliamentary services and public work. His nephew, the late Sir Ian Zachary Malcolm, K.C.M.G., who was also a Member of Parliament and had a distinguished record of public service, married the daughter of the famous beauty, Lily Langtry. Their son, Colonel G. I. Malcolm, the present owner, succeeded in 1944, and later commanded the 8th Bn. Argyll and Sutherland Highlanders for the last eighteen months of their active service. Colonel Malcolm, who now farms, breeds part-bred Arab ponies and writes, is Chief of the Clan Malcolm.

Duntrune claims to be the oldest continuously inhabited castle in Scotland. Some years ago Colonel and Mrs. Malcolm transformed the interior from its Victorian trappings to a house of great distinction and originality. In the little courtyard leading to the entrance, the dovecot (fully occupied) has been restored with a charming curved roof, and two low rounded turrets built into the northern angles of the house—all features without exact forebears but with a traditional flavour. At this ground level the old rooms have been skilfully converted to small bedrooms—one is formed from part of the old kitchen, containing the original entrance and spiral stair—a dining room, a tiny but perfectly fitted-up kitchen, bathrooms and cupboards. The angled dining room, built up from a once open courtyard, is supported by a central pillar, and white painted plastered walls show to advantage family portraits and a glass cupboard. On the first floor the original Jacobean great hall makes a delightful drawing room with its large open chimneypiece, the enchanting views across land and sea framed by the windows, and the vivid colours of flowers and paintings against bare stone walls. The little withdrawing room at the south end of the great hall, which has the most superb outlook in the house over Crinan Bay to the Atlantic, has been completely modernised.

On five days every year, including Anzac Day, April 25th, the Australian flag, given by the Royal Military College of Australia, is flown from Duntrune Castle. The college building, acquired by the Australian Government some years ago, was once the home of Robert Campbell, one of a cadet branch of the Duntrune family, who settled in Australia at the end of the 18th century. He became a prosperous sheep farmer and eventually built on his land a large house which he called Duntroon. A coloured print of Duntrune Castle hangs in the Officers' Mess of the college today.

ABOVE: *The dining room on the ground floor.*

LEFT: *Colonel Malcolm's dressing room is converted from the kitchen of the Jacobean house.*

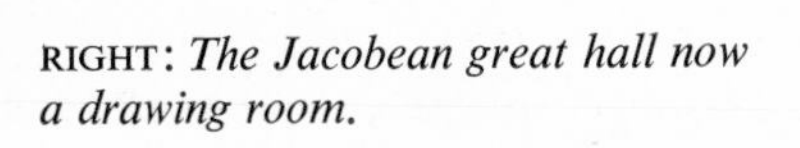

RIGHT: *The Jacobean great hall now a drawing room.*

Inveraray Castle, on the shores of Loch Fyne.

Inveraray Castle

"*CEUD mille Failte de'n Bhan Rhighinn do Inerara*" (A hundred thousand welcomes to the Queen to Inveraray), was the inscription, written above an archway, which greeted Queen Victoria as she approached the Castle in September, 1875. "When we reached the gate, there were two halberdiers," the Queen recorded in her diary, "whilst others were posted at intervals along the approach, dressed in Campbell tartan kilts with brown coats turned back with red, and bonnets with a black cock's tail and bog myrtle (the Campbell badge)."

Until the early nineteen-fifties, Inveraray Castle was little known to the general public. From the town, its grey turrets and pointed pinnacles could be glimpsed through the trees. By name it was as famous as the House of Argyll, but the castle itself remained remote, secluded and withdrawn for many years. But, on the second of May, 1953, it was officially opened. Set among a great regiment of trees, between high hills and the long sweep of Loch Fyne, it commands a splendid position.

Mock-Gothic architecture became a raging fashion towards the end of the 18th century and lasted more than a hundred years. But Inveraray, on the solitary reaches of western Argyllshire, is one of the last places in Great Britain one would expect to find the first example of this Romantic Revival. History gives us the answer. The 3rd Duke of Argyll, born and brought up in England, imbued with the liberal and progressive ideas for which his family was well known in the 18th century, and virtually the "Ruler of Scotland" from 1743 to 1761, decided to make a clean sweep of his ancient town and castle of Inveraray. When he succeeded in 1743, he abandoned the old keep built by Sir Colin Campbell of Lochow in the 15th century (it was later pulled down) and demolished the entire town which then clustered round it. The present castle was begun in 1746 and the town rebuilt where it now stands on a nearby promontory jutting into Loch Fyne.

For the building of his new castle, the Duke employed Roger Morris, a London architect, under whose direction William Adam was clerk of works. Most fortunately, the original plans of the castle and the architect's letter book survive. After Morris's death in 1749 the building was completed by John Adam, and about 1770 the interior decoration, also largely by Adam, was partly altered by Robert Mylne, the last of a celebrated family, who for generations had been Master Masons to the Crown of Scotland. The interior holds another surprise for the curious. Except for the towering height of the great hall, it is as classical and elegantly Georgian as the outside is " Gothick." The magnificent reception rooms, with their richly ornamented ceilings, delicate friezes, and wealth of fine English and French furniture, are superbly decorated. The present Duke has carried out extensive repairs and renovations although these have been strictly in keeping with the original design. Rearrangements, fresh colour, light and space have all brought new life to a masterpiece of two centuries ago.

Among the innumerable treasures of art and antiquity at the castle are family portraits by Allan Ramsay, Gainsborough and Cosway, some beautiful tapestries, remarkable collections of old weapons, china, books and silver and the famous Conway gold plate dessert service. Rob Roy's dirk and sporran and embroidery by Mary Queen of Scots are three of the countless interesting relics.

In 1745 the Duke rallied Argyllshire to the Hanoverian cause, and Inveraray became the headquarters of anti-Jacobite resistance in the north-west. Scott has drawn an unsympathetic picture of Argyll in *The Heart of Midlothian*, but, in fact, he worked hard and successfully for the improvement of industry and transport in Scotland. The Argyll family has long been powerful in the western Highlands. Lord Colin Campbell, who was Lord High Chancellor of Scotland, was created Earl of Argyll in 1457, and among his descendants have been many men outstanding in the pattern of Scottish history. The tragic careers of the 8th and 9th Earls (father and son) are well known, the former executed in 1661 for his Covenanting sympathies and his compromise with Cromwell, and the latter brought to the scaffold twenty-four years later for his part in Monmouth's Rebellion. The dukedom dates from 1701, and the present Duke, who served in the Argyll and Sutherland Highlanders during the last war, succeeded in 1949. His new venture in opening Inveraray Castle to the public may well prove as important a tribute to Scotland as many of his ancestors' feats of arms.

When Dr. Johnson visited the castle in 1773 on his return from the Hebrides with Boswell, he was " much struck with the

ABOVE: *The north-east drawing room, where Johnson and Boswell were received on their visit in 1773. The walls are covered in French 18th century Beauvais tapestries and the furniture of the same period in Aubusson tapestry.*

LEFT: *Part of the interesting collection of old weapons in the great hall are the "Brown Besses" over the fireplace, used by the Argyll militia at Culloden in 1746.*

grandeur and elegance of this princely seat.' Curiously enough, his suggestion that it might be improved by the addition of another storey was realised a century later after a fire had destroyed the roof of the central hall. Whether this is an improvement, however, is doubtful, as the original proportions are somewhat distorted by the extra height and the conical roofs which were added at the same time. " What I admire here," said Dr. Johnson, " is the total defiance of expense." He spent an evening of animated conversation with the family, much to Boswell's joy, who noted that " The Duke of Argyle was exceedingly polite to him, and upon his complaining of the shelties which he had hitherto ridden being too small for him, his grace told him he should be provided with a good horse to carry him next day." Famous travellers' accounts have so far given us most of the existing intimate and informal glimpses of Inveraray Castle. Today, it is open house to anyone who has the opportunity and good fortune to make the journey there.

Barcaldine, looking across Loch Creran to the hills beyond.

Barcaldine Castle

BARCALDINE, THE "BLACK CASTLE" OF Benderloch, stands today softly white and tall, its knife-edge roof of dove-grey Ballachulish slate touched with golden lichen. In fact, it seems to be the only white object in the widespread landscape. On all sides there are prospects of extravagant beauty—in the foreground Loch Creran backed by the great mountains above Glencoe and further north the distant pointed peaks of Ardgour beyond Appin. South-west lie the still, glassy waters of Loch Linnhe stretching to the widening Firth of Lorne, blue-grey on the finest day, with the darker blue heights of Mull in the background.

But Barcaldine owes its superb position not to the builder's eye for beauty but to his design for defence. This was Sir Duncan Campbell, 7th Knight of Glenorchy, a Chief of great power and character, known to this day as Black Duncan. In more peaceful parts of Scotland towards the end of the 16th century, the need for defence was a dwindling consideration in castle and house building. Not so in Argyll, however, where turbulence and lawlessness had followed the break-up of the Lordship of the Isles, a

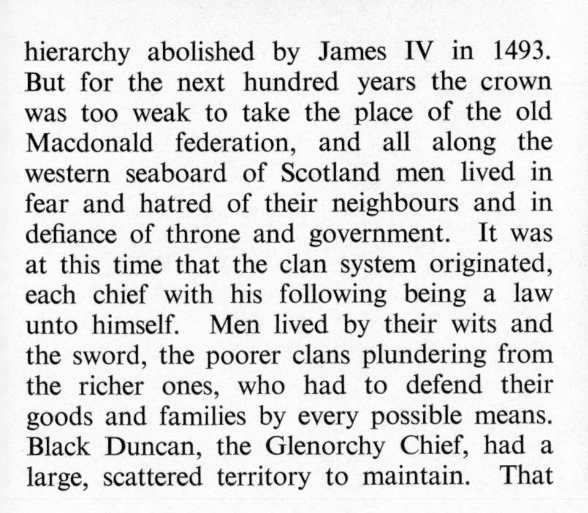

hierarchy abolished by James IV in 1493. But for the next hundred years the crown was too weak to take the place of the old Macdonald federation, and all along the western seaboard of Scotland men lived in fear and hatred of their neighbours and in defiance of throne and government. It was at this time that the clan system originated, each chief with his following being a law unto himself. Men lived by their wits and the sword, the poorer clans plundering from the richer ones, who had to defend their goods and families by every possible means. Black Duncan, the Glenorchy Chief, had a large, scattered territory to maintain. That he did so with such success was due partly to his strategically placed fortresses from Balloch Castle at the foot of Loch Tay to Barcaldine in Benderloch.

" Black Duncan of the Seven Castles " himself lived first at Kilchurn Castle on Loch Awe and later at Balloch. Although their main purpose was military, Sir Duncan did not entirely neglect the amenities of his castles, but " causit mak parkis . . . and saw ackornis and seid of fir thairin, and plantit in the samen young fir and birk." He also filled them with modern " plenishings " and even collected a library.

Barcaldine—derived from the Gaelic *Barr a challtuin*, meaning hazel knoll—was begun in 1579 and finished in 1601. Built on the usual L-plan, the main tower has a vaulted ground floor which housed the kitchen and cellars. On the first floor was the great hall or general living room, and at the same level in the projecting wing, the Laird's parlour, while his private apartments stood on the second floor under the garret. Over the entrance, Black Duncan's coat of arms, the motto " Follow me " and the date 1579, carved in the hard green local stone, remains in place today. The Chief himself never lived at Barcaldine, but installed his third son, John of Auchinryre, as baillie or lieutenant. It seems that John had no children, and it was his half-brother, Patrick Campbell, Para Beg (little black-haired Patrick) who founded the Barcaldine family. He died in 1678 and is buried in the ruined Priory of Ardchattan on Loch Etive.

For the next hundred years the Barcaldine family, as hereditary keepers of the castle, served their Glenorchy chiefs with loyalty and devotion in war and peace. Para Beg's eldest son, who fought with Argyll's Troop of Horse in the Civil War, married as his second wife a sister of the famous Sir Ewen Cameron of Lochiel. His eldest son Alasdair was one of the leaders of Glenorchy's invasion of Caithness in 1680. When the 6th Earl of Caithness died in 1677, he had mortgaged not only his property but his title to Glenorchy, whose ambitious claim to both was upheld by a politically pro-Campbell Government. Glenorchy's expedition with several hundred men, including 50 Barcaldine tenants, was a complete military success, but the Caithness people and the next Sinclair heir to the earldom soon made things so objectionable for Glenorchy that he was forced to sell out. The Laird of Barcaldine, however, was given a grant of land for his part in the business and Glenorchy himself created Earl of Breadalbane by Charles II.

Alasdair's son, Para Djarak (Red Patrick) succeeded to Barcaldine in 1720 when he was middle-aged with a large and growing family. While his father was still living at the castle, Para Djarak built the present Barcaldine House (then called Dalfure) at nearby Innerrergan, and just before his death in 1738 he returned to this more capacious, modern dwelling, abandoning Barcaldine Castle to wind and weather. Although his son Ian Du (black-haired John) was advised by his brother during the '45 Rising to " put your castle in a pouster of Defence without loss of time, and put in all your own and your friends' most valuable things," it is not known whether this was carried out.

Six years later the Barcaldine family were plunged into what eventually became a historic episode, by the murder of Ian Du's half-

ABOVE: *Copy of a portrait of Sir Duncan Campbell.*

LEFT: *Barcaldine from the south-east.*

brother, Colin Campbell of Glenure. The scape-goat for this murder was James Stewart of the Glen. Ian Du was put to much expense after the murder, yet he seems to have launched out on additions to his house and large-scale tree-planting far beyond his means. The inevitable crash came in 1775 and the Barcaldine estate was sold to Ian Du's shrewd and thrifty half-brother, Duncan Campbell of Glenure. Within five years the old Laird, Ian Du, and his son were both dead, and with them the senior branch of the Barcaldine family came to an end.

Raeburn painted Sir Duncan Campbell, 8th of Barcaldine, 1st Baronet, in military dress, after his distinguished service in the Napoleonic Wars. But, once again, extensive alterations to house and garden emptied the family coffers, and in 1842, on Sir Duncan's death, the entire property, some 30,000 acres, had to be sold. Meanwhile, the old castle, uninhabited and neglected since 1745, degenerated from farm house to bothy, and eventually to a shelter for a couple of tinkers who lived in the vaulted kitchen in mid-Victorian times. But the Campbells of Barcaldine had not lost sight of their old home. In 1896 Sir Duncan's grandson and namesake was able to buy back the now ruinous and roofless castle with about 400 acres of land. Slowly and carefully he rebuilt the castle on the original lines, but with a practical eye to comfort within, employing the architect, Mr. Butter of Perth, to carry out the restoration. The work was finished in 1910, and when Sir Duncan died in 1926 he left the property in trust for future heirs.

The occupants up to 1966 were Madame MacDougall of MacDougall, 30th Chief of the Clan MacDougall, herself a descendant of the Barcaldine family, and her husband, Mr. Leslie Grahame MacDougall, the well-known architect. They have now moved to the MacDougall family house of Dunollie. Today, Barcaldine, standing proudly once more in its grand natural setting, must surely look more lovely if less formidable than ever in the past. As a contemporary home, it has, for all its historic interest, a charming simplicity. The old entrance opens directly on to the wide spiral staircase leading up to the great hall on the first floor. This long, spacious room, with white painted walls above timber wainscoting and a beamed ceiling, easily accommodates both drawing room and dining room. In one of the windows stands a spinning wheel made for the last girl baby to be born at Dunollie Castle in 1741. Off the hall, the Laird's parlour, also panelled and painted white, is less formal with a cosy warmth which must be comforting when the silence is broken by Atlantic gales which rock the castle walls. Among other things of interest here is a memorable painting of Venice by Anne Redpath. The upper floors, of which no record of early times remains, have been made into several pleasant and unpretentious bedrooms, each with an incomparable view. A grant from the Historic Buildings Council in 1957 made it possible to bring the restoration of the castle up to date.

ABOVE: *The old entrance from the spiral stair, showing the original iron yett behind the door and an unusual stone ledge above the doorway.*

BELOW: *Part of the great hall on the first floor.*

Achnacarry

ACHNACARRY IS THE HOME OF COLONEL Donald Cameron of Lochiel, the 26th Chief. Since about 1660 his forefathers, the chiefs of the clan, have lived in this remote and beautiful part of Lochaber surrounded on three sides by high, rugged hills, the lower slopes of which are now thickly wooded. The present house, started in 1802, faces south over a long, green stretch of parkland, the north wall rising directly above the river Arkaig, so that from the windows of a tower on this side one seems to be on a peninsula in the very midst of the dark swirling waters, ruffled by white, crested rapids. The first settled home of the Camerons of Lochiel was at Tor Castle, on the River Lochy, built by the 13th Chief early in the 16th century. It was demolished by the famous Sir Ewen Cameron, who built the old Castle of Achnacarry, near the present site, soon after the Restoration. This, in turn, was entirely destroyed in 1746, after Culloden, by a party of Cumberland's soldiers. The house as it stands today was partly rebuilt in 1952 after a fire which severely damaged it during the last war while it was occupied by Commando troops.

Few families have emerged from the tangle of Highland history with such consistent honour as the Camerons of Lochiel. Romance, courage and some degree of tragedy, they share with the ancestors of other clan chiefs. But there is scarcely a historian in any age, who does not add some testimonial to Cameron of Lochiel. This is high praise over centuries of warring and clan feuds, adding up to much more than the outstanding qualities of two or three famous chiefs.

Most genealogists agree that the Camerons, with the Mackintoshes and other sects, are descended from "the aborigines of the ancient Scots or Caledonians that first planted the country." The Camerons of Lochiel assumed the chieftainship of the Clan about 1400, Black Donald (Donald Dubh) traditionally being the first to take up this position. His grandson, Ewen, however, was the earliest chief to be designated "of Lochiel" when in 1528 his lands were erected into the barony of Lochiel and a charter granted by James V. Ewen Cameron was the builder of Tor Castle, the first family home. He also built six chapels, now all ruinous, as part of a penance dictated by the Pope when this rich and powerful Chief resolved to "give up the world, and apply himself to the works of religion and peace."

Probably most eminent of all the chiefs was Sir Ewen Cameron of Lochiel (1629-1719). His life spanned the Civil War, the savage Killing Times, the Restoration of Charles II and the Protestant Revolution which brought William of Orange to the throne, and Lochiel was a leading figure in all these phases in Scotland. Educated with his kinsman, the Earl of Argyll, who headed the Covenanting Party in Scotland, Lochiel was converted to the other side by an interview with Royalist prisoners after the Battle of Philiphaugh. From this time he followed Montrose, being "always the first that offered himself in any dangerous piece of service, and in all that he undertook, acquitted himself with such conduct and valour that he gained great glory and reputation." Lochiel later supported General Monk against the English generals and helped him to restore Charles II to the throne. He was knighted by James VII in 1681 and fought with Dundee at the battle of Killiecrankie. By this time Sir Ewen had built the old Castle of Achnacarry. He retired in 1696, making over the greater part of his estates to his eldest son John.

John Cameron of Lochiel took part in the Jacobite Rising of 1715, after which he escaped to France, where he spent the rest of his life, leaving his son Donald in charge of the clan and the property. Donald, 19th Chief, known as "The Gentle Lochiel," was one of the most important Jacobites in the Highlands. Both James Stuart and his son, Prince Charles Edward, were in correspondence with him for many years before the '45 Rising. But Lochiel, unlike some of the Stuart supporters, was no unrealistic romantic. When he heard that the Prince had landed at Borrodale in the spring of 1745 without troops, arms or ammunition, he realised the expedition was bound to fail and made plans to visit Charles Edward in the hope of persuading him to give it up and return to France. He found the Prince adamant, however, and "determined to put all to the hazard . . ." "Lochiel, who my

Sir Ewen Cameron of Lochiel, 17th Chief.

ABOVE: *Donald Cameron of Lochiel, 23rd Chief in the uniform of the Grenadier Guards.*

ABOVE: *The long drawing room.*

LEFT: *Donald Cameron of Lochiel, 22nd Chief, by Raeburn.*

RIGHT: *Anne, wife of the 22nd Chief, by Raeburn.*

father has often told me was our first friend," he reproached him, " may stay at home and learn from the newspapers the fate of his Prince." " No," replied Lochiel, " I'll share the fate of my Prince, and so shall every man over whom nature or fortune has given me power." It is a curious fact that on this conversation depended the momentous decision to go ahead with the ill-fated Rising, for, without Lochiel's support, almost certainly the other chiefs would have refused to take up arms for the Prince.

The part played during the next 18 months by Lochiel and the Clan Cameron in the Jacobite triumphs and final defeat at Culloden is well known. Lochiel himself escaped with his life, being severely wounded early in the battle " with grapeshot in both ankles," when he was carried from the field by two henchmen. In the general confusion after the battle, Lochiel made his way back to Lochaber and some weeks later briefly entertained the Prince at Achnacarry. Knowing the King's army was near, the Camerons hid everything of value they could move in the surrounding woods and caves, killing as many cattle as possible. Lochiel's silver and jewellery were buried in the ground. Sure

enough, 320 men of Bligh's Regiment from Fort Augustus arrived on the scene soon after Charles Edward had gone. " The order was to set fire to his (Lochiel's) mansion house," records a contemporary account, " but the best of his moveables were carried off before the soldiers came; however, his fine chairs, tables, and all his cabinet goods were set afire and burnt with his house. His fine fruit garden, above a mile long, was pulled to pieces and laid waste. A beautiful summerhouse that stood in the pleasure garden was also set on fire, and everything valuable was burnt or destroyed." Another later account describes the way Cumberland's troops treated Lochiel's gardener and cook, who were dragged from their hiding place in a " mean hut." " They were ordered to tell the soldiers where the gold and the silver and the jewels had been buried, but the frightened old men would not say or did not know, though they were flogged again and again by the drummers. With their backs cruelly flayed, they were finally sent in irons to Inverness."

It is said that Lochiel with some of his men watched the burning of Achnacarry as they lay in hiding on a hill above the house and that he saw many of the beech saplings he had been thinning when he was called to arms trampled underfoot by the soldiers' heavy boots. In that same beech avenue, grown to maturity today, may be seen how Lochiel had to abandon the work and the unthinned trees have grown up as they were planted. The Chief himself eluded his enemies

ABOVE: *The dining room.*

RIGHT: *The central hall.*

BOTTOM RIGHT: *The staircase leading from the hall to a gallery on the upper floor.*

and with Prince Charles Edward and several other chiefs, "in all 23 gentlemen and 107 men of humbler rank," sailed in two frigates for the coast of Brittany. Lochiel died in France in 1748.

It was the Gentle Lochiel's grandson, the 22nd Chief, who built the present house. The forfeited estates had been restored to him by the Government when he was a minor of seven years old, but born and educated in France and unknown to his people and the customs of his country, this Chief had no liking for life in the Highlands. When the house was practically finished he "became disgusted with the place, left it and never returned." He married a daughter of the celebrated General Sir Ralph Abercromby and died in England in 1832. Nor did his son, a Captain in the Grenadier Guards who fought at Waterloo, live at Achnacarry. Ill health influenced his choice to remain in England when he retired from the army, leaving his property in the charge of a kinsman, Sir Duncan Cameron. A visitor to Achnacarry in 1837 wrote: "The house had been built some 35 years previously . . . We found that the plaster ornaments of the ceiling lay all that time on the floor ready to be fixed, and the doors of the rooms, of beautiful Highland pine, grown brown with age, leaned against the wall ready to be screwed on. They lay in that position for 35 years. The present year Lochiel arranged to have the house completed, which he has done, and it is now a handsome residence worthy of the Chief." Donald Cameron, 24th Chief and grandfather of the present Lochiel, was the first to make the new house his home. After retiring from the Diplomatic Service he was M.P. for Inverness-shire for some years and Groom-in-waiting to Queen Victoria. He was succeeded in 1905 by his eldest son, the late Colonel Sir Donald Cameron, K.T., C.M.G., who had a distinguished army career, serving in the Boer War and the First World War. In 1939 he became Lord-Lieutenant of Inverness-shire.

Today the setting of Achnacarry is magnificent, for many of the great woods are in their prime. The house, square and two-storeyed, with a semi-basement and attics, is built of a greyish-brown whinstone flecked with golden and slate-blue lights. On the north and west sides round towers are built up above first floor level and finished with a castellated parapet which is continued round the house, punctuated by turrets. On the south front, two narrow Gothic windows flank the front door below three larger oval-topped windows on the first floor. Lochiel employed the architect James Gillespie (1777-1855) to build Achnacarry, which must have been one of his first compositions. Later known as Gillespie-Graham, after he had added his wife's name to his own, he became an enthusiastic supporter of the early romantic Gothic revival. His churches in Edinburgh and Glasgow are among the first examples of Gothic facades built on to classical foundations. Achnacarry, in fact, is

The beech avenue.

just such an example of a domestic building where the proportions and design are classical with Gothic detail and decoration. In 1952 the house was reconstructed after war damage, on the original pattern, under the direction of the well-known architect, Mr Ian G. Lindsay, R.S.A.

The interior, high-ceilinged and lit by many large windows, has a lightness and sense of space which is emphasised by the imaginative colour schemes used in redecorating the house. A wide staircase leads out of the central hall to a gallery running round the upper floor. This arrangement, as it were, gathers the whole house round one focal point. Most striking is the long drawing room, its five huge windows curtained in buttercup yellow damask and the walls painted arctic white, reflecting the ice-blue glass of the handsome chandelier. Stronger colour is introduced by an olive green carpet and dusty pink furnishings. Regency furniture mixes well with older and newer pieces, and part of an entrancing collection of Dresden china is shown in a recessed alcove painted Wedgwood blue. In the dining room, with its curved bow overlooking the river, bold crimson curtains are splashed against pale green walls on which are hung many portraits of past chiefs. Of the five long windows in the library, four frame different enchanting views of the river set among woods and high hills. Above a wide chimneypiece of topaz-coloured marble hang three Dutch landscapes, and on another wall two portraits by Raeburn of the 22nd Chief, who built the present house, and his wife.

Perhaps most interesting of all is the rich collection of family treasures and relics in the house from almost every century of Cameron history. Among these are a claymore of 1585, a gun *circa* 1700 with which Sir Ewen Cameron, 17th Chief, is said to have shot the last wolf in Lochaber, a broadsword with scabbard and silver hilt used by the Gentle Lochiel during the '45 Rising and a pistol and miniature portrait of Charles Edward given to him by the Prince.

The present and 26th Chief, Colonel Donald Cameron of Lochiel, who succeeded his father in 1951 and now lives at Achnacarry with his wife and family, is, among other things, a director of the Royal Bank of Scotland, a Crown Estate Commissioner, Chairman of the Scottish Railway Board, and Hon. Colonel of the 4/5th Bn. of the Queen's Own Cameron Highlanders.

The library.

ABOVE: *The famous Fairy Flag.*

BELOW: *Rory Mor's Horn.*

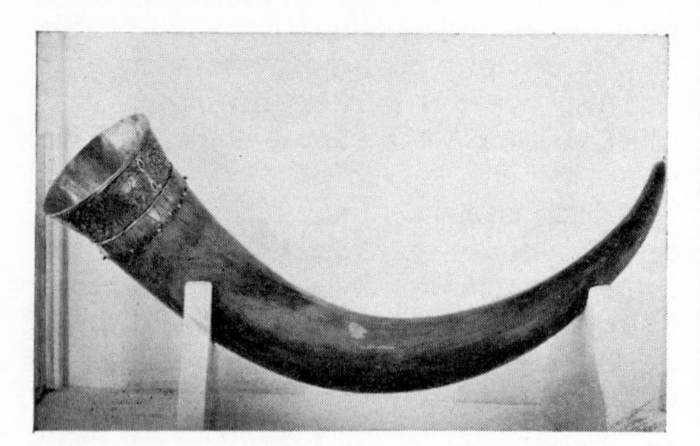

Dunvegan Castle

FROM THE MAINLAND, THE JOURNEY to Loch Dunvegan in Skye is adventurous and commendably slow. While the road winds between steep, rocky hill-sides and ink-dark sea and over bare, remote moors, there is time to remember Dunvegan Castle's long past and to imagine today's setting.

From the landward approach, the building itself is not spectacular. Since the MacLeods acquired Dunvegan some 700 years ago, additions and alterations have continually changed the shape of the castle which, in almost every century, presents a different picture. Although much of the medieval work and some earlier building remain, these are partly masked today by later reconstructions. Anyone who thinks, however, that the mock-Gothic turrets and battlements of the 19th century are indicative of a pseudo-baronial cult would be quite wrong. In 1549 the castle was described as "Ane starke strengthe biggit upon ane craig" and in the words of Dr. Douglas Simpson, the greatest living authority on the architecture of Dunvegan, "It is at once the greatest and most renowned among Hebridean strongholds."

In 1266, after a long struggle, the Hebrides were ceded to Scotland by Norway. About this time, Leod, first of the MacLeod Chiefs of Dunvegan, married the heiress of its early owners, the Macarailts, and established himself there. The Macarailts were descended from the Norsemen who had invaded the Hebrides in the 8th century and later settled there, and Leod's father-in-law was Governor of Skye under the King of Norway. Leod himself, the son of Olav the Black, King of the Isle of Man, was also of Norse descent, his ancestor being King Harald Hardrada. Leod, who owned Harris, part of Lewis and North Uist as well as much of Skye, has been described as "the most powerful Chief in the Islands." It is believed that he built the oldest portion of the castle—the sea-gate and the curtain wall.

Surrounded on three sides by the waters and beaches of Loch Dunvegan, the castle rock in those days was separated from the east landward side by a deep, wide ditch. The sea-gate, at the top of a steep flight of steps cut out of the rock, remained the only entrance to the castle till 1748. From here, a narrow passage led up to the oval shaped platform encircled by Leod's fortified stone and lime wall. Without written records of this early period, the living quarters within the courtyard must be reconstructed in imagination.

Next in age comes the massive four-storeyed keep, rising at first alone, a mighty bulk above rock and curtain wall. Malcolm, 3rd Chief (circa 1320-70), who is reported to have been "the greatest hero of his race," is thought to have built the keep under the direction of a royal architect. By two marriages, he was connected to important families on the mainland and it seems likely he was in a position to start building an up-to-date castle. The outline of the keep still forms the most solid exterior feature of the castle today and the present drawing room, almost completely modernised inside, now occupies the place, on the first floor, of the medieval great hall.

The MacLeods held their island properties as vassals, first of the Earls of Ross and later of the Lords of the Isles. After the latter office had been abolished, the crown granted charters to the MacLeod Chiefs of their Hebridean estates, and the first document at Dunvegan is a grant of their lands in Skye and Harris by James IV in 1498, in return for maintaining "One birlinn of 26 oars and two of six oars for the service of the King in peace and in war."

Soon after this, early in the 16th century, the Fairy Tower at the south end of the rock was built, probably by Alastair Crottach, 8th Chief. The least altered and most captivating of the range of buildings today, the tall Fairy Tower with its crow-stepped gables and midget windows is a complete entity. Whether it was

RIGHT: *A print of Dunvegan in 1790 by Grose.*

finished when James V called at Dunvegan, it is said in 1536 and 1540 on his Hebridean voyages, is not known. In 1557 the castle was seized by the wicked usurper, Ian Dubh, who was eventually expelled by his own clansmen, escaping first to Harris and then to Ireland where the O'Donnels "disposed of the wretch by thrusting a red hot iron into his bowel."

In 1623 Rory Mor, 16th Chief, built a long house between the keep and the Fairy Tower. One of the most powerful of the Highland chiefs, Sir Rory, who in his early years had often been on the wrong side of the law, was in his latter days knighted by James VI for his part in keeping order in the north-west. His building was altered greatly in the 19th century but the Renaissance balustrade, added in 1665, may still be seen today. Ten years later Ian Breac, 19th Chief, built out the south-west wing, the interior of which was gutted in the fire of 1938, when modern kitchens, bathrooms and offices were installed.

Earlier in the century the MacLeods of Dunvegan had supported the Royalists in the Civil War and sent a force to fight for Charles II at the Battle of Worcester in 1651, where they were killed almost to a man. The other clans agreed that this tragedy should exempt the MacLeods from further battles till they regained their strength. Possibly this was why the MacLeods took no part in the Jacobite Rising of 1715; while in the '45 they fought on the Hanoverian side, apparently from political pressure rather than conviction.

Except for the opening of the landward door in 1748, little building was done during the 18th century. A delightful print by Grose shows Dunvegan as it stood in 1790. This was the castle which Dr. Johnson and James Boswell saw when they paid their memorable visit in 1773. The account of their stay at Dunvegan, which by now holds an unassailable place in English literature, is also fascinating history. Boswell's report of their conversation with Lady MacLeod at breakfast concerned the castle rock:—"The lady and I got into a warm dispute. She wanted to build a house upon a farm which she had taken about five miles from the old castle, and to make gardens and everything fine there . . . the lady insisted that the rock was very inconvenient. That there was no place near it where a good garden could be made; that it must always be a rude place; that it was a Herculean labour to make a dinner here. . . . 'Madam,' said I, 'if once you quit this rock, this centre of gravity, there is no knowing where you may settle. . . No, no; keep to the rock. It is the very jewel of the estate.' "

At the turn of the century, General MacLeod, 23rd Chief, whose portraits by Raeburn and Zoffany hang in the castle today, made some changes to the building, including repairs to the keep which had become ruinous, and the addition of a north wing. He also planted many of the trees which now flourish on what was a bare moor and laid out the castle policies. But it was the extensive alterations of the 19th century, carried out in two stages,

ABOVE: *1819 print of Dunvegan by Daniell.*

RIGHT: *The entrance front.*

BELOW: *The ancient dungeon in the keep.*

RIGHT: *The dining room.*

which transformed the castle, both inside and out, to its present "Gothick" aspect. Daniell's print of 1819 shows the first stage, completed by the 24th Chief who was host to Sir Walter Scott in 1814. An enthusiastic guest, Sir Walter's visit inspired one of his best known poems, "The Lord of the Isles." During the 1840s, Norman MacLeod, 25th Chief, employed Robert Brown, an Edinburgh architect, to make the final and still more drastic alterations. The tower at the north end of the keep was heightened and embattled, Rory Mor's house was raised a storey and given a flat roof in place of the original steep roof and gables, windows were enlarged and the pepper-pot turrets added along the new roof-top at a cost of £100 each, while the interiors were extensively reconstructed.

Dunvegan is the only one of the old Hebridean castles to have been continually lived in for as long as seven centuries—and by the same family. Their long and varied history is vividly illustrated by one of the most remarkable collections of relics and treasures in Scotland, ranging from the Fairy Flag to the framed bread-and-butter letters written by Dr. Johnson and Sir Walter Scott after their visits to Dunvegan. The Fairy Flag, which is believed by all MacLeods to have magic powers of bringing the clan victory in battle, is today a frail spider's web of weathered brown silk, meticulously darned in red, and is now framed in the drawing room. According to recent expert opinion, this is of Syrian origin and may have been a saint's garment before it was a flag, brought back from the East by Harald Hardrada and taken after his death at Stamford Bridge in 1066 to the Isle of Man, whence it was taken to Dunvegan by Leod, son of Olav the Black, King of the Isle of Man.

Another important possession is the Dunvegan Cup, a mazer of wood, mounted with filigreed silver work and set with precious stones, traditionally associated with Niall of the Black Knees, King of Ulster in the 10th century. The present workmanship dates from 1493 and the cup was probably brought from Ireland as a gift by an Irish Chief, Shane O'Neill, when he visited Rory Mor at Dunvegan. In the drawing room also is Rory Mor's Horn, a giant ox horn decorated with Celtic designs in silver. Each chief, to pass the test of manhood, had to drain it of the half-gallon of claret it held at a single draught. It was last drained "without setting down or falling down" by Dame Flora's grandson, John, on his 21st birthday in 1956. The richly carved sideboard in the dining room also belongs to Rory Mor's period and is said to have been brought by him from London in 1613. In this room, too, are portraits by Allan Ramsay and Raeburn of various MacLeod Chiefs and their wives, and Sir William Hutchison's painting of Dame Flora, presented to her in 1952 by clansmen and friends throughout the world.

Since Dame Flora succeeded to the chieftainship in 1935, she has entertained thousands of guests at Dunvegan, among the most distinguished, Her Majesty the Queen, Prince Philip and Princess Margaret. Dame Flora, who was created D.B.E. in 1953, was a County Councillor for Inverness-shire and does much public work besides her gigantic task, not only as hostess to the MacLeod clan all over the world, but as honoured guest of clan societies in many countries. In 1963, in her 85th year, she visited Japan, America, India and Persia. Today, Dame Flora, uses her powers and responsibilities to the full in forging international goodwill as a MacLeod ambassador.

ABOVE: *Dame Flora MacLeod of MacLeod by Denys Ramsay.*

ABOVE RIGHT: *The Dunvegan Cup.*

RIGHT: *In the entrance hall hang banners of the MacLeod Fencibles, raised as a Home Guard in the Napoleonic Wars.*

Houses & Castles
OPEN TO THE PUBLIC

* indicates a National Trust for Scotland property.

Abbotsford
March 20-October 31
Weekdays 10-5 : Sundays 2-5
Adm.: Adults 2/6 : Children 1/6

Airlie Castle
By arrangement with owner
Castle and Gardens open once a year under Scotland's Garden Scheme

House of Aldie
By arrangement with owner

Arbuthnott House
By arrangement with owner

Barcaldine Castle
By arrangement with J.A. Campbell and Lamond, C.S., 1 Thistle Court, Edinburgh, 2.

Barra Castle
By arrangement with owner

***The Binns**
Throughout the year
Saturdays and Sundays 2-5
Mid-June to mid-September
Daily 2-5
At other times by arrangement
Adm.: Adults 1/- : Children 6d

Blair Castle
Easter weekend and Sundays and Mondays in April
May 1-October 8
Weekdays 10-6 : Sundays 2-6
Adm.: Adults 3/6
Children half-price

Borthwick Castle
By arrangement with tenant

***Brodick Castle**
Easter weekend: May-September
Daily (except Sundays) 1-5
Gardens open 10-5
Adm.: Adults 3/-: Gdns. only: 2/-
Children half price
Car park 1/-

Broughton Place
Gardens open occasionally under Scotland's Garden Scheme

***Craigievar Castle**
May-September
Weds., Thurs. and Suns. 2-7
Adm.: Adults 2/- : Children 1/-
Car park 1/-

***Crathes Castle**
May-September
Daily 2-7
October and April
Wednesdays and Sundays 2-7
Gardens open throughout the year from 9.30-dusk
Admission to Castle and Gardens:
Adults 4/- : Children 2/-
Castle only: 2/6 : Children 1/-
Gardens only: 2/6 : Children 1/-

Culross Abbey House
Please note that **Culross Abbey House** is NOT open to the public

***Culzean Castle**
March-October
Daily (including Sundays) 10-dusk
Admission to Castle and Grounds:
Adults 4/- : Children 2/-
Grounds only: Adults 2/6 : Children 1/-

Darnaway Castle
Open once a year for charity

Drum Castle
June, July, August
Sundays 2.30-6
Admission to House and Grounds:
Adults 2/6 : Children (under 15) half-price
Reductions for parties of 20 or more by previous arrangement

Drumlanrig Castle
Open occasionally for charity

Dunrobin Castle
June 12-July 31
Daily (except Sundays) 2-6
August 1-September 15
Daily (except Sundays) 11-6
Admission to Castle and Gardens:
Adults 3/- : Museum only: 1/-
Gardens only: 1/-
Children (under 14) half-price
Special rates for families and for parties of over 20 : Free car park

Duntrune Castle
By arrangement with owner

Dunvegan Castle
April 1-October 14
Daily (except Sundays) 2-5
Adm.: Adults 3/- : Children 1/-

***Falkland Palace**
April-October
Daily 10-6 : Sundays 2-6
Admission to Palace and Gardens:
Adults 2/6 : Children 1/-
Gardens only: 1/-
Reduced rates for previously arranged educational parties

Floors Castle
Open once a year for charity
Gardens open each Wednesday during summer months

Glamis Castle *May-September*
Weds. and Thurs. 2-5.30
July, August, September
Sundays only 2-5.30
Adm.: Adults 3/- : Children 1/6
Grounds only: 1/- : Bus and car park free

Gribloch *Gardens open occasionally under Scotland's Garden Scheme*

Haddo House *Sundays, June 18, 25; July 2, 9, 16, 23, 30; September 17, 24; 2.30-5*
Organised parties on any date from May to July
Adm.: Adults 2/6 : Children reduced rates

***Hamilton House** *By arrangement with tenant*

The Hirsel *Gardens open throughout the year*

Hopetoun House *April 29-October 1*
Daily (except Thursdays and Fridays) 1.30-5.45
Admission to House, Grounds, Gardens:
Adults 3/6 : Children 2/-
Grounds, Gardens, Deer park: 2/-
Special terms for organised parties of over 20

Inveraray Castle *April 1-June 25*
Daily (except Fridays)
June 26-October 8
Daily
Weekdays 10-12.30, 2-6 : Sundays 2-6
Adm.: Adults 4/- : Children 2/-
Gardens open May 13-July 30
Saturdays 10-6 : Sundays 2-6
Adm.: 1/-
Bus and car park free

Kilkerran House *By arrangement with owner*

Kinross House *By arrangement with owner*

***Leith Hall** *May-September*
Daily 11-6 : Sundays 2.30-6
Rock gardens on show all the year round
Daily 9.30-dusk : Sundays 2.30-dusk
Adm.: House 2/- : Gardens 1/-
Children half price

Lennoxlove *Coach and private parties (minimum of 10 persons or 30/-) from May-end of September*
Adm.: Adults 3/- : Children 1/6

Castle Leod *By arrangement with owner*

Maxwelton House *By arrangement with owner*

Mellerstain *May-September*
Daily (except Saturdays) 2-5.30
Adm.: Adults 3/6 : Children 1/-
Grounds: Adults 1/6 : Children 6d
Special terms for organised parties, apply curator

Paxton House *Open occasionally for charity*

Penicuik House *By arrangement with owner*

Pinkie House *Throughout the year Tuesdays 2-4*

Thirlestane Castle *Large parties only by arrangement with owner*

Traquair House *July-September*
Daily 2-5.30
Easter Sunday, Monday, Spring bank holiday (May 29) and all Sundays following Easter
Parties at other times by arrangement
Adm.: Adults 3/6 : Children 1/6
Grounds only: 1/6 : Library: 1/-
Reduced rates for parties

Yester House *By arrangement with owner*

Please note that dates and times of opening, etc.,
are subject to alteration and should be checked locally.

Index

Entries in **bold** *type indicate houses and castles described in the text*